A STATE UNDER SIEGE

A State Under Siege

The Establishment of Northern Ireland,
1920–1925

BRYAN A. FOLLIS

CLARENDON PRESS · OXFORD
1995

Oxford University Press, Walton Street, Oxford OX2 6DP
Oxford New York
Athens Auckland Bangkok Bombay
Calcutta Cape Town Dar es Salaam Delhi
Florence Hong Kong Istanbul Karachi
Kuala Lumpur Madras Madrid Melbourne
Mexico City Nairobi Paris Singapore
Taipei Tokyo Toronto
and associated companies in
Berlin Ibadan

Oxford is a trade mark of Oxford University Press

Published in the United States
by Oxford University Press Inc., New York

British Library Cataloguing in Publication Data
Data available

Library of Congress Cataloging in Publication Data
Data applied for

ISBN 0–19–820305 5

1 3 5 7 9 10 8 6 4 2

Typeset by Graphicraft Typesetters Ltd., Hong Kong
Printed in Great Britain
on acid-free paper by
Biddles Ltd., Guildford and King's Lynn

To
MY MOTHER
and in memory of
MY FATHER

Acknowledgements

I wish to thank the staffs of the following institutions for their assistance: the Archives Department of University College Dublin, the Public Record Office (London), the National Archives of Ireland (incorporating what was formerly the State Paper Office), the House of Lords Record Office, the Assembly Library at Stormont, the National Library of Ireland, and in particular the Public Record Office of Northern Ireland where the great bulk of my research was carried out.

For permission to quote from papers deposited in the Public Record Office of Northern Ireland I wish to thank Dr A. P. W. Malcomson, the Deputy Keeper of the Records, and also express my gratitude to Miss Nancy Clark, Viscount Craigavon, the family of the late Sir Wilfrid Spender, the trustees of the estate of the late F. H. Crawford, and the Ulster Unionist Council. I wish to thank the Mulcahy Trust for permitting me to consult and quote from the Mulcahy Papers in the Archives Department of University College Dublin. Quotation from the Lloyd George Papers is by kind permission of the Clerk of the Records, House of Lords Record Office, and the trustees of the Beaverbrook Foundation. A special thanks is due to Mr Brian McClintock who generously allowed me to consult his research on relations between the governments of Northern Ireland and the Irish Free State.

This book is based on my Ph.D. thesis and I wish to thank my supervisor, Dr A. T. Q. Stewart, for his guidance and unfailing kindness, and my external examiner, Professor D. G. Boyce, for his very helpful comments.

I am grateful to many people whose encouragement helped sustain my interest and motivation, thus ensuring the completion of the research and the subsequent writing-up. In particular, I wish to record my deep sense of debt to Miss Esther Hewitt, who not only provided enthusiastic support but also read and offered advice on various drafts. Her practical assistance was indispensable in making my thesis suitable for publication. Though many friends made suggestions about the text, the views (and mistakes) in the book are entirely my own. I also wish to take this opportunity to thank my publisher and in particular Tony Morris for guiding me into print.

The typing of the original thesis and a large part of this book was undertaken by Miss Ruth Dickson, and I greatly appreciate her accuracy and promptitude.

Finally, I mention my family with gratitude for their patience, loyalty, and support. It was through the gift of books from my parents that I acquired as a child my interest in history, and it is to my parents that this book is dedicated.

Note on Terminology

Although Northern Ireland constituted only two-thirds of the province of Ulster, the term 'Ulster' was widely used by many contemporaries, as was the phrase 'the North'. Meanwhile the Irish Free State was often referred to as 'the South' or 'Southern Ireland'. While I have endeavoured to use the formal titles for the two territories, on some occasions I have used alternative terms, but no significance is attached to the use of any term.

A small initial letter has been used when referring to Ulster unionism in general terms but a capital has been used for all references to the Ulster Unionist Party and its members. In general references to the governments in Belfast, Dublin, and London, a small initial letter has also been used. However, capitals have been used for all references which give the proper title, for example 'Government of Northern Ireland'.

Contents

List of Abbreviations

The following abbreviations are used in the notes:

HLRO   House of Lords Record Office, London
NAI   National Archives of Ireland, Dublin (incorporating what was formerly the State Paper Office of Ireland)
NLI   National Library of Ireland, Dublin
PRO(L) Public Record Office, London
PRONI   Public Record Office of Northern Ireland, Belfast
UCDAD   University College, Dublin, Archives Department

1

Introduction

On 23 December 1920 the Government of Ireland Act, 1920, received the Royal Assent and thus became law. The Act provided for the setting up of two legislatures in Ireland, one for Northern Ireland and one for Southern Ireland. The parliaments, each consisting of the Sovereign, Senate, and House of Commons, were based on the Westminster model which they were devolved from and subordinate to. The northern parliament was responsible for the defined area of the parliamentary counties of Antrim, Armagh, Down, Fermanagh, Londonderry, and Tyrone, and the parliamentary boroughs of Belfast and Londonderry.

The devolved parliaments were given 'power to make laws for the peace, order and good government'[1] of their respective areas subject to certain limitations. The Act set out a list of 'excepted' matters over which the Irish parliaments had no powers of legislation. These matters included the Crown, war, the armed forces, treaties with foreign states, treason, coinage, and trade with any place outside that part of Ireland under their jurisdiction. In addition to the 'excepted' matters, there were other 'reserved' matters on which the parliaments of Southern and Northern Ireland had not yet the power to legislate. These included the Supreme Court, the postal service, the imposition and collection of major taxes such as customs duties and income tax, the registration of deeds, and for up to three years the management and control of the Royal Irish Constabulary. The transfer of 'reserved' matters to the parliaments of Southern and Northern Ireland was deferred in view of the possibility of a united parliament for all Ireland being established as provided for under the terms of the Act.

To help give substance to its declared hope of eventual Irish unity, the Act envisaged a single Lord-Lieutenant to represent the King in both parts of Ireland, and proposed the establishment of a Council of Ireland. This was to consist of a President nominated by the Lord-Lieutenant, along with twenty representatives from each parliament in Ireland. Among the matters for which the Council of Ireland was given responsibility were railways and the administration of the Diseases of Animals Acts. It was also hoped that it would provide for the

[1] A. S. Quekett, *The Constitution of Northern Ireland* (Belfast, 1928–46), ii. 7.

discussion of other topics of mutual interest and for the development of common programmes of action by the southern and northern parliaments. It was through the work of the Council of Ireland that the dream of the peaceful evolution of a single parliament for all Ireland was to be realized. The Council was to:

make recommendations to the Parliaments of Southern Ireland and Northern Ireland as to the advisability of passing identical Acts delegating to the Council the administration of any such Irish services, with a view to avoiding the necessity of administering them separately in Southern Ireland or Northern Ireland, and providing for the transfer of any such reserved services at the earliest possible dates.[2]

In addition to the legislative limitations created by the designation of certain matters as 'excepted' and 'reserved', Section 75 of the Government of Ireland Act laid it down, as a kind of blanket provision, that the supreme authority of the United Kingdom parliament at Westminster remained undiminished. Furthermore, it was stipulated that Southern and/or Northern Ireland statutes would be void to the extent that they were repugnant to the United Kingdom statutes passed after the appointed day and extending to Southern and/or Northern Ireland.[3] As many fundamentally Irish matters were being 'reserved' by, or 'excepted' to, Westminster, the Act provided for the continuation, albeit reduced, of Irish representation at Westminster.

If the British Government had hoped for an enthusiastic acceptance of its Government of Ireland Act by Irish nationalists and Ulster unionists, it was to be bitterly disappointed. The Act had been a genuine attempt at compromise designed to grant Irish nationalist demands for Home Rule and meet Ulster unionist insistence that they should not be forcibly placed under the rule of a Dublin parliament. The 1920 Act was the fourth attempt by Westminster to introduce legislation establishing Home Rule in Ireland, but it was the first legislation in which the British Government took account of the determination of the Ulster unionists not to submit to a Dublin parliament. It was hoped that the Act would contribute to the solution of a problem which for forty years had dominated the Irish political scene and, at times, had also dominated the national political scene.[4] Yet the proceedings at Westminster which led to the Bill's becoming law were conducted in

[2] Government of Ireland Act, 1920, Sect. 10.

[3] R. J. Lawrence, *The Government of Northern Ireland: Public Finance and Public Services 1921–64* (Oxford, 1965), 167.

[4] For an account of the campaign for Home Rule and the opposition of Ulster unionists to it, see P. Buckland, *Ulster Unionism and the Origins of Northern Ireland 1886 to 1922* (Dublin, 1973).

an atmosphere of unreality, and the Act stood little chance of success. The nationalists repudiated the Bill and adhered to the principles of earlier legislation which had proposed Home Rule for Ireland on a unitary basis. Furthermore, the nationalists had largely been replaced by the more militant Sinn Fein (Ourselves) as the representatives of Gaelic Roman Catholic Ireland. Committed to the achievement of an Irish republic outside the United Kingdom, Sinn Fein completely rejected the limited powers offered by the 1920 Act.

It was ironic that Ulster unionists who had vigorously opposed Home Rule for the previous forty years should accept, albeit grudgingly, the 1920 Act. When the new Home Rule scheme with two Irish parliaments had first been proposed at Westminster, the then Ulster Unionist leader, Sir Edward Carson, had opposed it. He clearly stated unionist objections to the scheme and advised 'against forcing upon Ulster a parliament it had not sought and did not want'.[5] Unionists preferred to be governed by Westminster as an integral and equal part of the United Kingdom. However, the establishment of a northern parliament in which they could confidently expect to form the government did hold some attraction for the Ulster unionists. It was felt that a separate Northern Ireland administration would strengthen their position and serve as a defence against any future hostile new proposals suggested by Westminster. Carson came to recognize the additional security afforded by a parliament of Northern Ireland against absorption into an all-Ireland parliament. He stated that 'you cannot knock Parliaments up and down as you do a ball, and, once you have planted them there, you cannot get rid of them'.[6] If total union could no longer be preserved and if some form of Irish Home Rule was to be granted, Ulster unionists concluded that the scheme proposed in the Government of Ireland Act would cause the least diminution of their Britishness.

Meanwhile Sinn Fein, having won a majority of Irish seats in the 1918 Westminster General Election, had embarked upon a strategy designed to achieve an Irish republic. Boycotting Westminster, they formed an alternative parliament, Dail Eireann, and attempted to subvert the British administration with their own illegal courts, police, and so on. An integral part of their strategy was the waging of a terrorist campaign by the Irish Republican Army (IRA) against the British administration.[7] At first, with the bombings and shootings only taking place in Southern Ireland, Ulster escaped the rising violence. However, it was not long

[5] D. W. Harkness, *Northern Ireland Since 1920* (Dublin, 1983), 2.

[6] *Parl. Deb.* (House of Commons) (UK), 123, 22 Dec. 1919, col. 1202.

[7] For an account of the campaign by Sinn Fein and the IRA against the British administration, see W. A. Philips, *The Revolution in Ireland 1906–1923* (London, 1926).

able to escape the growing tension created by the terrorist incidents. The results of the local government elections in January and June 1920 confirmed the rout of the Irish nationalists by Sinn Fein. In the eyes of the Ulster unionists it vindicated their suspicion that the Roman Catholics not only endorsed Irish republicanism but also supported the terrorist action of the IRA. As the IRA and Sinn Fein attempted to increase their operations and activities in Ulster, so the fear among loyalists of the republican threat and inter-communal tensions both increased.

Serious public disorder broke out in Belfast in July 1920, leaving forty-eight people dead and 300 wounded. In a fit of hysteria, fearing that their Roman Catholic fellow-workers had associations with subversive elements and in retaliation for the expulsion of Protestants from the Londonderry shipyards, Protestants expelled some 8,000 Roman Catholics from the Belfast shipyards and from other industries. Alarmed about the deteriorating political and security situation, and concerned that control of grass-roots unionists was slipping away from the unionist leadership towards extreme and lower-class elements, Sir James Craig took action. After Carson, Craig was the most important figure in the Ulster Unionist movement, and on 23 July he appointed Colonel Wilfrid Spender Chief of Staff to the Ulster Volunteer Force (UVF), with the task of reactivating it on a six-county basis. He also pressed the British Cabinet for official recognition of the UVF or, alternatively, for a new official peace-keeping force to be drawn from the UVF. As law and order deteriorated further, and with police resources in Ulster below the normal peacetime establishment, the London government became more sympathetic to the creation of a new police reserve. However, Craig wanted such a force to be independent of the Dublin Castle administration and to be placed, along with the regular Royal Irish Constabulary (RIC) in Ulster, under an RIC Commissioner who would have exclusive command in the area which would become Northern Ireland. In addition, Craig wanted the creation of an administrative authority based in Belfast which, by reporting directly to the Irish Chief Secretary and bypassing the Dublin civil servants (whom Ulster unionists disliked and accused of disloyalty),[8] could act as the administrative foundation for the new state of Northern Ireland.

On 2 September 1920, with fighting going on in Belfast, Craig attended a conference of ministers in London and argued his case with vigour and conviction. Pressing the government to grant his objectives so that he might retain the confidence of the people and prevent

---

[8] J. McColgan, *British Policy and the Irish Administration, 1920–22* (London, 1983), 25.

grass-roots extremists from precipitating civil war, Craig won the day.[9] As Dr McColgan has pointed out, the creation of a 'new administrative centre in Belfast responsible exclusively for the six counties, together with government agreement to establish a special constabulary, amounted to an impressive coup for Craig. The British were conscious of this and of the political embarrassment it could cause to themselves.'[10] Craig, who had wanted to announce the good news upon his return to Belfast, was requested to maintain a public silence until the government had made a statement. The government was keen to appear to be acting independently.[11] However, whether in practice the agreement would provide Ulster unionists with the sense of security they sought or contribute towards the establishment of Northern Ireland remained to be seen. Indeed, it was questionable whether Northern Ireland, even assuming it could be established, could survive as an entity.

[9] Conclusions of a Conference of Ministers, 2 Sept. 1920, London, Cabinet Conclusions, PRO(L) CAB23/22.
[10] McColgan, *British Policy*, 26.
[11] Bonar Law to Lloyd George, 2 Sept. 1920, HLRO, Lloyd George Papers, F/31/1/43.

2

Planning for Self-Government

In making provision for the establishment of a parliament and government of Northern Ireland, the Government of Ireland Act made possible the creation of Northern Ireland. However, at the stage when the Act became law, Northern Ireland existed not as an entity but only in name and on paper. Not only had Northern Ireland no parliament and no government: it had no civil service to support and serve it, no police or defence force to enforce whatever laws it might make, protect its people, or defend its territory from possible (and indeed likely) attack, nor had it a judiciary to uphold its laws and administer justice. The problems involved in the creation of Northern Ireland must have seemed daunting, and the sheer size of the task to be undertaken almost overwhelming. Yet within six months of the passage of the Act, a government of Northern Ireland had been formed and had taken office.

With the election of a local parliament and the formation of a government, a parliamentary democracy had been established within Northern Ireland. The administrative machine to serve it had also been created, for not only had ministries been constituted, but some staff were selected and plans for full recruitment made; office accommodation was arranged and all necessary equipment, from desks and cupboards to files and forms, was organized. One man more than any other made possible this swift and highly efficient formation of Northern Ireland—Sir Ernest Clark. Clark was appointed in September 1920 as additional Assistant Under-Secretary in the Irish Office, with particular administrative responsibility for the area that was to form Northern Ireland. It was his energy and enthusiasm which made possible the creation of Northern Ireland much sooner than had been considered possible.

The son of a government schoolmaster, Ernest Clark was born in England on 13 April 1864, the youngest of five children. At the age of 17 he entered the Imperial Civil Service, taking fourth place in a competitive examination of about 600 candidates.[1] After two years in

---

[1] From an unpublished biographical account of Sir Ernest Clark written by his niece, Miss Nancy Clark, in 1983: 'Sir Ernest Clark', fo. 3.

the National Debt Office, with further study at King's College, London, he obtained the position of an Inspector of Taxes in the Inland Revenue Department of the Treasury. Clark served the Inland Revenue in various parts of the United Kingdom, rising to become deputy chief inspector of taxes as Assistant Secretary to the Board of Inland Revenue. In 1904 he had been seconded to the Cape Government (in what was to become part of the Union of South Africa) to inaugurate a new system of income tax. In 1919 he was appointed to the Royal Commission on Income Tax which conducted a comprehensive enquiry under the chairmanship of Lord Colwyn. The Commission's Report was presented in March 1920, and Ernest Clark was knighted on the recommendation of Lord Colwyn.

A very meticulous, hard-working, and hard-driving individual, Clark was also a man of great social charm. He had risen in society by sheer hard work and believed that the Victorian era gave great opportunities to the talented, ambitious, and energetic—and this was undoubtedly how he saw himself.[2] While still a teenager Clark had come under the influence of the Evangelical movement and become a committed Christian, taking part in street-preaching and tract distribution. Although Sir Ernest was later to lose his religious fervour, many of the Evangelical influences remained with him, guiding his moral outlook and philosophy of life, including his views on hard work. He felt that one of the greatest joys in life was to tackle a difficult job and to do a hard day's work, once declaring his belief 'that really hard work, even to the point of exhaustion, is not an evil, but a benefit to a vigorous constitution'.[3]

Sir John Anderson, chairman of the Board of Inland Revenue, became joint Under-Secretary for Ireland in May 1920. Shortly after Sir John had gone to Dublin, Sir Ernest offered to go over if the former felt he could be of any help. However, Sir Ernest heard no more about his offer until September 1920 when he received a letter from Anderson 'asking me whether I was still in a mind to come to Ireland and if so, whether I would take the position at Belfast of Assistant Under-Secretary for Ireland, a position which had been newly created under pressure from the Members of Parliament of Northern Ireland'.[4] The letter ended by telling Clark to see the Irish Chief Secretary, Sir Hamar Greenwood,

[2] From an interview with Miss Nancy Clark, the niece of Sir Ernest Clark, at her home in Hadley Wood on 21 Jan. 1988.
[3] A quotation from Miss Clark's account (see n. 1 above), second chap., fo. 6, in which she draws from Sir Ernest's own autobiographical notes.
[4] Unpublished autobiographical notes written by Sir Ernest Clark about his services in Northern Ireland, Clark Papers, PRONI D1022/2/2.

at his London office if he was interested in the post. Visiting Sir Hamar, Clark was told that the post was to prepare the way for the new administration in Northern Ireland, but was given no details of what might be involved.

A second meeting was held the following day at Greenwood's office, and Clark was introduced to Sir James Craig, Colonel Fred Crawford, the 1914 UVF gun-runner, and Richard (later Sir Richard) Dawson Bates, Secretary to the Ulster Unionist Council. Sir Ernest's autobiographical notes record that:

They were full of grievances, and painted to Sir Hamar Greenwood a picture of the deathly peril which threatened all loyalists (including themselves), in the North of Ireland. At the time I failed to sympathise with them and indeed hardly understood what they were talking [about, so] widely did the conditions they described differ from my notions, and previous experience of an ordered government.[5]

Clark realized that he was 'on show' before the Ulster Unionists, since naturally Greenwood wanted to secure the approval and thus achieve the co-operation of Craig to ensure the success of the man sent to Belfast. Clark had lunch with Crawford and Spender and the full meeting resumed in the afternoon. It was then taken for granted, Craig having made no objection, that Clark would go to Belfast as the new Assistant Under-Secretary. Recalling the meeting some years later, Clark declared: 'I remember vividly that Sir James Craig walked across to me and towering above this little man said "Now you are coming to Ulster you must write this one word across your heart," and he tapped out with his finger on my chest "ULSTER".'[6]

Later the same day, following the meeting with Craig, Clark was asked by Greenwood to take up the post in Ireland. That evening he took the night train to Edinburgh to visit Sir John Anderson, who was on leave, to be briefed about his new duties and the political and administrative situation in Ireland. Anderson explained to Clark the role he was to play in helping to plan for the creation of self-government in Northern Ireland. Immediately after this meeting Clark travelled to Holyhead and crossed by the night boat to Dublin. Arriving under armed escort at Dublin Castle, he was briefed by civil servants and military commanders. Clark also examined the general system of records and correspondence at Dublin Castle, in order that the branch of the Chief Secretary's Office in Belfast which he was to head might be conducted along the same lines. Early next morning he was escorted to the railway station to catch the Belfast train. Only five days after

[5] Ibid.   [6] Ibid.

receiving the letter from Sir John Anderson, Sir Ernest Clark was about to arrive in Belfast and take up his new post as Assistant Under-Secretary.

The additional post of Assistant Under-Secretary had been created as a result of Craig's meeting with ministers on 2 September. The first reports about the creation of the new post broke on 13 September, and by 15 September the name of Sir Ernest Clark had been announced as the person to fill the post. Belfast nationalists were hostile to the creation of the office, regarding it as 'preparation for partition',[7] but it was this very thought that delighted the Ulster unionists. However, the delay between the conference of ministers and the official announcement on 13 September allowed speculation and rumour to increase. Ulster unionists had begun to expect the complete realization of their objectives, and early statements appeared to confirm that they had achieved all they wanted. However, as details became clear about exactly what was proposed, the Ulster unionist reaction became guarded and, following the appointment of Clark, even cool. As mentioned earlier, the London government realized that by conceding a local civil authority for Belfast and a police auxiliary, they could be accused of surrendering to Craig's demands. In an effort to retain its appearance of impartiality, the government was attempting to find a compromise which would prove acceptable to both unionists and nationalists.

The Ulster unionists had wanted the appointment of an Under-Secretary specifically for the area to form Northern Ireland, since he could bypass the Under-Secretary in Dublin and report directly to the Irish Chief Secretary. However, the government appointed an Assistant Under-Secretary who was to be subordinate to the Under-Secretaries in Dublin and had to report to them. Unionists were disappointed by the new post's lack of autonomy from Dublin, believing that the nationalist 'sympathies of the permanent official staff at Dublin Castle are a matter of common knowledge'.[8] The disappointment of the Ulster unionists was all the greater when they realized that the person appointed to the post was to be from an administrative background. Indeed, the unionists really seemed to have been talking—publicly at least—about the appointment of a Parliamentary Under-Secretary. There had even been intense speculation that Charles Craig MP, brother of Sir James, would be appointed.[9]

Unionist disappointment turned to dismay when, after his appointment, Sir Ernest Clark, in Dublin for a briefing before proceeding

---

[7] *Irish News*, 14 Sept. 1920.   [8] *Belfast Newsletter*, 16 Sept. 1920.
[9] *Pall Mall Gazette*, 14 Sept. 1920; *Daily Mirror*, 15 Sept. 1920; and *Western Morning News*, 15 Sept. 1920.

to Belfast, stated that he would be sending his reports to Sir John
Anderson and added that his appointment was purely administrative
and had no political significance, and that to 'say that his appointment
was a preliminary step towards the partition of Ireland is quite untrue'.[10]
During his first few days in Belfast, Clark realized that there was a
certain resentment and opposition in political circles to his appointment—from nationalists, who opposed the creation of the post, and
from unionists, because of its limited role. However, it was not long
before the fears and suspicions of the Ulster unionists were allayed.
After all, Clark had not been imposed on Ulster against their wishes—
Craig himself had made no objections to his appointment. Ulster
unionists realized that at least a locally based administrator could look
after local interests.

Our interests are frequently neglected, either because Parliament is too busy
or there is no Minister charged with the duty of pressing them upon the consideration of the Government. The state of primary education in Belfast is an
example. The want of school accommodation in Belfast is notorious, and the
failure to provide it is an administrative scandal.[11]

As he travelled from Dublin to Belfast by train, on 18 September
1920, to take up his new post, Clark reflected on

the magnitude of the task, which I was to attempt to accomplish [and which]
rather appalled me[.] I had realized in my talks with Anderson and with Cope
and other officials at Dublin Castle, that for the moment, I was literally alone
and that [on] my shoulders lay heavy responsibilities, not only for inaugurating
the work of the new office of Assistant Under-Secretary which had been created,
but also for those preparatory measures which would be necessary for ultimately bringing into existence the separate government of Northern Ireland.[12]

Arriving in Belfast, he was met by the general commanding military
forces, Sir Guy Bainbridge, the chief of police, J. F. Gelston, and the
Lord Mayor of Belfast, William—afterwards Sir William—Coates. The
Lord Mayor not only provided Clark with an office but also made
available his private apartments at the City Hall and supplied him with
a clerk and a shorthand writer. Thus equipped, Clark was able immediately upon his arrival to begin work and take up his duties (no doubt
the very reason why the Ulster Unionist Lord Mayor and the unionist
establishment in general were keen to provide all possible assistance,
assistance which Clark himself acknowledged).

Clark met various local dignitaries on his first day, lunched with the
Lord Mayor at the Ulster Club, made arrangements for a permanent

---

[10] *Irish News*, 17 Sept. 1920.   [11] *Belfast Newsletter*, 14 Sept. 1920.
[12] Clark's autobiographical notes, PRONI D1022/2/2.

office, and selected as his personal assistant/private secretary Captain
C. H. Petherick. Petherick, then an assistant inspector of taxes in one
of the Belfast districts, had previously served during the war with an
Ulster regiment, the Inniskilling Fusiliers. Clark was later to say that
Petherick was 'specially suited for the post as Private Secretary on
account of his general tact and ability, and also owing to his army
service in a North of Ireland Regiment. His general knowledge of
Northern Ireland has also been very useful.'[13] The appointment of
Petherick helped restore unionist confidence in the administration and
thaw many unionists' initial coolness towards, and suspicion of, Clark.

On the evening of his first day in Belfast, Clark had a late dinner at
his hotel with the Belfast Police Commissioner, Gelston, and his principal District Inspector, Harrison. Among other business, they discussed
security arrangements to protect Sir Ernest from terrorist attack and,
talking till late at night, they also heard, as he observed:

occasional firing in the neighbourhood for York Street was one of the disturbed
areas, but that did not seem to worry my visitors. It was an instance common
to most evenings, as I afterwards found out, for someone to start firing and for
some of 'the other side' to reply, generally doing no damage, but sometimes
producing more or less serious casualties.[14]

Sir Ernest spent the first few days meeting prominent citizens and
the various interest groups in Belfast. By 30 September he had opened
a permanent office at the Scottish Provident Buildings situated in
Belfast's city-centre, in what had previously been the office of the Land
Valuation Department. Alterations were carried out to the suite of
offices while the police put up steel shutters and placed an armed guard
at the entrance.[15]

On 12 October the Under-Secretary, Sir John Anderson, wrote to
Clark further defining his duties. He pointed out that the Chief Secretary's Office was the political headquarters of the Irish government,
and in addition exercised supervisory authority over services such as
education, prisons, and local government. He added:

Your office functioning for the six counties will be concerned primarily with
the former and only incidentally with the latter category of work. Matters
arising out of the political situation of the six counties and in connection with
the special measures to be taken for the raising of a Force of Special Constabulary will, I anticipate, practically monopolise your time and that of your staff.
In addition you will, of course, be available as the principal representative of

---

[13] Clark to Sir John Anderson, 20 Oct. 1920, PRONI D1022/2/1.
[14] Clark's autobiographical notes, PRONI D1022/2/2.
[15] Clark to the Secretary of the Board of Works, Dublin, 26 Mar. 1921, Assistant
Under-Secretary's Papers, PRONI AUS1/2.

the Civil Government in Ulster to deal with any special problems that may arise in connection with the services which are administered for Ireland as a whole, but in such a case there will be no shifting of the responsibility here.

There will be no decentralisation of general services such as Education, Local Government, Public Health etc which are administered for the country as a whole; but the Assistant Under Secretary in his capacity as the principal representative of the Civil Government in the six counties will be available for consultation and reference on such matters.[16]

The last sentence in Anderson's letter left the door open for Clark's involvement in the organization of such services as the steps to separation were carried out. The references by Anderson to Clark's being responsible for the 'six counties' were a clear indication that the government was already pushing ahead with its plans for the creation of a six-county Northern Ireland, over two months before the Bill became law.

On 18 September Clark had received a telegram from the Irish Chief Secretary, Sir Hamar Greenwood, reminding him that it was 'a matter of paramount importance that the Catholic workers in Belfast area who had been expelled from employment should be restored and your most urgent duty is to get in touch with employers and leaders of public opinion and do all in your power to insure the restoration of normal employment'.[17] Clark, writing to the Chief Secretary on the same day, reported that he had already met a number of prominent persons, while on 21 September he indicated that he was taking every practicable step to help secure the reinstatement of expelled workers. Clark identified the causes of the expulsions of Roman Catholic workers as an emotional reaction, a desire for retaliation for the expulsion of Protestant workmen from the Londonderry dockyards, and anger (if not fear) at the spread of the IRA murder campaign into Ulster, but he found no evidence of a conspiracy organized by the unionist leadership to create a systematic 'pogrom' (as has often been alleged by nationalists).[18] Indeed, he found that when the first violence of the rioting had calmed down, many of the expelled workers, especially those in the linen industry, returned to work. Peace committees, containing representatives of all factions, and including the loyalist workers' Vigilance Committee, were formed and several conferences took place, but a solution could not be found. Clark met a delegation from the Ulster Unionist Labour Association on 21 September, to encourage them to use what influence they had with the Vigilance Committee to persuade it to accept the return of the expelled workers.

---

[16] Anderson to Clark, 12 Oct. 1920, Treasury Division Papers, PRONI FIN18/1/87.
[17] Sir Hamar Greenwood to Clark, 18 Sept. 1920, PRONI FIN18/1/176.
[18] D. Macardle, *The Irish Republic* (London, 1937), 437.

While the loyalist workers had long been prepared to accept Roman Catholics back into the shipyard, the stumbling-block to any settlement had been the proposed declaration of loyalty. The Protestant workers had demanded as a condition before the reinstatement of the expelled men that they sign a declaration renouncing any association with Sinn Fein or the IRA. However, the Expelled Workers' Union rejected such a condition.[19] It was through Clark's negotiating skills that agreement was reached whereby the expelled workers could be reinstated on the understanding that they were not, on their honour, associated with Sinn Fein. Clark was worried that the workers as a body would not accept the conclusions of the conference, and felt that:

it would greatly add to the chance of a general return to work if action in regard to the enlisting of a Special Constabulary throughout Ireland—to which I referred in my report yesterday—were taken without any further delay. The Loyalists having proved better than their word will expect an early fulfilment of what they regard as an absolute pledge by the Government, viz to form an armed Constabulary at once. I am seeing General Tudor tomorrow.[20]

The murder of two policemen and the wounding of a third by the IRA in Belfast, which caused further fighting at the end of September between unionists and nationalists, largely nullified the agreement and prevented a full return to work as tension and tempers rose once again. Many felt the IRA had committed the murders in order to polarize society, to prevent the reinstatement of expelled workers, and so to make propaganda capital out of the plight of these workers and the hardships which they were enduring.[21]

The fresh outbreak of trouble convinced Sir Ernest Clark, if he needed further convincing, that action to form an armed force of special constables should be taken immediately. The formation of such a force would provide the badly needed psychological protection which unionists required to calm their fears of a full-scale IRA offensive against an Ulster which was apparently unguarded and undefended. It was felt that eliminating such fears would thus remove the potential for spontaneous action by grass-roots loyalists, such as that which led to the shipyard expulsions. Writing to Sir John Anderson, Clark reported that there 'exists in Belfast a feeling of insecurity . . . due to the recent developments of Sinn Fein activity . . . but the secret information in

[19] Mr E. Gullery, Hon. Sec. of the Expelled Workers' Union, to Clark, 24 Nov. 1920, PRONI FIN18/1/176.
[20] Clark to Anderson, 23 Sept. 1920, PRONI FIN18/1/176.
[21] Meeting of the Ulster Unionist Labour Association with Clark on 5 Nov. 1920, PRONI FIN18/1/176.

the possession of the Government, of which the Police Commissioner here has had notifications, affords justification for the feeling'.[22]

Recognizing the need, as well as the demand, for a Special Constabulary, Clark applied himself to the planning and organizing of such a force. By 22 October 1920—less than five weeks after his appointment—the details of the new Special Constabulary, which was to comprise three categories, were published. Class A, or 'A' Specials, were to be paid and full-time, but would only serve within the division where they were recruited. They would have the same arms and equipment as the RIC. Class B, or 'B' Specials, were to be part-time and unpaid, apart from a small allowance for service and wear and tear of clothes. Their arms and equipment were to be determined by the police county commander. The 'B' Specials were to do 'occasional duty, usually one evening per week, exclusive of training drills, in an area convenient to the members, day duties being required only in an emergency'.[23] Class C, or 'C' Specials, were to be a reserve force and were to be called out in case of emergency. Initially recruitment, which commenced on 1 November, was confined to Belfast and County Tyrone, but it soon extended to all the counties that were later to form Northern Ireland.

Clark did not so much establish the Special Constabulary as create it. Using powers available under the Special Constables Act, 1832, he enthusiastically and energetically set about forming the new force. He designed and arranged for the production of application and enrolment forms, prepared the oath which was to be taken by the new special constables, decided what uniforms, if any, should be worn by the different categories of special constables, and arranged for the supply of uniforms, arms, and equipment. So meticulous was Clark in his preparations for the new force that, when planning the Special Constabulary Training Camp at Newtownards, County Down, he even organized the camp kitchen, including the ordering of kettles, knives, and frying-pans.

Although Clark was keen to establish the Special Constabulary, he was also anxious to ensure that the new recruits were of a good character and that hordes of undesirable people did not flood in. Consequently, he set up an elaborate recruitment procedure including the appointment of local selection committees (composed of justices of the peace), whose choice in turn was vetted by the local police District Inspector, and he directed that 'only men of unquestionable fidelity and efficiency' were to be recruited.[24] Contrary to the view of nationalist writers,[25] applicants were not accepted merely because they were loyalist, and many loyalist applicants, who in the eyes of a selection committee lacked a sufficiently good character, were turned down.[26] Clark also arranged for the formation of local advisory and disciplinary boards to help regulate the conduct of the special constables, and issued a memorandum forbidding the wearing of political or party emblems or badges.

On 9 December he wrote to Lieutenant-Colonel Wickham, the police Divisional Commissioner for the province, that with recruitment for the Special Constabulary going well and with no difficulties in the administrative machinery, he proposed to transfer responsibility for the force to him with effect from 15 December. Wickham had been appointed at the beginning of November, having just returned from Russia where, as a regular officer, 'he had been on the staff of General Knox's expedition fighting the Bolsheviks'.[27] The Ulster unionists had been pushing for the appointment of a new police Divisional Commissioner responsible for the six-county area alone, and Wickham was appointed in preference to Gelston, the Belfast Commissioner who, it was felt, lacked organizational experience.[28] Wickham was partly answerable to General Tudor in Dublin but also partly to Sir Ernest Clark, while greater autonomy was given to the army commanders in Belfast who were instructed to liaise with Clark and Wickham on security and police matters.[29] A minute from Clark, dated 10 December 1920, suggested that in order to overcome the strong anti-Dublin attitudes in Ulster, the commander of the Special Constabulary (that is, the Ulster Divisional Commissioner) should 'have the powers of the Inspector-General . . . as this concession will maintain the local territorial connection with the six counties which is a point they make very strongly on all occasions'.[30] This proposal by Sir Ernest that the Divisional Commissioner should have the powers, if not the status, of an Inspector-General appears to have been accepted, and it was a key step in the path towards the creation of a new police force independent of Dublin in what was to become Northern Ireland. Writing on 5 January 1921,

[24] Memorandum issued by Clark to Selection Committees, 4 Nov. 1920, PRONI FIN18/1/2.

[25] e.g. M. Farrell, *Arming the Protestants: The Formation of the Ulster Special Constabulary and the Royal Ulster Constabulary, 1920–27* (London, 1983).

[26] Monthly returns for recruitment to the Special Constabulary for each county, PRONI FIN18/1/123. One return for County Antrim reveals that for 298 'A' Specials appointed, some 121 applicants had been rejected.

[27] Farrell, *Arming the Protestants*, 40.

[28] Clark to Gen. Tudor, 20 Oct. 1920, PRONI FIN18/1/40.

[29] Farrell, *Arming the Protestants*, 40.

[30] Lt.-Col. Wickham to Tudor, 10 Dec. 1920, PRONI FIN18/1/2.

Anderson told Clark that Dublin would 'leave you and Wickham a very free hand' with security matters, but that Dublin should still be kept informed of important developments.[31]

The transfer of responsibility for the Special Constabulary to Wickham freed Clark from a major burden and allowed him to concentrate on preparing for the administrative separation of Northern Ireland. However, his work in creating this Special Constabulary was not so much a diversion from the task of planning for self-government as a contribution to it, a fact recognized by both the nationalists and the unionists. The main Belfast nationalist newspaper, the *Irish News*, stated that Sir Ernest was 'commissioned to clear the way for legislative partition by inaugurating a new system of administration and enrolling a "new force" to take the place of the RIC'.[32] When recruitment began for the Special Constabulary on 1 November the *Irish News* declared:

It should be clearly understood that the enrolment of Special Constables in connection with the proposed imposition of a bogus Parliament on six Ulster counties . . . is to emphasise and embitter the artificial divisions between two integral parts of an indivisible and hitherto undivided country.

However, this view conveniently ignored the reality of the Belfast riots, the expulsions of nationalist workers, increasing IRA terrorism in Ulster, and political polarization, none of which suggested that unionists and nationalists were an 'integral' and 'indivisible' people, or that Ireland before the Special Constabulary was hitherto an 'undivided country'. The Special Constabulary, established to help maintain the public peace after serious public disorders between two communities who saw themselves as representing rival political, ethnic, and religious cultures, was a product or a symptom of the divisions, and not the cause.

The nationalists were on somewhat firmer ground when they alleged that the creation of the Special Constabulary was to 'place a standing army at the disposal' of the Ulster unionists who, once they became the Government of Northern Ireland, could make separation 'permanent—thus shattering the Irish National Ideal'.[33] This was the very hope of the Ulster unionists, who regarded the Special Constabulary as a defence force which would not merely contribute to the restoration of public order but could also protect the new entity of Northern Ireland from attack by republican forces. The UVF Commander in Londonderry City, Lieutenant-Colonel Moore-Irvine, stated in a letter to his men that, in recruiting to the Special Constabulary, it was 'essential that

---

[31] Anderson to Clark, 5 Jan. 1921, PRONI FIN18/1/5.
[32] *Irish News*, 20 Sept. 1920.   [33] Ibid. 1 Nov. 1920.

those selected shall be men of integrity and strength of character', because the 'establishment of an armed Special Constabulary Force marks the beginning and foundation of our own rule in the province, and the success of the undertaking will prove our fitness to govern'. The Specials, he added, could be the 'chief controlling agency during the forthcoming transition stages of government'.[34]

In October 1920 the prospect of major troop withdrawals from Ireland to other trouble-spots of the empire worried the Ulster Unionist Council, which was, as Clark told Sir John Anderson, 'evidently getting frightened',[35] particularly about the possibility of an IRA offensive against Ulster. Clark hoped that the Special Constabulary could fill any vacuum created by the reduction of troops, a hope which was fulfilled as it soon became the key weapon against terrorist attack. By the end of 1920 the Special Constabulary totalled

nearly 3,500 'A' Constables, over 1,000 'C' and 16,000 'B' Constables, the latter being especially useful in the border areas where terrain and opponents were familiar to the local part-timers. These men, however, were themselves vulnerable to attack in their homes and at work in areas where traditional sectarian hatreds exacerbated the political ambitions of nationalists and unionists. Born of the brutal clashes of the previous year, this force had been increasingly deployed in support of the RIC, the barrage of hostile propaganda mounted against it being in part a measure of its very effectiveness.[36]

Having transferred responsibility for the Special Constabulary to Wickham, Sir Ernest once again tackled the problem of the expelled workers. He was, however, unable to find a formula which would satisfy both unionists and nationalists and allow a return to work. Although the creation of the Special Constabulary had provided the grass-roots loyalists with psychological—and physical—protection against IRA attacks, tensions and antagonism remained. The question of the return of the expelled workers was further complicated by the deteriorating economic situation. Writing to Sir Hamar Greenwood on 20 December 1920, Clark reported:

When I saw Sir James Craig in Belfast some time since, he thought that I was beating the air in endeavouring to bring about a reconciliation and expressed the opinion that at the bottom of the opposition of the workers in the yards to the return of their fellows, was a knowledge on their part that the shipbuilding industry had less prosperous times before it and that to bring back the workers would only lead to discharges later on.[37]

[34] Lt.-Col. Moore-Irvine to Londonderry City UVF, 26 Nov. 1920, PRONI FIN18/1/65.
[35] Clark to Anderson, 19 Oct. 1920, PRONI FIN18/1/131.
[36] D. Harkness, *Northern Ireland Since 1920* (Dublin, 1983), 18–19.
[37] Clark to Greenwood, 20 Dec. 1920, PRONI FIN18/1/176.

While this economic fear among the workers gave rise to no rivalry at an individual level, it led to increased group solidarity, setting loyalist workers collectively against the republican workers. As most of the latter had only been recruited to the shipyards during the war, when the regular workers had volunteered for military service, they were clearly recognizable as a group.[38]

The 'Belfast Boycott', which began shortly after the expulsions, also served to heighten tension and make a reinstatement of workers more difficult. The campaign, which was supported by the Roman Catholic Church and the whole spectrum of nationalist opinion, was designed to undermine economically Belfast and other predominantly loyalist towns by means of financial isolation and commercial boycott. The policy against the Belfast banks created pressures which, as the Ulster Bank acknowledged, became 'so acute that steps have been taken to ask the British Government to declare a moratorium against withdrawals'.[39] An 'Advisory Committee for Belfast Trade Boycott' operated from St Mary's Hall, the main Roman Catholic hall in Belfast. A police Crime Special report felt the work 'is being done by the members of the Expelled Workers' Committee, who sit in St Mary's Hall'.[40] The 'Belfast Boycott' campaign was regarded by many loyalists as another attempt to destabilize Ulster and prevent the establishment of a Government of Northern Ireland. Sir Ernest Clark felt that 'the Boycott was probably at the present moment one of the main causes of the bitter feeling between the North and South'.[41] It certainly created a form of economic partition, driving a wedge between Belfast and Dublin even before parliamentary partition.

Many observers have noted that 'long before May 1921 the unionists had begun to acquire a degree of effective power in Northern Ireland',[42] and that psychologically and even administratively they had 'seceded from Dublin Castle rule almost as thoroughly as their southern Catholic counterpart'[43] who had been fighting a terrorist campaign for separation. Clark worked hard to achieve a separation of administrative services, or rather made the preparations whereby an early separation

---

[38] Minute written by Clark, dated 12 Jan. 1921, relating to a recent meeting he had with John Andrews, PRONI FIN18/1/176.

[39] Circular letter from Ulster Bank Head Office to all branches of the bank, 12 Oct. 1920, PRONI FIN18/1/185.

[40] A 'Crime Special' report prepared by Sergeant Terence Kelly of the RIC Belfast Detective Branch, 24 Dec. 1920, PRONI FIN18/1/185.

[41] Rough notes drafted by Sir Ernest Clark for his autobiographical notes, PRONI D1022/7/10.

[42] M. Laffan, *The Partition of Ireland 1911–1925* (Dundalk, 1983), 70.

[43] D. Miller, *Queen's Rebels: Ulster Loyalism in Historical Perspective* (Dublin and New York, 1978), 128.

was possible. As he tackled his task of preparing for the establishment of Northern Ireland, Clark often found that in order to discharge his duties in an efficient manner he had to modify an existing administrative machine which was too cumbersome, inadequate, or outdated. Many of the administrative changes which he either carried out or requested were simply intended to improve efficiency, but in the event their effect was to produce an embryonic administrative machine which was to serve the new Northern Ireland state.

One such measure was the proposal concerning the Board of Works. Writing to Sir John Anderson on 22 December 1920, Clark suggested that if he could direct the 'Board of Works, as a temporary measure, to greatly enlarge their official's power here, I think it would help in the solution of some of these problems of office accommodation'.[44] Such a move meant that in Belfast the Board of Works had adequate authority and ability to deal with accommodation and related matters, and that the establishment of the Northern Ireland Civil Service was not hindered by an accommodation shortage. Indeed, Clark was aware of the need to prepare and arrange additional accommodation for the new administration before the 'appointed day' and the transfer of power to a Government of Northern Ireland. Another step towards administrative separation from Dublin concerned application for and issuing of passports. In cases where a passport was required at short notice, Belfast people were now to be allowed to apply directly to the Chief Passport Officer in London by way of the Assistant Under-Secretary in Belfast, rather than having to go through the normal Dublin Castle channels.[45]

Clark received many deputations representing a variety of interest groups to discuss or protest about some aspect or other of government policy. Among these was the Ulster Unionist Council, which sent a major deputation to meet him on 'Ulster Day', 28 September 1920. The deputation—some twenty-three strong—met Clark for a major briefing and discussion about the Ulster situation, at which they made their views quite clear. Clark was also involved with a meeting between the Council and the Irish Chief Secretary, Sir Hamar Greenwood, who was accompanied by Sir John Anderson on a visit to Belfast on 13 October 1920. The fifty-eight men who comprised the Ulster Unionist Council delegation on that occasion included those who had formed the Provisional Government of 1912 and the six men who were to form the first Cabinet in 1921 following the establishment of the

---

[44] Clark to Anderson, 22 Dec. 1920, PRONI FIN18/1/87.
[45] See correspondence in PRONI AUS1/15.

Government of Northern Ireland—Sir James Craig, Mr H. M. Pollock, Mr J. Andrews, Sir R. Dawson Bates, Lord Londonderry, and Mr E. Archdale—along with the man who was to be the Cabinet Secretary, Colonel W. Spender, previously UVF Chief of Staff.

At the meeting with Greenwood—the first the Ulster Unionist Council ever had with the Chief Secretary in Belfast—the unionists left him in no doubt as to their disillusionment, anger, fear, resentment, aspirations, and intentions. The official minutes give a detailed account of the meeting and confirm the depth of unionist feelings of isolation and of mistrust against the Dublin Castle administration. Mr Garrett, a former President of the Belfast Chamber of Commerce, stated that there was 'no use my mincing matters. We have not the smallest confidence in the officials in Dublin Castle . . . We say Dublin Castle has seen this Sinn Fein movement go from bad to worse and has absolutely failed to deal with it.' John Andrews, who was to serve as Northern Ireland's first Minister of Labour, attacked the Under-Secretary in Dublin, James McMahon, who 'may or may not be in sympathy with Sinn Fein, but we know Sinn Fein looks upon him as a friend and therefore we cannot consider him very favourable to this province'.[46]

The Ulster unionists' mistrust of Dublin Castle and their belief that official contacts had been established with Sinn Fein—the political wing of the IRA who were engaged in a terrorist campaign—were not paranoid illusions. They had long been unhappy about the Dublin Castle administration and the Under-Secretary 'Sir James McMahon was a particular focus for concern, allayed only by the presence of the strongly unionist Assistant Under-Secretary, Sir John Taylor. In May 1920 Taylor was replaced by [Alfred] Cope, who was soon rumoured to be in contact with Sinn Fein, and the Ulster Unionists' suspicions were multiplied.'[47] Coalition Liberals in the government at Westminster, such as H. A. L. Fisher MP, had pressed the government for a conciliatory Irish policy, and while it did not accept Fisher's political policy, his arguments for administrative reform of the Irish Office were adopted, if only in part.[48] One tangible result of the reforms was the appointment to Dublin of a new team of senior civil servants from Britain.

These new men, nearly all of whom held similar views to Fisher, made political accommodation with Sinn Fein possible by laying

[46] Minutes of a meeting on 13 Oct. 1920 between the Irish Chief Secretary and a delegation from the Ulster Unionist Council, PRONI FIN18/1/125.

[47] Farrell, *Arming the Protestants*, 36.

[48] J. McColgan, *British Policy and the Irish Administration, 1920–1922* (London, 1983), 9.

discreet yet solid foundations for later negotiations, and it was their appointment which worried the Ulster unionists. Following upon the appointment of Sir John Anderson as joint Under-Secretary came that of Cope, Mark Sturgis (who acted as Anderson's private secretary), G. G. Whiskard, and T. D. Fairgrave. In common with Sir James McMahon and W. E. Wylie, legal adviser to the Irish government, they believed in Dominion Home Rule for Ireland and began to develop a new policy towards this end. They assumed that the IRA could not be defeated by military measures, and therefore concluded that only a political settlement could be achieved. The removal from within Dublin Castle of senior civil servants who believed in the military defeat of the IRA was the first stage in the plan of the newcomers. Some officers were transferred 'on loan' to various departments in London, while the nature of Sir John Taylor's 'retirement', as well as his actual departure, alarmed unionists. Taylor was on leave when he learned of his 'retirement', and 'he made attempts to be retained in the civil service, but was refused and awarded £3,000 gratuity in the "special circumstances" '.[49]

Cope soon made contact with Sinn Fein, and though it is difficult to know how far he was acting on Lloyd George's specific instructions, he appears to have worked closely with Tom Jones,[50] the Assistant Secretary to the Cabinet and a close confidant of Lloyd George, who, it may be assumed, kept the latter informed, albeit unofficially. The contact with Sinn Fein was intended to produce the declaration of a truce as a necessary prelude to a political settlement. Speaking in the House of Commons on 10 December 1920, Sir Hamar Greenwood offered a truce to Sinn Fein but only if the IRA would surrender their arms. Although this attempt to reach a truce failed, Lloyd George, still seeking to find the basis of agreement for the negotiation of a settlement, kept up his indirect and informal links with Sinn Fein. Ever conscious of the influence of the United States, Lloyd George had received depressing reports from the British Ambassador about the effect of the Irish situation on Anglo-American relations.[51] As Sinn Fein realized, the government's policy in Ireland had 'been most damaging to England's prestige' abroad, and they felt that it was inevitable that the government would again seek a truce, this time offering better terms to help secure it.[52] As rumours of the early contacts between the

[49] Ibid. 11.

[50] K. Middlemas (ed.), *Thomas Jones Whitehall Diary: Ireland 1918–1925* (London, 1971), 25.

[51] S. Cronin, *Washington's Irish Policy 1916–1986: Independence Partition Neutrality* (Dublin, 1987), 43.

[52] Report prepared by the Sinn Fein Publicity Department, Jan. 1921, NAI DE2/10.

government and Sinn Fein reached the Ulster Unionist Council, its members were—as has been pointed out earlier—not only worried and apprehensive but also angry and resentful. The Ulster unionists were concerned that the government, in its search for a settlement with Sinn Fein, contemplated scrapping plans to establish a parliament and government in Northern Ireland. The unionists warned the government that they would 'strenuously oppose' any attempt to replace the Government of Ireland Bill.[53]

It was against this backdrop that Clark was appointed with the task— apart from other important duties—of calming the fears of the unionists. Although he wanted, and needed, to woo the unionists, he was equally keen to maintain a 'just and impartial administration'. He achieved the difficult balance of seeking to gain the confidence and co-operation of the Ulster Unionist Council while preserving his loyalty as a civil servant to his Dublin Castle superiors. When an Ulster unionist delegation pressed him to request additional powers so that he might be independent of Dublin Castle control, Clark—as he later informed Sir John Anderson—'told the deputation that it was a matter which I could neither discuss nor control, but I gave them to understand the condition laid down (and implied in the name), namely, that I was an Assistant Under-Secretary only'.[54] Despite the anti-Dublin Castle attitudes of the unionists, he continued to liaise on a regular basis with Dublin (as his correspondence files reveal) and he paid frequent visits there.[55] Nevertheless, by his ability to identify with the aspirations of the Ulster unionists, he retained their confidence.

In making preparations for the establishment of a local parliamentary system and planning the creation of Northern Ireland, Sir Ernest Clark faced an immense task. Starting from scratch, he declared that: 'Once more I found myself, as I had done a quarter of a century before, setting out to form a new "administration" armed only with a table, a chair and an Act of Parliament . . . with a "clean slate" upon which to help write history.'[56] In creating a rudimentary staff structure, Clark sought the help of his old department, Inland Revenue. As mentioned earlier, his first recruit was Captain C. H. Petherick, an assistant inspector of taxes in Belfast who was appointed as Clark's private secretary and confidential assistant. Although Clark filled many of his key posts from the Inland Revenue, he also drew upon the Chief Secretary's Office for people such as J. A. Kirkpatrick, a staff clerk who possessed

[53] Minutes of meeting on 13 Oct. 1920, PRONI FIN18/1/125.
[54] Clark to Anderson, 1 Oct. 1920, PRONI D1022/2/9.
[55] For details, see PRONI FIN18/1/85–90.
[56] Clark's autobiographical account, PRONI D1022/2/2.

'considerable knowledge of the various branches of work of the Irish administration'.[57] Kirkpatrick would have thus proved invaluable in guiding Clark through the work of the various branches of which he had no prior experience. Many of those who joined Clark's staff were later absorbed into the Northern Ireland Civil Service. One such person was W. D. Scott who, after serving Clark in the Assistant Under-Secretary's office as a confidential assistant, joined the newly founded Northern Ireland Civil Service and eventually rose to become its head.[58] As the office expanded so Clark requested the transfer or loan of officials from the Irish Land Commission, the Treasury, or the Irish Local Government Board to tackle specific duties in preparation for the implementation of the Government of Ireland Act. He suggested that such staff could, at the appointed day, return to their normal duties if they wished or stay on in Belfast to be employed by the new government.

The monthly staff returns for the office of the Assistant Under-Secretary show that in October 1920 (the first figures available for a full month) Clark had a staff of fifteen. Over the next few months, as the work-load in relation to the preparations for the establishment of Northern Ireland increased, his staff numbers expanded but the establishment never rose above twenty. It was with this small team that Sir Ernest planned, co-ordinated, and carried out those preparatory measures by which Northern Ireland became an entity. Though he worked his staff hard, he worked himself even harder (toiling away for sixteen hours a day, every day of the week), but even then he had difficulty in meeting his targets. He often felt that he was not receiving adequate administrative support from Dublin Castle, and more than once had to ask Cope to ensure that his letters requesting information, advice, or assistance were 'dealt with more expeditiously'.[59]

The administrative problems Clark encountered in dealing with Dublin Castle resulted from bureaucratic incompetence rather than obstacles erected because of policy disagreement regarding the establishment of Northern Ireland. The fact that Dublin Castle still favoured the implementation of the Government of Ireland Act at an early stage is shown by two circulars issued in January 1921. Issued to all departments, the circulars asked them to consider how their operations would be affected by the introduction of devolved government. In order to make certain that the relevant legislation for the functions

---

[57] Clark to Anderson, 20 Oct. 1920, PRONI D1022/2/1.
[58] W. D. Scott was a Tax Inspector 2nd class, a Bachelor of Law of Edinburgh University, and was reading for a London University Doctor of Law degree: Clark to Anderson, 2 Nov. 1920, PRONI FIN18/1/87.
[59] Clark to A. Cope, 28 Oct. 1920, PRONI FIN18/1/92.

of existing departments was adapted so as to ensure that the new departments would be legally invested with the necessary statutory powers for the administration of the different services, the second circular declared:

It will be necessary, therefore, to examine carefully every statute which has any bearing upon each existing department and its functions, and to make a list of the provisions which appear to be inconsistent with the new conditions and to require to be adapted to those conditions.[60]

These circulars made possible the essential preparations facilitating the early enactment of self-government and the separation of Northern Ireland which Clark had been working towards since October 1920. Dublin Castle was acting at the behest of a Cabinet dominated by British Conservatives and Unionists who wanted to protect the interests of their Ulster unionist allies by safeguarding the position of Ulster. However, as has been pointed out:

The traditional alliance of the previous thirty years between Ulster Unionists and British Conservatives had long begun to crack. The surging power of a more extreme nationalism after 1916 had made devolutionists of the Conservatives. Were it not for the long-standing association with the Unionists, the Tories would now gladly trade the Orange Card for a settlement.[61]

The Ulster unionists realized that the 'Conservative Party's swashbuckling days were over', and that the latter no longer required Ulster 'as a patriotic issue which might help them back into office'.[62] Indeed, British Conservative support for the Ulster unionists lacked enthusiasm and was more like the somewhat unwilling settling of a long-standing debt. It was the realization that their allies were now lukewarm that spurred on the Ulster unionists to secure the early establishment of a self-government which allowed them to control their own destiny.

---

[60] 'Suggestions as to Departmental Work preparatory to the Adaptation of Enactments', 26 Jan. 1921, PRONI FIN18/1/134.
[61] McColgan, *British Policy*, 49.   [62] Laffan, *Partition of Ireland*, 61.

3

Preparing for Self-Government

In tackling the problems relating to the creation of Northern Ireland, and in making preparations for the establishment of self-government, Clark had to work from scratch. His efforts to build a suitable administrative service for Northern Ireland were further handicapped in that the existing all-Ireland system was bureaucratic, cumbersome, and quite unsuited to modern needs. Consequently, it did not provide Clark with a sound basis on which to work nor could it simply be conveniently divided into two parts to serve the new governments. Among the more important measures which Clark carried out in anticipation of the administrative separation of Northern Ireland was the drafting of a scheme for a civil service. Before devising the scheme, he and his staff sought, through an exhausting series of meetings in January 1921, the opinion and advice of civil servants in Dublin and London. By 7 February 1921 he was able to forward to Sir James Craig a detailed scheme for the organization of ministries, with an accompanying staff-chart for the proposed Northern Ireland government and administration. At Craig's request a copy of the draft scheme was passed to Adam Duffin, chairman of Belfast Chamber of Commerce, for his comments.

Although Sir James Craig held no office in the Irish administration, and thus had no official status, Clark consulted regularly with him on a range of topics. Sir Edward Carson had made it quite clear to an Ulster Unionist delegation which visited him in London on 25 January that, in view of his age and poor health, he could not accept responsibilities which would arise from the creation of Northern Ireland, and so could no longer continue as leader of the Ulster Unionist Party. His obvious successor was Sir James Craig, and the Ulster Unionist Council formally elected him on 4 February. Craig, as the leader of the largest party in Ulster, and the party acknowledged by most people as destined to form the first Government of Northern Ireland, was regarded as a type of prospective prime minister. It was, therefore, perfectly natural that Clark should consult with him, and indeed the Civil Service trade union, the Association of Executive Officers of the Irish Civil Service, referred to Craig as the 'prospective Head of the Government of Northern Ireland'.[1]

---

[1] R. Clarke and M. Smithwick, joint hon. secretaries of the Association of Officers

Craig's Ulster roots were deep, his ancestors having settled there in the seventeenth century, and it is not surprising that his primary concern was for the Ulster people. The son of a whiskey distiller and millionaire, he entered parliament in 1906 after a short career as a stockbroker and after having served in the second South African War.[2] While Carson was the public face of Ulster unionism during the Ulster Crisis, it was Craig who masterminded the campaign. In those 'years as a potential rebel leader he showed prodigious energy and ingenuity in promoting the Ulster Unionist cause. His stability and geniality complemented Carson's mercurial temperament and powers of imagination'.[3] Craig was involved in planning the various demonstrations, the signing of the Ulster Covenant, the gun-running, and the drafting of the constitution for the proposed Provisional Government.[4]

The outbreak of the First World War brought a temporary end to the Ulster Crisis, with a general cessation of political activity, the Ulster unionists devoting their energies to the war effort. It was Craig who convinced the War Secretary that the UVF should form the core of a distinctive Ulster Division within the British Army. Poor health prevented him from serving abroad with the Ulster Division, and his contribution to it had to be confined to recruitment and the provision of equipment. When Lloyd George formed a new Cabinet in December 1916, Carson was appointed First Lord of the Admiralty, while Craig received minor office as a junior whip and Treasurer of the Household. In the 1917 New Year's Honours List Craig's public services were further recognized when he received a baronetcy. However, during the Irish Convention in January 1918 when it looked as if Lloyd George was going to coerce Ulster unionists into a settlement with the Irish nationalists, Carson and Craig resigned from the government.[5]

Following a resolution of their political differences, Craig was appointed by Lloyd George in January 1919 to his new peacetime coalition as Parliamentary Secretary of the Ministry of Pensions. Craig tackled his new duties with enthusiasm and, in recognition of his success, was promoted in April 1920 to the post of Financial Secretary to the Admiralty. Walter Long was the First Lord, but as he 'was gravely ill for much of the latter part of 1920, Craig was in effect First Lord, and

of the Irish Civil Service, to Rt. Hon. Sir James Craig MP, 15 Apr. 1921, Treasury Division Papers, PRONI FIN18/1/234.

[2] For details about Craig's early life and family background, see P. Buckland, *James Craig* (Dublin, 1980) and St John Ervine, *Craigavon: Ulsterman* (Aberdeen, 1949).

[3] P. Buckland, *A History of Northern Ireland* (Dublin, 1981), 12.

[4] For details, see A. T. Q. Stewart, *The Ulster Crisis: Resistance to Home Rule 1912–14* (London, 1967), 47–8, 61–4, 119, 151–4, and 177.

[5] H. Montgomery Hyde, *Carson: The Life of Sir Edward Carson, Lord Carson of Duncairn* (Surrey, 1953), 429.

his handling of business underlined his administrative ability'.[6] However, the setting up of a Parliament of Northern Ireland required a leader who would be Ulster-based and who could serve as the new Prime Minister. Having just succeeded Carson as leader of the Ulster Unionist Council, Craig believed that as an Ulsterman his duty called him to Belfast and thus he 'decided to go home'.[7]

In the draft scheme for the Northern Ireland administration which Clark submitted to Craig, he proposed the creation of five departments —Finance, Education, Agriculture and Public Works, Health and Local Government, and Commerce and Labour. He made no provision for a separate Department of the Prime Minister, as he believed that Craig would probably take responsibility for one of the ministries.[8] Clark envisaged two main divisions within the Ministry of Finance—Treasury and Home Affairs—and assumed that the executive head of this department should have general control of the Civil Service. The Ministry of Education was to be a homogeneous department with oversight of all aspects of the educational system ranging from primary school to university level. For the first time, education was to be directed from one office rather than, as under Dublin Castle administration, by six offices. The proposed Ministry of Agriculture and Public Works had two divisions. The Agriculture Division was to be responsible for all agricultural matters, while the Public Works Division inherited the functions previously carried out by the Board of Public Works and the Irish Land Commission, as well as a few miscellaneous duties. The work of the National Health Insurance Commission and of the Inspector of Lunatics was to be undertaken by the Health Division in the Ministry of Health and Local Government, while the work previously carried out by the Local Government Board was to go to the Local Government Division. Clark proposed that within the Ministry of Commerce and Labour the Trade Division should look after the functions of the Board of Trade, while the Labour Division was to be responsible for Unemployment Insurance, Employment Exchanges and Trade Boards, and industrial relations generally.

On 18 February 1921 Clark forwarded to Craig a staff-chart and statement for the Ministry of Finance. In this paper he had worked out the staffing necessary to operate the department and had costed the scheme. Over the next few days he submitted proposals for the other departments. His original scheme proposed a staff complement of eighty-five for the Ministry of Finance, eighty-four for Education, ninety-six

---

[6] Buckland, *Craig*, 37.

[7] St John Ervine, *Craigavon*, 372.

[8] Original scheme drafted by Clark for 'Government of Northern Ireland: Department and Staff Scheme', PRONI FIN18/1/90.

for Agriculture and Public Works, and ninety-six for Health and Local Government, while Commerce and Labour was to have a staff of forty-eight, excluding the clerical and typing staff and messengers for that department. He deemed that 'it ought to be possible by a reorganisation of the existing Labour Ministry staff in Belfast, (which includes several hundred persons) to provide for the clerical, typing and messenger staff of the proposed ministry'.[9] The cost of the scheme amounted to 30 per cent of the Salary List of the Central Departments in Dublin and London then carrying out the duties which were to fall to the new administration in Northern Ireland, and Clark was satisfied 'that the cost of the proposed staff does not err on the side of extravagance, seeing that the population of Northern Ireland is 28 per cent, its Revenue 32 per cent, and its expenditure 28 per cent of the whole'.[10]

On behalf of Belfast Chamber of Commerce, Adam Duffin proposed the establishment of eight ministries—departments of the Prime Minister, Treasury, Labour, Education, Agriculture, Commerce, Law and Justice, and Civil Government—which would look after such functions as health, housing, local government, and old-age pensions. Craig largely accepted the scheme proposed by the Belfast Chamber of Commerce, seeing it as representing the views of the people who would be the principal contributors to the exchequer for Northern Ireland and were thus unlikely to promote a proposal for eight departments if it was considered to be extravagant. He influenced Clark to do likewise. Although designed to achieve the greatest cost-effectiveness, Clark's initial scheme might have proved counter-productive in terms of administrative efficiency, in that conflicts of interest could have arisen within the different departments. For example, if the Ministry of Finance had comprised a Home Affairs Division and Treasury Division, the responsible minister would have found himself unable to represent to Cabinet the interests of his entire department. Requiring substantial amounts of public funds, the Home Affairs Division would inevitably have clashed with the Treasury, whose aim was to restrict public expenditure to an absolute minimum. Over the next few months there were regular consultations between Clark and Craig as they considered various amendments to the proposed administrative scheme at departmental, divisional, and branch level. Clark kept his superiors at Dublin Castle fully informed of all developments and of the changes which were agreed in the scheme.[11]

[9] Chart drafted by Clark for Ministry of Commerce and Labour, PRONI FIN18/1/190.

[10] Sir Ernest Clark to Sir James Craig MP, 23 Feb. 1921, PRONI FIN18/1/190.

[11] See correspondence between Clark and Sir John Anderson, PRONI FIN18/1/191.

The final scheme as agreed and adopted consisted of seven depart-ments.[12] The Department of the Prime Minister was to be the channel of communication between the Lord-Lieutenant and the Cabinet of Northern Ireland, and between that Cabinet and the various ministries of Northern Ireland. The Ministry of Finance, in addition to adminis-tering the financial and taxation business of the government, would have responsibility for public works and statistics. The Ministry of Home Affairs was to have two major divisions, one to deal with its Home Affairs duties (such as law, justice, and prisons), while its Local Government Division would look after those functions previously carried out by the Local Government Board and by the Inspector of Lunatics. Art, science, and education at all levels were to be the responsibility of the Ministry of Education, which was to have two major branches covering primary and advanced education. The Ministry of Agricul-ture, with no apparent breakdown into divisions, was to look after all aspects of agriculture and other rural industries. The Ministry of Labour, responsible for industrial relations, working conditions, and national health insurance, was to have two main divisions—Labour and National Health Insurance. The smallest ministry, and the most junior, was Commerce, which was to administer services in connection with companies and commercial matters generally. However, the scheme did not please everyone:

The number of government departments was a source of vocal complaint during the early years of the state . . . Yet the Northern Ireland departments were grouped together more efficiently than under the Dublin Castle system, and it is difficult to see how the number of departments could have been reduced without jeopardising major interest groups and creating undue tensions within departments.[13]

The final administrative scheme for the organization of the North-ern Ireland departments was only agreed as late as 25 May 1921, but had it not been for the work carried out some four months earlier by Clark, the formation of the Government of Northern Ireland would have been delayed by some months. Such a delay could have had momentous repercussions, not only for the Government of Northern Ireland but also for the fledgeling entity of Northern Ireland itself. With-in a month of the formation and appointment of the Government of Northern Ireland, the United Kingdom Government managed—after many months of effort—to secure a truce and arrange preliminary

[12] 'Government of Northern Ireland: Department and Staff Scheme (Amended Scheme)', PRONI FIN18/1/191.

[13] P. Buckland, *The Factory of Grievances: Devolved Government in Northern Ireland 1921–39* (Dublin, 1979), 10.

discussions with Sinn Fein and the IRA about the constitutional destiny of Ireland. Given Sinn Fein's antipathy to Northern Ireland, its creation was certain to be an issue in the negotiations. Although much consultation—and amendment—followed the completion of Clark's original proposals, it was his draft which proved the basis of discussion and it was its preparation at an early stage and final completion by May which made possible the formation of the Government of Northern Ireland at what hindsight would discern as a crucial time.

While devising an organizational scheme for the Civil Service, Clark tackled the problem of accommodating the new civil servants. He realized that in a growing city such as Belfast there was a shortage, not only of office but also of the housing accommodation which would be needed for the additional civil servants employed by the new administration. As a solution to the problem, he wanted the Board of Works to grant greater freedom of action to their local officials in Belfast.[14] By his early and prompt attention to the resolution of a potential major problem, Clark initiated a series of actions which allowed the Northern Ireland administration to commence its duties without unnecessary delay. He also addressed the problem of finding suitable housing for all the new civil servants and suggested the provision of a hostel.[15] However, this idea was not looked upon favourably by the Civil Service staff representatives, and it was not pursued. Those civil servants transferred to Northern Ireland managed to find their own individual accommodation in one form or another.

Clark was keen to preserve the administrative continuity of the government in Northern Ireland, thus preventing any interruption of service to the public and avoiding detrimental changes in the internal administrative process during the hand-over to the Government of Northern Ireland. He wished to ensure that the new Northern Ireland administration functioned smoothly, especially in its first few difficult months, and that the traditions of the Imperial Service would be preserved and continued. He had his staff write to a variety of branches of the government in Dublin and London requesting copies of the various forms and booklets used by them.[16] Clark was not only interested in acquiring a range of specimen forms which could be adopted by the Northern Ireland administration; he also wished to obtain information about the organization and administration of the other branches which could help guide the new Northern Ireland departments.

---

[14] Clark to Anderson, 22 Dec. 1920, PRONI FIN18/1/87.

[15] Clark to Craig, 12 Feb. 1921, PRONI FIN18/1/93.

[16] See correspondence by Clark's Clerk of Stationery to various Civil Service branches in Assistant Under-Secretary's Papers, PRONI AUS1/3.

To this end he collected copies of all publications issued by the Stationery Office relating to the appointments and conditions of employment in the government service. He also wrote to various departments for copies of the general instructions on the administration of the different branches within each department. He had batches of files relating to a range of government services brought from Dublin Castle to Belfast so that he could study them.[17] Reading these various files gave him a clear insight into how the different departments were organized and managed, and allowed him to become acquainted with the variety of problems with which they had to cope (many of which Clark and the Northern Ireland administration would soon have to face).

In addition to forms and booklets and offices to work in, the new Civil Service would need office furniture and equipment; this too Clark arranged. Most of the equipment was obtained from the government stores in Dublin or England, and where there was insufficient stock available the shortage was overcome by supply from the private sector, the contracts being issued by Dublin Castle. Belfast businessmen were bitterly disappointed at not being able to supply the new government with the necessary furniture and equipment, but Clark defended the use of Dublin suppliers on grounds of financial efficiency. He believed that, in the interests of economy, the furniture should be obtained to a standardized design.[18] As the Belfast merchants could not supply the office furniture in a standard form in the quantity the new administration required, Dublin was able to benefit commercially from the creation of the new Civil Service in Northern Ireland. It was while he was making detailed plans and carrying out preparations whereby the Northern Ireland administration would not only be created but also sustained, that Clark remarked to a colleague: 'At the present moment I am more like John the Baptist than any other person I can think of, with an unknown Saviour, who has only one chance in a hundred of bringing peace and goodwill on the earth (or this portion of it), whoever he may be.'[19]

Having prepared a detailed staff-chart for the manning of each department, Clark now had to make arrangements for the recruitment and appointment of persons to fill the actual staff places. The Government of Ireland Act laid down that Irish civil servants concerned solely with work in what was to become Northern Ireland were to be allocated to the new Government of Northern Ireland. Those Irish officers

[17] See correspondence between Clark and/or W. D. Scott with Dublin Castle, PRONI FIN18/1/240.

[18] Clark to Craig, 18 Feb. 1921, PRONI FIN18/1/190.

[19] Clark to Mr Hopkins, Treasury, Whitehall, 12 Apr. 1921, PRONI FIN18/1/195.

engaged on general duties over the whole of Ireland (and by definition stationed at the central office in Dublin) were to be allocated to the northern
government or the southern government by a statutory civil service committee
consisting partly of persons nominated by the British, the Southern and the
Northern governments.[20]

Clark expected that most of the staff required for the Northern Ireland
departments would be assigned from Dublin. Indeed, he assumed that:

sufficient staff will be available by assignment to fill the various Civil Service
offices, and it is suggested most emphatically that future recruitment in the
Civil Service should be by means of competitive examination, which not only
gets the best material, but gives an equal opportunity to men in every rank of
life, and avoids the inevitable political friction which arises from disappointed
candidates if any other method of selection is adopted.[21]

Clark had believed that, as a sufficient number of civil servants
would be assigned by or transferred from Dublin to the new Northern
Ireland administration, it would be able to undertake its duties without
delay. However, as this main source of recruitment was in the hands
of the Irish Civil Service Committee, the Government of Northern
Ireland was dependent upon the willing co-operation of this committee
to secure the staff it required. As long as the establishment of the
Government of Northern Ireland remained a priority of the London
government, the Ulster unionists could rely upon the co-operation of
the authorities in Dublin Castle in this matter. However, as the attitude of the London government changed—as it attempted to reach a
truce with Sinn Fein and the IRA—so the vulnerability of the prospective government for Northern Ireland increased. As Lloyd George took
definite steps to reach a settlement in Ireland with both the unionists
and the republicans, albeit attempting to do so at this stage through
separate negotiations, Sir John Anderson was acutely aware of the
delicate position in which the British Government was placing itself.
As Dr John McColgan has observed: 'a new phase emerged in which
the task of transferring full powers [and staff] to the government of
Northern Ireland was subordinated to the requirements of the larger
Irish policy—the need to reach agreement with the South.'[22]

Anderson advised Clark that, if he was concerned about safeguarding
the interests of Northern Ireland, the most prudent course was to appoint
the Permanent Secretary of each Northern Ireland department and

[20] J. A. Oliver, *Working at Stormont* (Dublin, 1978), 55.
[21] Clark to Craig, 18 Feb. 1921, 'Government of Northern Ireland: General Notes as
to proposed Ministers and Departments', PRONI FIN18/1/190.
[22] J. McColgan, *British Policy and the Irish Administration, 1920–1922* (London, 1983),
58.

then to rely mainly upon him to see that Northern Ireland was not prejudiced in the allocation of staff.[23] Clark agreed that the first posts to be settled were the senior positions. The new government was to be served at its centre by Lieutenant-Colonel Wilfrid Spender as the Secretary to the Northern Ireland Cabinet. Although he had been closely associated with the Ulster unionist resistance campaign, Spender brought with him a wide experience of life outside Ulster. Prior to the formation of the Northern Ireland government and the appointment of the Cabinet, Spender worked alongside Clark in the organizing of the new administration.

Spender, an Englishman, had become in 1911 the 'youngest officer on the general staff, marked for accelerated promotion, and secretary to one of the subcommittees of the Committee of Imperial Defence, that which was concerned with home defence'.[24] It was because of what he regarded as the strategic importance of Ireland that he became involved in opposition to Home Rule. His support for the Ulster unionists caused trouble for him with the military establishment, and he resigned from the army in 1913. As soon as Spender left the army, he accepted a post at Unionist Headquarters in Belfast, becoming Assistant Quartermaster General to the Ulster Volunteer Force. Following the outbreak of war, Spender was appointed as a General Staff Officer to the Ulster Division, and in the years following was to be awarded the DSO and MC. After the war he was selected by Lord Haig to organize the Officers' Friend Branch at the Ministry of Pensions in London. Spender returned to Belfast in 1920 to re-form and command the UVF, which was later absorbed into the Special Constabulary.

Having resigned as Parliamentary Secretary to the Admiralty, Craig returned to Ulster on 5 April 1921 to prepare for, and assist in, the establishment of the Government of Northern Ireland. He was accompanied by Charles H. Blackmore, who had served him in both the Ministry of Pensions and the Admiralty and who now took up the post of Private Secretary to the prospective Prime Minister of Northern Ireland. Although the formal appointments of the Permanent Secretaries to the various Northern Ireland departments were not to be made until after the Government of Northern Ireland had taken office, Clark was at this stage busily engaged upon identifying and selecting suitable persons for appointment at the appropriate time. Clark himself agreed to serve the new Belfast administration and was to accept the post of

[23] Anderson to Clark, 23 Apr. 1921, PRONI FIN18/1/88.
[24] Stewart, *The Ulster Crisis*, 83.

Permanent Secretary to the Ministry of Finance, the most senior post in the new Northern Ireland Civil Service.

Samuel Watt, an Ulsterman transferred from the Irish Office to the Admiralty in London when Cope moved into Dublin Castle in 1920, was selected for the post of Permanent Secretary to Home Affairs. It was no doubt reassuring for the Ulster unionists to see such a person as Watt, who had strong anti-terrorist views, appointed to the key post which would have responsibility for the administration of law and order. His service at the Admiralty at the time when Craig was the Parliamentary Secretary no doubt also helped to re-establish his links with Ulster. J. C. Gordon, Chief Inspector in the Irish Department of Agriculture and Technical Instruction, was to be the Permanent Secretary to the Northern Ireland Ministry of Agriculture, while another Ulsterman, Cecil Litchfield, was to be Permanent Secretary in the Ministry of Commerce, having previously served in the Imperial Civil Service. J. A. Dale, who was to be appointed as Permanent Secretary to the Ministry of Labour, also came from the Imperial Civil Service. He was a friend of Sir John Anderson, and the Irish Under-Secretary may have suggested him to Clark for the post since Clark did not know him until his appointment.[25]

Lord Londonderry, who was to be Northern Ireland's Minister of Education, was particularly active among the prospective Northern Ireland ministers in lobbying for the transfer from Dublin of specific civil servants whom he felt would make a positive contribution to the new ministry.[26] Lewis McQuibban was appointed Education's Permanent Secretary. He was a former Scottish civil servant with a fair degree of experience in drafting legislation. An interesting appointment in the Ministry of Education was that of Andrew Napoleon Bonaparte Wyse. His transfer from Dublin was a 'coup for Lord Londonderry because in all probability [he] was the most able and widely experienced Irish civil servant in educational affairs'.[27] A Roman Catholic from a southern Irish background, Wyse was to rise to become the Ministry of Education's Permanent Secretary. Meanwhile, in 1921, C. A. C. J. Hendricks was appointed Private Secretary to the Minister of Education, following his transfer from service in Dublin to his native Ulster.

Clark continued to press the authorities in Dublin Castle to give information about those civil servants wishing to transfer to Northern Ireland, but he encountered further obstruction and delay. When he

---

[25] Clark to Anderson, 17 Aug. 1921, PRONI FIN18/1/90.

[26] See correspondence in PRONI FIN18/1/90 and 238 for details.

[27] D. H. Akenson, *Education and Enmity: The Control of Schooling in Northern Ireland 1920–50* (Newton Abbot, 1973), 43.

was told that no list of such staff had been drawn up by Dublin Castle,
Clark reminded them of the circular issued on 20 January 1921 to all
branches which had requested them to ensure that such a list was
prepared. However, Anderson told him on 1 July 1921 (after the actual
appointment of the Government of Northern Ireland) that:

while Heads of Departments were asked to prepare a provisional distribution
of staff we did not ask them to send in the particulars into the Irish Government. The omission was quite deliberate. The matter is rather a delicate one,
and I do not think it should be the subject of official correspondence at this
stage.[28]

No doubt Anderson was thinking of the political manœuvres by the
London government to reach a truce with the IRA and begin negotiations with Sinn Fein. He did not want to upset the republicans by
helping the Ulster unionists to establish their administrative machinery. However, Clark was still able to write to Craig that: 'So far as
I am able to judge, the number of men likely to be transferred from
Dublin exceeds the numbers which we might require with due regard
to economy and efficiency. This is especially so in the case of Junior
officials, viz Assistant Clerks and Temporary Clerks.'[29]

In Clark's memorandum to Craig about staff classification and
grading, recruitment, and conditions of employment in the new Civil
Service, he had suggested four main bands of grading—administrative,
executive, clerical, and typing. He believed that the administrative
grades (Permanent Secretary, Assistant Secretaries, Principal Clerks,
and Assistant Principals) could be filled by officers from the Imperial
Civil Service, while the executive class (Staff Clerks and Senior Second
Division Clerks) would be 'practically wholly recruited from the existing
Civil Servants in Irish Services'.[30] Clark also believed that the clerical
grades (Junior Second Division Clerks and Assistant Clerks) could be
filled by those civil servants who had been 'assigned' to Northern Ireland,
and that any remaining posts could be filled by means of competition
open to all local ex-servicemen. The existing Civil Service, Clark
considered, could not supply the people to act as typists or shorthand
typists, and he envisaged that many posts in the typing bands would
have to be filled by local recruitment.

One nationalist newspaper carried the headline 'No Catholic Need
Apply' in relation to the appointment of civil servants in Northern
Ireland, and alleged that the Ulster Unionist government was excluding

---

[28] Anderson to Clark, 1 July 1921, PRONI FIN18/1/238.
[29] Clark to Craig, 26 Aug. 1921, Clark Papers, PRONI D1022/2/17.
[30] Clark to Craig, 7 Apr. 1921, 'Government Departments of Northern Ireland. Civil
Service: Transfer and Recruitment of', PRONI FIN18/1/238.

Roman Catholics from its administration.[31] This view has also been taken up by Irish academics, who allege that from its beginning the Northern Ireland 'government became partial to recruits with local and "loyal" origins, and regarded with suspicion the majority of existing Irish officers who could have been compulsorily allocated to Belfast under the 1920 Act'.[32] A study of the Northern Ireland state by three Marxist academics maintains that 'clear instances of discrimination against well qualified Catholics occurred from the beginnings'[33] of the Northern Ireland Civil Service. However, none of the writers produces any evidence to substantiate the allegations of anti-Roman Catholic discrimination.

As has been observed, it was certainly not

[the unionist] government's original intention to have an overwhelmingly Protestant governmental service. When planning the structure of the civil service in 1921, Clark had raised with Craig the question of reserving a proportion of posts for Catholics, but there is no record of a quota being decided upon. There was, however a hope that all creeds would join the government service.[34]

Although the Ulster unionist leaders did not want to accept an ethnic or religious quota, a concept alien to the British public service, they were keen to ensure equality of opportunity for the individual candidate seeking a job in the administration. Clark drew up proposals which would in practice provide such equality of opportunity for individuals regardless of their religion. In the introduction to the paper (about Civil Service recruitment) which Clark drafted and which he forwarded to Craig on 7 April 1921, he pointed out how Section 5 of the Government of Ireland Act prohibited the making of any laws by the Parliament of Northern Ireland which gave preference to anyone because of religious belief. It was sufficient, he believed, to prevent possible discriminatory legislation which could penalize persons seeking Civil Service employment. He also wanted to guard against political interference in Civil Service appointments, and suggested that any 'attempt on the part of a candidate to enlist support for his application should disqualify him for an appointment'.[35]

As most posts in the new Northern Ireland administration were to be filled by civil servants drawn from either the Irish Civil Service or the Imperial Civil Service, there was—as noted earlier—to be initially

---

[31] *Freeman's Journal*, 5 Sept. 1921.   [32] McColgan, *British Policy*, 133.
[33] P. Bew, P. Gibbon, and H. Patterson, *The State in Northern Ireland 1921–72* (Manchester, 1979), 77.
[34] Buckland, *Factory of Grievances*, 21.
[35] Clark to Craig, 7 Apr. 1921, PRONI D1022/2/17.

little recruitment. There was thus little scope for discrimination in the allocation of jobs, even assuming that the Government of Northern Ireland had any such wish (of which there is, in any case, no evidence). Any posts not filled by transferred civil servants were to be filled by ex-soldiers 'selected under the reconstruction regulations of the British Civil Service'.[36] The ex-soldiers were to sit a competitive examination and be interviewed by a selection board composed of senior civil servants and chaired by the Permanent Secretary to the Ministry of Finance. The committee, Clark proposed, should be empowered to co-opt representatives of the Queen's University of Belfast and of Belfast Technical College to assist on the Selection Boards. Whether the theoretical equality of opportunity offered to all people seeking posts in the Northern Ireland Civil Service would be upheld in practice, only time and testing would tell.

In addition to preparing a regional government structure in Northern Ireland, Clark had to face the problem of relating it to the existing institutions of local government. Responsibility for the administration of the transferred services in Northern Ireland was to be shared between the new government and over seventy local authorities, most of which were created by the Local Government (Ireland) Act, 1898. The Government of Ireland Act, 1920, did not pay any attention to the relationship between the new Northern Ireland government and the subordinate local authorities. Unfortunately, as the government in Belfast was soon to discover, the local authorities were so limited—in both resources and vision—that they were unable to assist with policies for regional development. The main preoccupation of the local authorities was not the development of services, but how to keep rates to a minimum. It has been stated that:

The most serious defect of the three-tier system of government established in Northern Ireland was . . . the uncomfortable position the regional government occupied between an imperial authority with an exacting Treasury and a multitude of parsimonious local authorities. These imperial and local perspectives were often at variance with their regional perspective, and thus severely restricted the Northern Ireland government's will and capacity for developing satisfactory regional policies.[37]

Nevertheless, the local authorities did not present problems for those preparing for the establishment of Northern Ireland and its separation from the Dublin administration. The establishment of Northern Ireland and the drawing of a boundary between it and Southern Ireland—

---

[36] Clark to Craig, 7 Apr. 1921, paper on Civil Service recruitment, PRONI FIN18/1/238.
[37] Buckland, *Factory of Grievances*, 4.

which, with the latter seceding from the United Kingdom in 1922, became an international frontier—caused difficulties for any local authorities whose area straddled the border. However, these were very few. As the two county boroughs (Belfast and Londonderry) and six counties (Antrim, Armagh, Down, Fermanagh, Londonderry, and Tyrone) all lay entirely within Northern Ireland, there was no need to adjust their boundaries to correspond to the border. Given that rural-district, urban-district, and borough councils were normally territorial subdivisions of the county councils, the border did not pose any problems for these types of local authorities either. Indeed, the only authorities whose area straddled the border were the Poor Law Unions, and only a few of these, such as Londonderry and Strabane, were affected.

As there had not been any decentralization of local-government services to the Assistant Under-Secretary in Belfast, the responsibility for redrafting the boundaries of local authorities came within the remit of Dublin Castle's Local Government Board. Consequently, Clark was not directly involved in the work to prepare local authorities for the establishment of Northern Ireland. On 13 January 1921 a letter from the Local Government Board was issued to local authorities affected by the terms of the Government of Ireland Act. The letter informed the authorities concerned that their present boundaries would be altered and that a new estimate and financial demand would need to be submitted. Apart from preparing new estimates, each of the affected Poor Law Unions also had to arrange for the transfer from its workhouse of inmates belonging to the area to be detached from its administrative unit.

In preparing for the establishment of self-government, Clark also turned his attention to the issue of reserved services as provided under the Government of Ireland Act. The Ulster Unionist Council led by Craig, increasingly anxious about the implications for Northern Ireland in a possible peace deal between the British Government and Sinn Fein, and also concerned about the lack of definitiveness in the Government of Ireland Act, extended their campaign for separation from Dublin to include a demand for the reserved services. Writing to an Inland Revenue official in London on 25 March 1921, Clark said that people 'could hardly appreciate how intense the feeling is on the subject here, and with what horror communications with Dublin on the subject of income tax would be regarded after there is a government here to manage its own affairs'.[38]

Following the formation of the Government of Northern Ireland in June 1921, Clark was directed by the Cabinet to inform Dublin Castle

[38] Clark to Mr Harrison of the Inland Revenue, 25 Mar. 1921, PRONI FIN18/1/195.

that it wanted all reserved services in Northern Ireland to be self-contained, with offices in Belfast, and to correspond directly with their London head-office. Aware that this would be the view and policy of the Government of Northern Ireland once it took office, and conscious of the need to harmonize administrative relations and services between Belfast and London, Clark had already taken preliminary action regarding the administration of reserved services.

In January 1921 Clark met various officials of the different offices scheduled to become reserved services. These discussions were also a useful way to clarify which duties within a particular office or department were to be transferred or were to remain reserved services. For example, the Secretary of the General Post Office in London pointed out that, although the postal service was a reserved matter under Section 9(2) of the Act, 'the expression "postal service" does not include duties with respect to Old Age Pensions or National Health Insurance undertaken by the Postmaster General or such other duties of a similar character as may be excluded by Order in Council'.[39] Those services undertaken by the Post Office on behalf of the Government of Northern Ireland were to be paid for out of that government's revenue.

Following his election as leader of the Ulster Unionist Council on 4 February 1921, Craig had been unable to proceed directly to Ulster owing to his existing Admiralty commitments. However, once the estimates were passed he resigned the Westminster post and returned to Ulster on 5 April. The following day he held an important meeting with Clark to discuss preparations for the establishment of Northern Ireland. Although Craig had been kept busy in London with Admiralty duties, he had continued to protect Ulster's interests and in particular had liaised with Clark about the steps necessary to enact the Government of Ireland Act.[40] Now Craig could give his undivided attention to the creation of Ulster self-government, and in particular to mobilizing the loyalists to fight and win the first General Election for the Parliament of Northern Ireland from which the new government would be formed.

Craig had been pushing for an early election and arranged to 'be summoned to the Cabinet meeting when the matter comes up for discussion'.[41] The British Government continued to be apprehensive at the prospect of a Sinn Fein-dominated Parliament of Southern Ireland, which might obstruct a peace settlement. Rumours soon circulated

[39] Letter from the Secretary GPO London, to Anderson, 3 Mar. 1921, PRONI AUS2/8

[40] See correspondence in Dept. of Prime Minister's Correspondence, PRONI PM1/11–20.

[41] Craig to Sir Richard Dawson Bates, 24 Feb. 1921, PRONI PM1/16.

that the government was once again considering postponing the elections in both Southern and Northern Ireland. Furious at such a possibility, Craig refused to participate in a Westminster debate about possible postponement of the elections. Meanwhile Sir Edward Carson wrote to Lloyd George on 27 April that Craig was 'extremely anxious that there should be no delay' of the elections.[42]

A Cabinet meeting was held on 27 April to determine the government's attitude in the forthcoming debate on postponement. The meeting was told that the southern unionists urged postponement and Sir Hamar Greenwood, the Irish Chief Secretary, reported that all his officials were against proceeding with the elections. However, Denis Henry, the Irish Attorney-General and an Ulster Unionist MP, argued the case for the elections to go ahead. He declared that if a Sinn Fein-dominated parliament in Southern Ireland would not function, it should be dissolved and Crown Colony government be established. Lloyd George stated that he had come to the meeting favouring postponement but had been very much influenced by the discussions and was now, on the whole, against it. He added, however, that a 'great deal depends on the semi-official negotiations going on' with the IRA, but that he had 'an idea that the North will be able to look after themselves'.[43]

With the threat of postponement averted the Ulster unionist leadership breathed a sigh of relief, and Craig was able to turn again to the preparations for creating self-government. While he had been fighting politically to preserve the elections, Clark had continued his administrative work to make the elections for Northern Ireland possible, whenever they might be held. As they were to take place under the proportional-representation voting system, with new multi-member constituencies, there were many additional administrative problems to tackle. Although the 1921 General Election was to be the first parliamentary election in the United Kingdom using this system, the Irish local-government elections of 1920 had used it and it was from the experience of that election that Clark hoped to learn. As early as 6 January 1921, Clark had written to Anderson requesting that J. W. Drury, the senior Local Government Board auditor, who had drawn up regulations for the 1920 local elections, be enlisted to prepare Orders in Council for the forthcoming elections.[44]

---

[42] Sir Edward Carson to Rt. Hon. David Lloyd George MP, 27 Apr. 1921, PRONI PM1/22.

[43] K. Middlemas (ed.), *Thomas Jones Whitehall Diary: Ireland 1918–1925* (London, 1971), 60.

[44] Clark to Anderson, 6 Jan. 1921, PRONI FIN18/1/90.

The provisions in the Government of Ireland Act, 1920, for constituting the Senate were rather vague, with Section 15(2) simply allowing the King 'by Order in Council, [to] make such provisions as may
appear to him necessary or proper for making any provisions of the
election laws applicable to elections of members of the Senate'. Clark
tackled this problem and suggested practical ways of implementing an
election system for the Senate. He proposed that the Commons would
elect the Senators under a cross-voting system which would be a reflec-
tion of the proportional representation in the lower house.[45] At their
meeting on 6 April Craig and Clark discussed and agreed this proposal.
The procedures were to be given in the Election of Senators (Northern
Ireland) Order, 1921, and the Senators were elected by the House of
Commons under regulations made by the Speaker of that House after
his appointment.

Although Clark and his staff in Belfast were making most of the
preparations for the elections, it is clear that Dublin Castle was retain-
ing the reins of power in its hands and only allowing Clark to operate
within the parameters it set.[46] At times Dublin Castle acted unilaterally, keeping Belfast so much in the dark that it only learned of certain
developments at second-hand, sometimes only from press reports. One
of Clark's staff had to write to Dublin Castle requesting copies of the
Orders in Council which, 'according to the press was made on Thursday
last fixing appointed days for bringing the Government of Ireland Act
into operation'.[47] No doubt Dublin kept the Belfast office in the dark
because of the delicate semi-official discussions with Sinn Fein, which
might have necessitated the postponement of the elections. Nevertheless, Clark continued to prepare for self-government, forwarding to
Craig on 15 April a 'chronological list of events in setting up the
Government of Northern Ireland'.[48] In it he included plans for the
Local Government Board to instruct returning officers in the workings
of proportional representation. On 4 May the new Lord-Lieutenant,
Viscount FitzAlan of Derwent, set 24 May as the date for elections and
summoned the new Northern Ireland parliament to meet on 7 June.

Clark was very concerned that subversives might attempt to destroy
ballot-boxes after polling had closed: in an election under proportional
representation such an act, committed during the counting stages when
majorities between candidates were sometimes wafer-thin, could cause

[45] Clark to Anderson, 16 Mar. 1921, PRONI FIN18/1/90
[46] Anderson to Clark, 12 Apr. 1921, PRONI FIN18/1/217.
[47] Mr Kirkpatrick to Mr Martin Jones, 28 Mar. 1921, PRONI FIN18/1/212.
[48] Memo prepared by Clark for the attention of Craig, 15 Apr. 1921, PRONI D1022/
2/17.

a party to lose a seat. Writing to Craig, Clark declared that there was no clear provision in the Act to render an election void should a box be destroyed.[49] It was, however, agreed not to raise the matter further but rather to direct the police to make every effort to guard polling booths and ballot-boxes. The Special Constabulary played a central role in guarding the polling stations and enabling citizens to cast their votes in peace. Clark arranged that the part-time 'B' Force of the Special Constabulary 'be increased in numbers to any extent considered reasonably necessary in view of the imperative need of keeping order at the election'.[50] Lieutenant-Colonel Fred Crawford, a District Commandant in the Special Constabulary in Belfast, noted in his diary that in one police station alone 180 'B' Specials turned out for duty on election day, and it was acknowledged by Clark that, 'if it were not for the special constables, it would have been impossible to hold the elections'.[51]

In addition to working with Clark towards the establishment of self-government, Craig, as leader of the Ulster Unionist Party, had a responsibility to prepare his party for the election, for victory, and for government. However, given his already hectic schedule, it was impossible for Craig to become personally involved in the organizational details, and he entrusted the settlement of such questions and problems to Herbert Dixon.[52] Dixon was Ulster Unionist MP for Pottinger at Westminster and, as an East Belfast MP in the Northern Ireland parliament, was to become Unionist Chief Whip. Since January 1921 most local Unionist associations had placed their organization on an election footing and begun to select candidates. Craig, on the whole, left the local associations to make their own decisions although he did sometimes suggest certain people whom he considered would maximize the Unionist vote in a particular constituency, or who would prove a useful asset to the new government. He was anxious to ensure that the team of Ulster Unionist candidates in each of the different constituencies was representative of the unionist people as a whole and representative of all socio-economic classes and the political diversity within the unity of unionism. Many people often overlook the political diversity. To some, unionism was a homogeneous monolith, but in reality, while there was agreement on the fundamental issues of the constitution and Ulster's right to self-determination, unionism was a coalition of personalities, ideals, and classes. However, Craig was able to boast to the Irish Chief Secretary, Sir Hamar Greenwood, that the candidates had been selected on the loyalist side without dissension, and that 'unanimity prevails'.[53]

In sharp contrast to Ulster unionism, northern nationalism was deeply divided. Although Sinn Fein was the dominant force throughout Ireland, in what was soon to be Northern Ireland it shared the leadership of the nationalist people with a northern rump of the United Irish League led by Joe Devlin.[54] Both Sinn Fein and Devlin's UIL agreed to fight the election but to boycott the new parliament in Belfast. Anxious to prevent a splitting of the anti-unionist vote, Devlin made a pact with de Valera[55] providing for an agreed number of candidates in each constituency and for the transfer of preferences between Sinn Fein and nationalist candidates. The UIL and Sinn Fein each nominated twenty-one candidates. Joe Devlin was selected to contest both West Belfast and County Antrim, while the rest of the UIL candidates were chosen because they were prominent men in their local nationalist communities. Sinn Fein put forward a number of its 'big-guns'—de Valera in County Down, Michael Collins in County Armagh, Arthur Griffith in Fermanagh and Tyrone, and Professor John MacNeil in County Londonderry. Many of the other Sinn Fein candidates were either 'on the run' or in prison.[56] Completing the electoral line-up were the four Independent Labour candidates nominated for constituencies in Belfast.[57] However, the Labour cause was seriously hindered by the decision of the Irish Labour Party not to contest formally any elections until the 'national question' had been settled.

Election day for the Northern Ireland parliament was Tuesday 24 May 1921, the date celebrated throughout the British Empire as Empire Day. Election fever appeared to grip the entire loyalist population, and the *Belfast Newsletter* observed: 'never at any period within the recollection of the present generation has there been such a profusion of flags or such a wonderful manifestation of patriotic feeling.'[58] An English newspaper describing the election-day scenes said that it was:

[53] Craig to Sir Hamar Greenwood MP, 7 Apr. 1921, PRONI PM1/20.

[54] Joseph Devlin had been MP for West Belfast at Westminster for the Irish Parliamentary Party since 1906 and was the undisputed 'boss' of the constitutional nationalists in the northern part of Ireland. Graham Walker has declared Devlin to be the consummate 'ghetto boss' who played the role of the 'broker' in his community, dispensing patronage on behalf of his party and receiving the solid support of the nationalist people.

[55] Eamon de Valera was the President of Sinn Fein and an IRA leader in the 1916 Easter Rebellion. He was sentenced to death but won a reprieve by claiming American citizenship by virtue of his parents.

[56] Official list of all candidates nominated and formally recording those who were returned, PRONI FIN18/1/217.

[57] G. Walker, *The Politics of Frustration: Harry Midgley and the Failure of Labour in Northern Ireland* (Manchester, 1985), 20.

[58] *Belfast Newsletter*, 24 May 1921.

the most extraordinary election in the history of Ulster. Scenes unprecedented in a land where politics are always taken seriously were witnessed in Belfast and all over the six counties, and in most districts over 90 per cent of the voters polled . . . Crowds were waiting for the polling booths to open, and at many of them there [were] long queues of voters . . . and decorated motors with the loyalist colours flashed to and fro in great numbers.[59]

The election was fought with great vigour and determination on both sides, but the results exceeded the 'wildest expectation'[60] of the most optimistic unionist. All forty Ulster Unionist candidates were elected, while Sinn Fein and the nationalists won six seats each. The Labour challenge ended in disaster, all candidates losing their deposits.[61] There had been an 89 per cent poll, and in highly marginal frontier constituencies, such as Fermanagh and Tyrone, there were 'scores of districts in which scarcely one available vote was left unpolled'.[62] The perceived threat of Sinn Fein and the nationalists to the emerging Northern Ireland had helped engender great enthusiasm and determination among the Ulster unionist people,[63] and this, combined with strong leadership and an excellent election machine, gave the Ulster Unionist Party its resounding victory.

The nationalists and republicans attributed the sweeping unionist election victory to intimidation and violence. The *Irish News* declared on 25 May 1921 that the scenes on election day were so 'utterly disgraceful that if the candidates on whose behalf the organised tyranny of the mob was exercised had any sense of decency they would decline to accept an electoral verdict secured by such methods'. In contrast, the *Belfast Newsletter* stated that election day 'passed off without any serious disorders'.[64] Although she provided no evidence to substantiate her allegations, Dorothy Macardle claimed that nationalist and republican 'agents in the polling booths were dragged out and beaten or waylaid on their way home'.[65] In his report to Dublin Castle about the elections, Sir Ernest Clark recognized that it was probable that there had been personation, but felt that, equally practised by both sides, it had no effect on the outcome. He concluded: 'I think the figures, taken in conjunction with the police reports, dispose of any accusation of intimidation.'[66]

[59] *Daily Telegraph*, 25 May 1921.
[60] Charles Blackmore to George Dunn, Admiralty, London, 31 May 1921, PRONI PM1/25.
[61] For a detailed account of election results, see Appendix 1.
[62] T. Moles, *Lord Carson of Duncairn* (Belfast, 1925), 101.
[63] Barry Meglaughlin of Simmons & Meglaughlin, Solicitors, Dungannon, to Craig, 25 May 1921, PRONI PM1/25.
[64] *Belfast Newsletter*, 25 May 1921.
[65] D. Macardle, *The Irish Republic* (London, 1937), 417.
[66] Clark to Sir Hamar Greenwood, 28 May 1921, PRONI FIN18/1/86.

The poor electoral result for the nationalists and republicans—who together had been expected to win twenty seats—was probably due to a weak organizational base and Sinn Fein–UIL rivalry and divisions. The *Irish News* admitted that the election had been fought under difficult conditions, in that nationalist organizations 'had become stale and ineffective within the past three years'.[67] Furthermore, despite their poll pact, there had not been harmony between the nationalists and republicans during the election campaign. Indeed, rioting had broken out in Seaforde Street, Belfast, between UIL and Sinn Fein supporters after rival election meetings. They rioted 'with as much vigour as though the opposition were loyalists, and there was much sniping from revolvers'.[68] Even in the marginal Fermanagh and Tyrone constituency, the UIL and Sinn Fein election efforts were hindered by the 'bad blood between them'.[69]

With the election over, the next step towards self-government was the convening and official opening of the newly elected parliament. Once again, as with the Civil Service, Northern Ireland had to start from scratch. It had no parliament building, no parliamentary staff to serve it, and no procedures under which to operate. However, the preparations to overcome these problems had begun long before the election was concluded. At their meeting in Belfast on 6 April Craig and Clark had discussed a suitable Parliament House. They agreed that Belfast City Hall would serve as the venue for the opening of parliament and suggested the Presbyterian Assembly Theological College as a temporary home until a permanent parliamentary building could be constructed. While Craig envisaged that a subcommittee would be established by the parliament to decide the permanent site of the new parliament, he wanted Clark to carry out the necessary preparations to enable the parliament to assemble in the first place. The officials who would serve the Northern Ireland parliament were to be obtained from Westminster on a 'loan basis' until the parliament had met and formally appointed its own officials.[70] It was recognized that the officials borrowed from Westminster could be retained by the Northern Ireland parliament, assuming that they would wish to accept such a post on a permanent basis. Craig, with his Westminster contacts, undertook to arrange for the loan of parliamentary staff.

Immediately the election was over, and even before the final result was declared, Craig wrote on 27 May to the Improvements Committee of Belfast Corporation requesting the use of Belfast City Hall for both

[67] *Irish News*, 28 May 1921.   [68] *Belfast Newsletter*, 20 May 1921.
[69] Barry Meglaughlin to Craig, 25 May 1921, PRONI PM1/25.
[70] See minutes of meeting, PRONI FIN18/1/237.

the preliminary meeting of the new parliament on 7 June and the formal opening on 21 June.[71] As early as 23 April Craig, along with Hugh O'Neill (who was to become the Speaker of the Northern Ireland House of Commons) and O'Neill's wife, had inspected the Presbyterian Assembly College, accompanied by Dr Lowe, the Moderator Designate, to study 'its capabilities as a combined House of Parliament and residence for the Speaker'.[72] Sufficiently impressed with what they saw, Craig later met the Presbyterian Church Trustees to discuss the details for leasing the college and confirmed and sealed the agreement.

Having won the election, Craig was formally invited by the Lord-Lieutenant to form the Government of Northern Ireland. The administration was formed on 7 June 1921 when, 'prior to the first meeting of the new parliament, the Lord-Lieutenant established the Departments of the Government of Northern Ireland and appointed a Minister as the head of each Department'.[73] Before the ministers took office, those not already members of the Privy Council of Ireland were, in compliance with the 1920 Act, sworn in as members. On 27 May the Privy Council had passed, by Order in Council, the Parliament of Northern Ireland (Disqualification Removal) Order, 1921, which prevented the possible disqualification of the new Northern Ireland ministers from the Commons or Senate by reason of their holding office under the Crown.

To allow for the publication of government notices in Belfast, Clark had made preparations for the establishment of the *Belfast Gazette*. However, Anderson informed Clark that while general notices could be inserted for 'information purposes' in the new *Belfast Gazette*, the *Dublin Gazette* 'must continue to be the official medium of publication as regards all statutory notices until the services to which they relate are transferred'.[74] Thus the formation of the Government of Northern Ireland was announced in both the *Belfast Gazette* and the *Dublin Gazette*. Sir James Craig became Prime Minister of Northern Ireland, Hugh Pollock was Minister of Finance, and Sir Richard Dawson Bates was Minister of Home Affairs. The post of Minister of Labour was taken by John Andrews and the Marquess of Londonderry was Minister of Education. Edward Archdale served as both Minister of Agriculture and Minister of Commerce. The first edition of the *Belfast Gazette*, which appeared on 7 June, also announced the assignment of specific functions to each of the new departments 'without prejudice to the powers and duties of existing departments and authorities pending the transfer

[71] *Irish News*, 31 May 1921.
[72] Craig to Hugh O'Neill MP, 23 Apr. 1921, PRONI PM1/22.
[73] A. S. Quekett, *The Constitution of Northern Ireland*, 3 vols. (Belfast, 1928–46), i. 20.
[74] Anderson to Clark, 1 June 1921, PRONI FIN18/1/88.

of services'. Craig and Archdale resigned their seats at Westminster so as to be able to take up their posts as Ministers of the Crown in Northern Ireland.

In the new Government of Northern Ireland the average age of the Cabinet members was 54: Pollock was 69, Archdale 68, Andrews and Craig both 50, Bates 44, and Londonderry 43.[75] The ministers were drawn from the upper echelons of Ulster society, and indeed it has been suggested that the first Cabinet 'read like an executive committee of Northern [Ireland] industry and commerce'.[76] However, as Dr Patrick Buckland has pointed out, 'while not representative of Ulster society, members of the government were of Ulster society. They had been born and educated there. They identified themselves with Ulster's problems and the preoccupations of the community.'[77] Furthermore, the Cabinet members were representative of the different strands of Ulster unionism and most loyalists were able to identify with the new government. It was an identification assisted by the appointment of members geographically representative of Northern Ireland.[78]

Craig had to form a Cabinet out of men not only without ministerial experience, but who also—in the majority of cases—lacked parliamentary experience. Fortunately, Craig had served at Westminster for some years, as had Archdale[79] and Londonderry,[80] the latter also having sat in the House of Lords. Like Craig, Londonderry had experience of junior government office, having served as the Parliamentary Under-Secretary for Air. Although Andrews, Pollock, and Bates had never

---

[75] Buckland, *Factory of Grievances*, 11.

[76] M. Farrell, *Northern Ireland: The Orange State* (London, 1976), 68.

[77] Buckland, *Factory of Grievances*, 12.

[78] Although in the Cabinet there were three ministers from County Down, one from East Belfast, and one from Fermanagh, this was balanced by other government appointments. The Lord Chief Justice was a former Unionist MP from County Londonderry, the Attorney-General represented County Armagh, and the Speaker of the House of Commons was from County Antrim. In addition, the various junior government posts were carefully spread across the country.

[79] Sir Edward Mervyn Archdale served in the Royal Navy for fourteen years, owned and farmed land in County Fermanagh, represented North Fermanagh at Westminster (1898–1903 and 1916–21), and was vice-chairman of Fermanagh County Council: McColgan, *British Policy*, 158; Buckland, *Factory of Grievances*, 12; and D. Harkness, *Northern Ireland since 1920* (Dublin, 1983), 15.

[80] Prior to inheriting his peerage, Lord Londonderry had represented at Westminster the constituency of Maidstone in Kent, 1905–16. Active in the Ulster unionist opposition to Home Rule, Londonderry was appointed as Secretary to the Ulster Unionist delegation to the Irish Convention. He had a somewhat broader perspective than some of his Ulster Unionist colleagues, but by devoting a lot of time to managing his substantial commercial interests in Britain he lost the opportunity to influence their outlook effectively: McColgan, *British Policy*, 166; Buckland, *Factory of Grievances*, 14–15; and Hyde, *Carson*, 212, 427.

served in parliament, they did have a record of public or political service. Andrews[81] had been active in the Ulster Unionist Council since its creation, was the Chairman of the Ulster Unionist Labour Association, and had served for many years on Down County Council. A prominent businessman, Pollock had been since 1900 a member of the prestigious—and commercially powerful—Belfast Harbour Commissioners.[82] Having served as Secretary of the Ulster Unionist Council since 1905, Dawson Bates had liaised closely with the Ulster Unionist Parliamentary Party, thus acquiring a useful insight into the workings of parliament. However, some commentators, including his Cabinet colleague Lord Londonderry, have expressed the view 'that Bates's previous work was no training for the duties of Home Secretary and his support and standing in the Six Counties was not high enough to give him that general support and confidence which are such factors in successfully controlling a Government office'.[83] However, while the ministers—or at least some of them—may have lacked parliamentary experience, they were at least competent, as they had clearly demonstrated by success in their respective careers.

Pursuant to the proclamation of the Lord-Lieutenant issued on 4 May, the first meeting of the Parliament of Northern Ireland took place on 7 June 1921. While all the newly elected Ulster Unionist MPs attended the opening session of parliament, the Sinn Fein and Nationalist representatives absented themselves. The nationalist Mayor of Londonderry, who was an *ex-officio* member of the Senate, also boycotted the proceedings, leaving the unionist Lord Mayor of Belfast as the only member of the Senate in attendance.[84] The chief business conducted on 7 June was the election of Hugh O'Neill as the Speaker

[81] As well as inheriting the successful family linen-bleaching company, J. M. Andrews & Co. Ltd., Andrews owned land in County Down. He also became a director of Belfast Rope Works and of the Belfast and County Down Railway Company. A leading Orangeman, he rose to become Grand Master of the Council of World Orange Institution: McColgan, *British Policy*, 158; Buckland, *Factory of Grievances*, 12; and J. Harbinson, *The Ulster Unionist Party 1882–1973: Its Development and Organisation* (Belfast, 1973), 139.

[82] Through serving as managing director of Shaw Pollock and Co.—a very profitable flour-import company—Hugh Pollock had earned a good reputation as a highly successful businessman. In addition to his service with Belfast Harbour Commission, a port which yielded a revenue to the customs authorities in 1920 of £8,878,850, Pollock was a past president of the influential Belfast Chamber of Commerce. He was thus familiar with the overall commercial interests and needs of the Belfast and Ulster businessman: *Belfast and Ulster Directory 1921–2* (Belfast, 1922), 57, and Harkness, *Northern Ireland*, 177.

[83] Buckland, *Factory of Grievances*, 14.

[84] Apart from the Lord Mayor of Belfast and the Mayor of Londonderry who were *ex-officio* members of the Senate by virtue of Section 13 of the Government of Ireland Act, 1920, the other twenty-four members of the Senate had yet to be elected by the Northern Ireland House of Commons.

of the House of Commons and the taking of the oath by the members. The newly elected Speaker announced that nominations were open for the Senate until 11 June, and that if a vote was necessary, it would be conducted by post. Parliament then adjourned until 22 June. The Ulster Unionist junior whip, T. H. Burn, submitted on 11 June the eighteen names for the Senate that their party strength in the Commons entitled them to claim. However, as neither of the opposition parties made any nominations, Burn then submitted another six names and the Speaker declared all twenty-four returned for the Senate. The election of these senators thus completed the composition of the new parliament in Northern Ireland.

At the first meeting of parliament on 7 June, the Lord-Lieutenant read a telegram from the King announcing that the Sovereign would conduct the official opening of parliament on 22 June. The formal opening closely followed Westminster ceremonial. The Senate met at Belfast City Hall under their speaker,[85] and opening prayers were led by the Church of Ireland Primate, the Moderator of the General Assembly of the Presbyterian Church, and the senior Methodist minister. The Roman Catholic Primate, Cardinal Michael Logue, declined Craig's invitation to attend the opening on the grounds that he had a previous engagement.[86] With the King on the throne, Black Rod summoned the Commons to attend the King in the Senate, where His Majesty delivered an address to both houses of parliament. After lunch —which Craig hosted at his own expense—the King received, in the Ulster Hall, loyal addresses from various organizations and local authorities.

The opening ceremony of parliament only occupied fifteen minutes, and the entire royal visit to Belfast barely lasted five hours. However, the royal visit evoked tremendous enthusiasm among the loyalist population, one English newspaper observing that 'the King was deeply touched by the fervour of his triumphant welcome, and on one occasion the Queen was seen to be smiling through happy tears'.[87] The opening of the Parliament of Northern Ireland appeared to signify the distinctiveness of the Ulster unionist people and marked the success of their claim to self-determination. A wave of loyalist fervour swept over the people and—just as on election day—streets were decorated in patriotic colours and a general holiday was observed by loyalists.

---

[85] Following the election by the House of Commons of the Senate, it had met on 20 June when members elected the Marquess of Dufferin and Ava as Speaker and took the oath. See *Parl. Deb.* (Senate), i, 20 June 1921, cols. 1–8.

[86] Buckland, *A History of Northern Ireland*, 35.

[87] *Daily Express*, 23 June 1921.

On 23 June the Senate met again when, with the Commons and their Speaker at the Bar, the Lord-Lieutenant read the King's Speech outlining, according to precedent, the government's programme for the session. After the King's Speech and upon their return to their own chamber, the Commons debated his address. Sir James Craig—now speaking as Prime Minister of Northern Ireland—declared that his Cabinet was:

at the disposal of the people of Northern Ireland. We have nothing in our view except the welfare of the people. Our duty and our privilege are from now onwards to have our Parliament well established, to look to the people as a whole, to set ourselves to probe to the bottom those problems that have retarded progress in the past, to do everything that lies in our power to help forward developments.[88]

Having elected representatives to serve on the Council of Ireland, both houses of parliament adjourned until 20 September 1921.

The speech delivered by the King at the opening of the Northern Ireland parliament was a 'plea for peace and reconciliation'[89] in Ireland. It appeared to confirm that the government in London was ready to open negotiations with Sinn Fein. He called on 'all Irishmen to pause, to stretch out the hand of forbearance and conciliation, to forgive and to forget, and to join in making for the land which they love a new era of peace, contentment, and goodwill'.[90] It was a key speech which accelerated negotiations between the British Government and Sinn Fein. The decision to use the opportunity offered by the opening of parliament to appeal for peace was 'due partly to the King himself, partly to General Smuts [Prime Minister of South Africa], who also used his influence with de Valera to promote a settlement'.[91] However, the input of Lloyd George's Cabinet into the speech should not be underestimated. The draft speech had been considered by the Cabinet and some of the more conservative (and unionist) members of the coalition were upset at the tone. Indeed, Craig was told that there 'was a meeting of the Cabinet at which this [that is, the speech] was altered'.[92]

Although the Parliament of Northern Ireland had been established and the Government of Northern Ireland had taken office, many believed that its long-term prospects were slight. Craig's first concern was thus to ensure the survival of his government. The 'very existence of

---

[88] *Parl. Deb.* (House of Commons), i, 23 June 1921, col. 36.

[89] M. Laffan, *The Partition of Ireland 1911–1925* (Dundalk, 1983), 70.

[90] *Parl. Deb.* (Senate), i, 22 June 1921, col. 11.

[91] J. C. Beckett, *The Making of Modern Ireland 1603–1923* (London, 1966), 452.

[92] Lord FitzAlan to Craig, 17 June 1921, PRONI PM1/28.

the Ulster administration involved it in that bitter conflict which was going on ... between the British Government and the republican organisation which claimed to be the true government of Ireland'.[93] The situation was somewhat alarming for the Ulster unionists, and one of Craig's grass-roots supporters told him that 'if it was not for the love of Ulster and the confidence that we have in our great leaders some of us would grow faint by the way'.[94] Sir Ernest Clark had 'prepared the way' for Craig's government extremely well, since it was because of his administrative efforts and meticulous preparations that the creation of self-government had proved possible without undue delay. However, only time and events would reveal if Craig could sustain self-government and consolidate Northern Ireland in the face of so many threats and dangers from both within and without.

[93] H. Shearman, *Northern Ireland 1921–1971* (Belfast, 1971), 22.
[94] Mr A. Saynes, Drumbeg, Lisburn, to Craig, 20 June 1921, PRONI PM1/28.

4

Implementing Self-Government

Within two days of the King's Speech to the Parliament of Northern Ireland and his call for peace and reconciliation, Lloyd George had invited de Valera and Craig to a conference. The ground appeared to be shifting under the very feet of the new government. Doubts increased as to whether the unionists could sustain self-government and consolidate Northern Ireland in the face of so many dangers. Craig called a meeting of his Cabinet and on 28 June 1921, with all ministers present, it unanimously agreed to accept Lloyd George's invitation to a conference in London. There was some concern that the British Government might grant Southern Ireland more favourable concessions than those granted to Northern Ireland.[1] Attendance at the conference was seen as a means of protecting Northern Ireland's interests.

De Valera had insisted that no settlement could be reached if it involved the separation of Northern Ireland from the rest of Ireland, and invited Craig to Dublin for talks.[2] Craig refused, but Lord Midleton, the leader of the southern unionists, and the four Unionist MPs elected to the non-functioning Parliament of Southern Ireland, attended a conference with Sinn Fein in Dublin on 4 July.[3] Some English newspapers criticized Craig for his refusal to meet de Valera in Dublin, predicting that it could wreck the prospect of peace between Sinn Fein and the London government. However, others felt that if he had 'agreed to go to Dublin at Mr De Valera's bidding, he would have demeaned himself as head of a self-governing community under the British Crown, and would have abandoned the whole position that the North of Ireland has taken up for centuries'.[4] Apart from wishing to preserve the

[1] Cabinet Conclusions, 28 June 1921, Cabinet Conclusions, PRONI CAB4/6/8.
[2] K. Middlemas (ed.), *Thomas Jones Whitehall Diary: Ireland 1918–1925* (London, 1971), 81.
[3] In the election for the Parliament of Southern Ireland, the United Irish League decided not to stand and Sinn Fein was returned unopposed for 124 out of 128 seats. Once again Sinn Fein did not attempt to take their parliamentary seats and at the first meeting of the new parliament only four Unionist MPs turned up. In these circumstances the attempt to put the Government of Ireland Act 'into operation in the south was abandoned': P. Buckland, *Ulster Unionism and the Origins of Northern Ireland 1886 to 1922* (Dublin, 1973), 126.
[4] Press cutting from *Sheffield Daily Telegraph*, 1 July 1921, in Lady Craig's press scrapbook, Craigavon Papers, PRONI D1415/A/11.

constitutional integrity of Northern Ireland, Craig may well have
thought that a meeting with de Valera could serve no useful purpose.
His previous meeting with him in Dublin, which Craig had undertaken
during the Northern Ireland election campaign at great political risk to
his leadership, had not yielded any beneficial results.

At a meeting on 16 July Craig's Cabinet considered the document
embodying the proposals which Lloyd George planned to offer de Valera.
It included four key points: acceptance of loyalty to the Crown; the
reserving of naval and air-force matters to the Imperial government;
complete freedom of trade between Great Britain and Southern Ireland; and no coercion of Ulster, whose rights were to be unimpaired.
Perhaps what was remarkable about this meeting was the restraint
shown by the Northern Ireland Cabinet. Although Andrews and
Londonderry took 'great exception' to Lloyd George's proposals, the
Cabinet limited its displeasure to merely deciding that it 'should take
no responsibility'[5] and, by maintaining a public silence, give no indication of what was going on behind the scenes. By remaining silent,
the Ulster unionists enabled Lloyd George to achieve the political
atmosphere which he required for his moves towards a settlement with
Sinn Fein. The question which might be asked is, why did the Ulster
unionists not leak what was going on and thus, by a premature disclosure,
scuttle Lloyd George's manœuvres? The answer, quite simply, would
appear to be that the Northern Ireland Cabinet, while not happy at
the prospect of the government in London negotiating with what they
regarded as a terrorist organization, was concerned first and foremost
with Ulster and the interests of her unionist people. Craig accepted the
assurance that there would be no coercion of Northern Ireland and
that the rights of the new government would be undiminished. He
had thus no wish to impede a settlement between Great Britain and
Southern Ireland; besides, it was after all in the interests of Northern
Ireland to have a politically stable neighbour.

By accepting Lloyd George's invitation, Craig no doubt felt that
he was serving the broader imperial interests by assisting His Majesty's
Government in London to outflank Sinn Fein. Certainly, during the
Imperial Conference in late June, Lloyd George had come under great
pressure to attempt some sort of settlement in Southern Ireland in
order to reduce tensions in and with the Dominions.[6] Craig appears to
have been prepared to go quite a distance to discharge Ulster's imperial
duty but, as the moves towards negotiations gained momentum, doubts

---

[5] Cabinet Conclusions, 16 July 1921, PRONI CAB4/8/3.
[6] Middlemas, *Thomas Jones Diary*, 79.

began to emerge as to the absolute permanency of the settlement which had established Northern Ireland. It was such worries that disturbed members of the Northern Ireland Cabinet. Although Craig had accepted Lloyd George's invitation, it was done 'somewhat reluctantly' by his Cabinet members, who were increasingly 'wondering what was behind the invitation [and who asked] why should not Ulster be left in peace to set its Parliament in order?'[7] While some of the Northern Ireland Cabinet may have had doubts and worries in private about the way the situation was developing, these were moderate and restrained compared to the anger and alarm expressed—and publicly expressed—by the unionist grass-roots.

Among the grass-roots unionists, there was a general outcry against Craig's meeting with Lloyd George and de Valera in London. One typical letter received by Craig from a rank-and-file supporter urged him to wash his hands of Lloyd George and de Valera and declared: 'how can we forget the happenings at our very doors—when one word, if de Valera is what some say he is, their leader—could have saved hundreds of lives—how can we forgive?'[8] In addition to the political concerns of many unionists about possible attempts to subvert Northern Ireland's constitutional position, there was a genuine moral outrage that the government in London should seek a settlement with terrorists. The grass-roots unionists regarded Sinn Fein not merely as political opponents but as the incarnation of evil. That the government should seek to 'negotiate at all with "rebels" whose hands were stained with the blood of their fellow citizens'[9] dismayed and disgusted many unionists.

Craig, however, believed that by attending the conference he could safeguard the rights and privileges which, under the Government of Ireland Act, 1920, granted Northern Ireland management of her own affairs. He stated that if he boycotted the conference it 'might be that the Prime Minister and de Valera would arrive at a settlement prejudicial to the interests of Ulster, and if we complained at any time, the answer would be that we were invited to a conference, and remained away'.[10] Nevertheless, it was recognized that if Craig stretched his support too far it could collapse,[11] and an Ulster Unionist MP, William Coote,

[7] Press cutting from *Yorkshire Post*, 2 July 1921, in Lady Craig's press scrapbook, PRONI D1415/A/11.

[8] Unionist supporter to Rt. Hon. Sir James Craig MP, 27 June 1921, Dept. of Prime Minister's Correspondence, PRONI PM1/29.

[9] H. Montgomery Hyde, *Carson: The Life of Sir Edward Carson, Lord Carson of Duncairn* (Surrey, 1953), 460.

[10] Craig to Mrs Woodside, Belfast, 28 June 1921, PRONI PM1/29.

[11] Press cutting from *Manchester Guardian*, 2 July 1921, in Lady Craig's press scrapbook, PRONI D1415/A/11.

addressing the County Tyrone Orange demonstration, reminded him that: 'No individual bound Ulster, even though he were Premier. Ulster's representatives in council assembled were the only exponents of her will, and she would hurl from power the man, no matter who he might be, who would for any consideration trifle with her liberties.'[12]

Lloyd George met de Valera on 14 July and telephoned Craig to come over to London. Arriving the next day, Craig met with Lloyd George and then summoned his Cabinet to join him in London. On 18 July Lloyd George met Craig and de Valera separately. That evening the Northern Ireland Cabinet returned to Belfast. Before leaving London, Craig issued a press statement 'which came as a surprise to the [parliamentary press] lobby'[13] but which brought some reality into the talks and checked the easy optimism which was current outside. Craig reminded everyone that while de Valera founded his claim on the basis of self-determination, the people of Northern Ireland had the same right to determine their own future. While the *Belfast Newsletter* felt that Craig's statement was a 'striking declaration', and that he had 'withdrawn for the time being from the London negotiations',[14] the *Irish News* headlines declared: the 'Six Counties Cabinet Fly from London! A dramatic end of their relations with English Prime Minister. A futile and sorry display of verbal acrobatics.'[15]

The Northern Ireland Cabinet had been placed under great pressure to make major concessions to the ideal—if not the reality—of Irish unity, but Craig had stood firm. On 20 July Lloyd George presented de Valera with detailed proposals, and by 22 July he 'was home in Dublin with an offer of "dominion home rule" to discuss with his cabinet, and subsequently with a full Dail Eireann'.[16] Lloyd George also sent a copy of their proposals to Craig, who discussed them with his Cabinet. In an accompanying letter, Lloyd George urged Craig to meet de Valera and, attempting to apply maximum pressure on Craig, appealed to his imperialism by saying that it would be bad for the Empire should the negotiations 'break on a refusal by Ulster to meet the representatives of Southern Ireland'.[17] Although the proposals for a settlement recognized that the existing powers and privileges of the Parliament and Government of Northern Ireland could only be abrogated with its own consent, it also declared that the British Government would welcome

---

[12] Press cutting from *Daily Telegraph*, 14 July 1921, ibid.
[13] *Belfast Newsletter*, 19 July 1921.
[14] Ibid.   [15] *Irish News*, 19 July 1921.
[16] D. Harkness, *Northern Ireland Since 1920* (Dublin, 1983), 10.
[17] Rt. Hon. David Lloyd George MP to Craig, 21 July 1921, PRONI CAB4/10/5.

unity, acknowledging that such unity could only be achieved by mutual agreement.[18]

While admittedly the British Government had stated that the rights of the Parliament of Northern Ireland could only be changed by consent, it had raised serious doubts about the basis of its existence. Indeed, Lloyd George, although apparently prepared to defend Northern Ireland against physical force, was quite happy to apply moral force on her government. His preferred option for settlement was that, while Northern Ireland would continue to have a parliament of her own, it would be subordinate not to Westminster but to a Dominion-status parliament in Dublin. Such a settlement would have placed the Ulster unionist people under the rule—albeit indirectly—of a Dublin parliament dominated by the Irish republicans. Given that the unionists had for forty years opposed the idea that a parliament in Dublin should have control over their affairs, it was not surprising that Craig's Cabinet rejected suggestions that they accept a Dublin parliament as the parent legislature from which Northern Ireland derived its right to self-rule. At their meeting on 22 July, the Northern Ireland Cabinet discussed the proposals and Craig stated that he did not think he could meet de Valera as requested by Lloyd George, unless 'it was previously made perfectly clear that Mr de Valera accepted the principle of Ulster's independent rights, and that he gave a written statement to that effect'.[19]

Unable to continue the difficult balancing act between the increasingly diverse interests of Ulster unionism and the broader imperial consideration, Craig plumped for Ulster. He was not merely giving in to the opinions of grass-roots unionists—although it must be stated that he had been under intense pressure to boycott any talks—but rather, as an Ulster unionist, he was acting in the interests of unionism. Craig had attempted to reconcile the particular interests of Ulster unionism with its responsibility as a member of the empire. During the preliminary talks with Lloyd George, Craig had refused to yield anything threatening the integrity of Northern Ireland's position. Nevertheless, he had been prepared to engage in discussions with Lloyd George in an attempt to contribute to the search for a settlement, though he was criticized by sections of his supporters for allegedly endangering the existence of the Northern Ireland parliament. However, with the changing attitudes of Lloyd George's government and the development of an imperial policy which appeared to threaten directly the Northern Ireland settlement,

[18] 'Proposals of the British Government for an Irish Settlement', 20 July 1921, PRONI CAB4/10/4.

[19] Cabinet Conclusions, 22 July 1921, PRONI CAB4/10/6.

Craig no longer felt bound to assist London in its efforts to reach a settlement with Southern Ireland. As an Ulster unionist, his first concern was the defence of Ulster's interests and the protection of her unionist people. His imperialism, though genuine, was only an extension of his unionism and a practical expression of his loyalty to the Crown. Normally the interests of unionism and imperialism coalesced in their loyalty to the Crown, and to such an extent that some observers have failed to grasp that they were distinct entities. However, it was natural for Craig that, when the interests of Ulster unionism and those of imperialism came into competition, he should act to defend Northern Ireland's integrity.

If the Ulster unionists were deeply disturbed at the political threat to the Parliament of Northern Ireland occasioned by the changing attitudes of the British Government, they were positively alarmed by the continued existence of the truce. Sinn Fein had insisted on a truce between the IRA and the security forces as a preliminary to negotiation, and it had come into operation on 10 July.

The truce gave official recognition to the IRA, establishing liaison officers to sort out details at a local level, and emasculated the Crown forces. The USC [Ulster Special Constabulary] was immobilised; the army withdrew from peace-keeping activities and ceased to exercise its emergency powers under the Restoration of Order in Ireland Act (ROIA), 1919, and the freedom of the RIC was severely curtailed.[20]

However, the truce did not bring peace to Northern Ireland, and after an IRA attack on police in Belfast on 14 July the city experienced its worst violence for several months.[21] For the rest of the summer Belfast was to suffer sporadic gun-battles and intensive outbreaks of full-scale rioting. Considerable damage was done to property and many citizens were injured or killed. Not yet having obtained any power for security matters, all that the Government of Northern Ireland could do was to call on the British Government to take firm action to restore law and order. Indeed, the role of Craig's Cabinet at this stage in relation to security matters was little more than a glorified pressure-group seeking, in competition with other interest groups, to influence the British Government. As Spender observed: 'The people cannot understand why, having elected a Parliament, and the Government having been set up, that the Government is not functioning.'[22] As Craig's government appeared increasingly powerless so its support crumbled.

[20] P. Buckland, *A History of Northern Ireland* (Dublin, 1981), 37.

[21] Cabinet Conclusions, 15 July 1921, PRONI CAB4/9/1.

[22] P. Buckland, *The Factory of Grievances: Devolved Government in Northern Ireland 1921–39* (Dublin, 1979), 187.

For Craig to consolidate the existence of Northern Ireland it was necessary for him to safeguard the interests of its parliament, and this meant achieving administrative, executive, and legislative control of those functions scheduled to be transferred. By building up the apparatus of government, Craig would not only be able to retain his hegemony over unionism, but would also be strengthened in his efforts to defend the general Ulster unionist position. Once Craig achieved actual power it would be difficult for the British Government to dislodge his government from office and force Northern Ireland under the authority of a parliament in Dublin. Immediately after the formation of the Government of Northern Ireland the Ulster unionists endeavoured to strengthen the administrative basis of the state. Indeed, as has been noted, even before the Ulster Unionist Party was elected to office, it had been pressing Sir Ernest Clark to ensure that firm foundations for the administration were laid. On 10 June 1921 Craig wrote to Sir Warren Fisher at the Treasury in London expressing his anxiety that those officers who had been selected to serve as Permanent Secretaries of the respective Northern Ireland departments should take up their posts at the earliest possible moment. Craig asked Fisher to 'let them come over on loan, if necessary, so that they can set the necessary machinery as regards the respective departments in motion and deal with the many pressing questions that are daily arising'.[23]

Craig had asked the Treasury to identify and lend to the Government of Northern Ireland senior officials who could assume key posts to enable the new administration to establish itself firmly. Although the attitude of the British Government to the consolidation of the administration in Northern Ireland would change as they developed their Irish policy *vis-à-vis* negotiations with Sinn Fein, in June they were co-operative. The Treasury endeavoured to obtain experienced officers who would be an asset to the Government of Northern Ireland. However, some officers, although very suitable, declined the 'challenge' of serving in Northern Ireland.[24] Apart from the IRA threat to senior civil servants, another factor which deterred some officers from transferring was uncertainty about their pension rights.

Although the Government of Ireland Act, 1920, provided that existing Irish officers who transferred to the new Civil Service of Northern Ireland should continue to hold their posts under the same

---

[23] Craig to Sir Warren Fisher, Treasury, London, 10 June 1921, Treasury Establishment Series, PRO(L) T162/74/E6968.

[24] In 'Northern Ireland Government: Arrangements for Loan of Officers', PRO(L) T162/74/E6968, see e.g. S. D. Waley to Sir Malcolm Ramsey, 23 June 1921, refusing the post in Northern Ireland of Comptroller of Finance.

terms and conditions as before, no provision was made for officers transferring from Great Britain. The Treasury suggested to Craig that his government should make provision to safeguard the pension rights of officers in such circumstances. This, however, would have meant imposing financial liability for the pensions of transferred officers upon the exchequer of Northern Ireland. The Treasury proposed that until the Government of Northern Ireland made legislative provision to secure pension rights (assuming of course that Northern Ireland was prepared to do so), it (the Treasury) would 'apply Section 4 of the Superannuation Act, 1914, by declaring employment under the government of Northern Ireland to be "approved employment" within the meaning of that section'.[25] The Treasury was also keen to protect the pension rights of those officers who would serve in Northern Ireland on a short-term loan basis, but wished to ensure that London did not have to accept any additional financial liability. They therefore proposed that the Government of Northern Ireland should, during the period of loan, make some contribution to the British exchequer in respect of their ultimate pension.

The financial complexities involved in the loan or transfer of staff to Northern Ireland illustrated the need for the new administration to obtain proper financial staff. Towards such ends, James Huggett, a member of the civil staff of the War Office holding the appointment of Audit Officer in the Irish Command, was appointed Comptroller and Auditor General for Northern Ireland.[26] With his appointment, the Government of Northern Ireland was able to establish its exchequer. In setting up the Northern Ireland exchequer and consolidated fund, Craig had cleared the way for the payment to his government of the necessary funds for sustaining the administration. Some £20,000 was advanced to the credit of Northern Ireland, and on 20 July he wrote to Anderson requesting authority on behalf of Pollock to transfer the £20,000 from the Northern Ireland exchequer into the account of the new Northern Ireland Paymaster-General as the payment of salaries of those civil servants working for the new administration fell due at the end of the month.[27] The fact that the Government of Northern Ireland had been formed, that it had appointed civil servants, but that it had no money to pay their wages and depended upon the approval of the Irish Office in Dublin to transfer the necessary funds, illustrated most vividly the administrative impotence and political vulnerability of

---

[25] Sir Malcolm Ramsey to Craig, 15 June 1921, PRONI PM1/28.

[26] Craig to Sir Warren Fisher, 5 July 1921, PRO(L) T162/74/E6968.

[27] Craig to Sir John Anderson, 20 July 1921, Treasury Division Papers, PRONI FIN18/1/90.

Craig's regime. Although Sir Ernest Clark had not yet been formally appointed as head of the Civil Service of Northern Ireland, he was already acting as the chief executive officer to the new government. However, the fact that Clark was still reporting to Anderson in Dublin reinforced the perception that Northern Ireland had not yet succeeded in separating from the influence of Dublin.

Just as the proposed negotiations with Sinn Fein stimulated the Ulster unionist desire to achieve executive and legislative power, so the British Government was anxious to ensure that the Ulster unionist position was not strengthened by building up the administration in Northern Ireland, as that might prove an obstacle to a settlement with Sinn Fein. The Government of Ireland Act, 1920, had made provision for the establishment of a Civil Service Committee to allocate existing Irish officers to the new administrations which it was envisaged they would staff. The Act had also proposed the creation of a Joint Exchequer Board to settle any financial questions arising between the British and the Southern and Northern Ireland governments, including determining any matter 'in connexion with the Irish residuary share of reserved taxes, or Irish revenue or expenditure, or the cost of any reserved service which may be referred to them for determination'.[28]

Recognizing that the formation of the Civil Service Committee and the Joint Exchequer Board was an essential prerequisite to enable them to obtain adequate staff and funding to consolidate Northern Ireland, the Ulster unionists pressed for their early establishment. The Northern Ireland Cabinet, at the meeting on 22 July 1921, had discussed the need to place the Northern Ireland administration on a firm basis as rapidly as possible. Craig thus undertook to 'write to the Chief Secretary in regard to the early appointment of the Civil Service Committee, which had been suspended pending the establishment of some form of Government in Southern Ireland'.[29] However, earlier in the year the British Government had been advised that, as the 1920 Act contemplated the simultaneous creation of governments in both Southern and Northern Ireland, the Joint Exchequer Board and the Civil Service Committee required both governments to be functioning before they could operate.[30] It was thus argued that, until governments had been established in Southern and Northern Ireland and had appointed their representatives to the Joint Exchequer Board and Civil Service Committee, neither tribunal could be constituted.

[28] Government of Ireland Act, 1920, Sect. 32.
[29] Cabinet Conclusions, 22 July 1921, PRONI CAB4/10/6.
[30] Memo by Sir Francis Greer, appendix to 'The Home Rule Act. Memorandum by the Chief Secretary for Ireland', 12 Jan. 1921, PRO(L) CP2444.

The delay in transferring responsibility to the Government of Northern Ireland for local services created financial problems for Craig's administration. The 1920 Act had envisaged that services would be transferred to both devolved governments within three months of their establishment, and during this period funds were to be made available to meet expenses. As has already been noted, the Government of Northern Ireland received an advance of £20,000 in July, and in August it received another £10,000. However, as the prospect of negotiations with Sinn Fein kept Northern Ireland in an administrative stalemate, with no sign of progress towards securing an adequate supply of funds for the government, Craig wrote to Sir Hamar Greenwood on 25 August. He stated that although the Parliament of Northern Ireland would be quite ready to assume financial responsibility when it assembled again on 20 September, he doubted whether his government could present Estimates. This was because, he explained, the transfer of departments, whose expenditure had to be included in the Estimates, had been delayed. He pointed out that it would be 'quite impossible for the Northern Parliament to be asked to vote supplies, seeing that, in the absence of the transfer of functions, they have no financial responsibility'.[31] In order to prevent a complete breakdown of the financial machinery in Northern Ireland, he requested that £130,000 be placed to the credit of his exchequer in addition to the £30,000 already granted. This money was eventually transferred and it enabled the Northern Ireland government to sustain its skeletal administration.

Meanwhile Craig had also been pressing the British Government to utilize the powers available in the 1920 Act to enable Northern Ireland to take over all its services. The Act had provided that, should a majority of the members of either Irish parliament refuse to take the oath to the Crown, then the Lord-Lieutenant could dissolve the defaulting parliament and establish 'Crown colony' government. However, while the establishment of Crown colony government in Southern Ireland would have facilitated the formation of the Civil Service Committee and the Joint Exchequer Board, it would have greatly offended Sinn Fein. This was recognized by the Irish Chief Secretary, Sir Hamar Greenwood MP, who warned the British Cabinet that the introduction of Crown colony government would prejudice proposed negotiations with Sinn Fein.[32] Craig therefore suggested an alternative which he thought would cause less offence. He proposed that the British Government should make an Order in Council under Section 69 of

---

[31] Craig to Sir Hamar Greenwood MP, 25 Aug. 1921, PRONI CAB4/22/6.

[32] Memo from Greenwood to the British Cabinet, 6 Oct. 1921, Cabinet Memoranda, PRO(L) CAB24/128.

the Government of Ireland Act, 1920, to 'empower the Lord Lieutenant to appoint the Southern representatives to the Civil Service Committee and Joint Exchequer Board'.[33] The British Government did not adopt this suggestion either, lest it antagonize Sinn Fein.

While high political drama had been going on with the British Government in an effort to secure the transfer of services to Northern Ireland, Craig's government had endeavoured to make what preparations it could in anticipation of transfer. By September 1921 there were twenty-seven officials in key posts who were on loan from United Kingdom departments.[34] Among the officers obtained on a loan or transfer basis to help establish the new administration was Sir Arthur Quekett. He was appointed as the Northern Ireland Parliamentary Draftsman and, as he was the man who, in his previous employment in the Local Government Board in Ireland, had been responsible for the drafting of the Government of Ireland Act, it was felt that 'his qualifications are unimpeachable'.[35] He immediately set to work drafting the legislation which the Parliament of Northern Ireland would have to pass preliminary to the transfer of executive authority.

When the Northern Ireland parliament reassembled on 20 September, Craig's government presented a Superannuation Bill to apply the Superannuation Acts, 1834 to 1914, to staff in the Civil Service of Northern Ireland. It was clearly a step to encourage civil servants to transfer to Northern Ireland by safeguarding their pension rights. During the summer of 1921 Quekett had also worked on the adaptation of enactments necessitated by the Government of Ireland Act, and on 27 September 1921 the General Adaptation of Enactments (Northern Ireland) Order was made under Section 69 of the 1920 Act.

Parallel to the efforts of Quekett to prepare the legislative foundations for the transfer of services, the other senior civil servants appointed since June 1921 worked hard to make the necessary administrative preparations. Clark's organizational and staff chart for the Civil Service had been necessarily of a general nature for those areas in which he lacked a detailed knowledge, such as Home Affairs. The appointment of staff to key posts, from June onwards, enabled the Northern Ireland government to undertake administrative preparations in a more comprehensive manner. For example, Samuel Watt, the new Permanent Secretary in Home Affairs, studied the different services to be

[33] J. McColgan, *British Policy and the Irish Administration, 1920–1922* (London, 1983), 63.

[34] *Parl. Deb.* (House of Commons), i, 22 Sept. 1921, col. 126.

[35] Wilfrid Spender to Mr Scott, Parliament Buildings, Edmonton, Canada, 27 July 1921, PRONI PM1/33.

administered by his department in order to calculate the staffing necessary to discharge these services effectively. He also identified a few
shortcomings in Clark's scheme—for example, there was no provision
for the appointment of auditors of the Local Government Board—and
endeavoured to rectify them so as to ensure that the scheme for the
administration was strengthened and ready for the transfer of services.
The Northern Ireland government also had its Civil Service team
consider any difficulties which might arise in the transfer or administration of services. The careful planning by the civil servants at this
stage, including liaising with the Irish Office in Dublin, overcame,
for example, many of the problems relating to the administration of
National Health Insurance.[36]

Meanwhile Sir Ernest Clark continued to make plans to ensure that
there would be sufficient office accommodation for the civil servants
who would move to Northern Ireland once the services were transferred.
In a minute dated 13 September he stated that, exclusive of staff in
Labour Exchanges and out-branches, Northern Ireland would require
accommodation for some 530 staff.[37] He had a survey carried out of all
available commercial premises in Belfast to ascertain whether they
could be used by the Civil Service. However, the rise in the projected
staff complement (Home Affairs, for example, proposed an increase
from eighty-six staff to 120) meant that by October Clark was outlining
accommodation needs for 620 staff.[38]

Although a temporary home had been found for the Parliament of
Northern Ireland by leasing the Presbyterian Assembly College, Craig's
Cabinet was keen to secure a permanent base. After rejecting possible
sites for the new Parliament Buildings at Belvoir Park and Orangefield,
the Cabinet settled on the Stormont estate.[39] By November Clark was
informed by the Office of Works, London, that the architects who
would design the new Parliament Buildings had been selected and
would shortly visit Belfast to look at the site. Meanwhile the furniture
and fittings for the temporary Parliament Buildings and other government offices in Belfast were supplied by the Commissioners of Public

[36] Anderson to Sir Ernest Clark, 1 July 1921, PRONI FIN18/1/270.

[37] Minute, 'Office Accommodation for the New Government', written by Clark,
13 Sept. 1921, PRONI FIN18/1/270.

[38] Clark to Captain Street, HM Office of Works, London, 26 Oct. 1921, PRONI
FIN18/1/404, giving details of the number of officers ultimately to be accommodated,
suggested that this would comprise: Ministry of Finance (130); Ministry of Home Affairs
(120); Ministry of Education (100); Ministry of Labour (100); Ministry of Agriculture
(70); Ministry of Commerce (40); Parliamentary Officials (40); Sundry Officials (20);
TOTAL (620).

[39] Cabinet Conclusions, 5 Aug. 1921, PRONI CAB4/13/21.

Works (Ireland). A District Office of Public Works had been established to facilitate liaison with the Northern Ireland government, but it obtained the furniture for the new administration through its existing suppliers and thus, as has earlier been mentioned, the Belfast business community did not gain the tenders. This caused considerable ill feeling among local businessmen, workers, and even some of Craig's Cabinet, who felt that all possible work should be provided in Belfast to help combat high unemployment.[40]

Clark wrote to the different Northern Ireland departments on 19 August requesting them to prepare Estimates for the sum required to meet departmental running expenses until 31 March 1922. Examining the Estimates for each department shows the small size of the Civil Service and the still-limited nature of the government. The Ministry of Finance, for example, prepared an Estimate of £8,850 for staff salaries and administrative expenses, while the Ministry of Home Affairs anticipated that £2,810 would meet their financial needs. The Ministry of Finance had a total staff of twenty (which included everyone from the Permanent Secretary to the two cleaners) while no other department had a staff of more than ten persons.[41] The total of the Estimates amounted to £43,690 which clearly did not provide for the full administrative expenditure to be borne by the Government of Northern Ireland once services were transferred.[42]

However, despite the best efforts of the Government of Northern Ireland to consolidate its administrative base in preparation for the transfer of services, the Ulster unionists were still in a very vulnerable position. As has been shown, the London government, while prepared to allow Northern Ireland to continue on a self-governing basis, wanted the local parliament to accept the sovereignty of a new parliament in Dublin. Indeed, the issue of Northern Ireland *vis-à-vis* Irish unity became more important and potentially more disruptive as a possible conference between the British Government and Sinn Fein drew closer. However, it has been suggested that the use made by Sinn Fein of the Northern Ireland question in the run-up to the formal conference was more a tactic than an expression of real concern. Identifying what they

[40] Rt. Hon. John Andrews MP to Rt. Hon. Hugh Pollock MP, 7 Sept. 1921, PRONI FIN18/1/341.

[41] For details of staffing level and each departmental Estimate see PRONI: FIN18/1/ 347 Ministry of Finance; FIN18/1/348 Ministry of Agriculture; FIN18/1/349 Ministry of Commerce; FIN18/1/350 Ministry of Labour; FIN18/1/351 Ministry of Education; FIN18/ 1/352 Ministry of Home Affairs; FIN18/1/365 Exchequer and Audit; FIN18/1/366 House of Commons and Senate; and FIN18/1/367 Cabinet Office.

[42] Milne Barbour MP, in the preamble to the Government of Northern Ireland Estimates, 1921/2, PRONI FIN18/1/391.

thought was a weak link in the armour of the London government, Sinn Fein perhaps put greater emphasis on Irish unity than they really felt it merited in order to outmanœuvre the London government on the issue of Irish independence. One writer has stated that, from 'the earliest efforts at negotiations it was clear that Irish unity was not sacrosanct and that for many in the Sinn Fein leadership it was theoretical rather than an essential concept'.[43]

Formal negotiations between the British Government and Sinn Fein opened in London on 11 October, and the question of Northern Ireland soon showed the differences in opinion between them. By 17 October Lloyd George was confiding to the Cabinet Assistant Secretary, Thomas Jones, that he thought preserving the territorial integrity of Northern Ireland was 'going to wreck [a] settlement' with Sinn Fein.[44] The moral pressure on Craig to compromise was increased as Lloyd George attempted to push him towards a settlement acceptable to Sinn Fein. Speculation grew that Northern Ireland would have to cede some of her territory to Southern Ireland, or alternatively that the parliament in Belfast would be required to give allegiance to a new all-Ireland parliament in Dublin. John Andrews encapsulated the Ulster unionist position when he stated on 4 November that it was 'unthinkable' to give up any part of Northern Ireland, nor could they 'submit to the Parliament of Northern Ireland owing allegiance or admitting the ascendancy of any Parliament other than Westminster'.[45]

The following day, as 'jolly as a sandlark', Craig and his wife went to London to visit their sons who were at school in England. Summoned from his hotel to a meeting with Lloyd George, Craig 'began to suspect there was something up, and as he put it later in the day, had the biggest shock he has ever had in his life, at finding so many "backsliders" among his old friends and colleagues'.[46] Lloyd George told Craig that he had led Sinn Fein to believe that if they agreed to accept the Crown, he would pressurize Northern Ireland into accepting an all-Ireland parliament. Regarding Lloyd George's proposals as an outrage against the Ulster unionist people, Craig summoned his Cabinet to meet in London, which it did on 9 November. On 10 November Lloyd George wrote to Craig to urge that the Northern Ireland parliament accept legislative subordination to a Dublin parliament. He pointed out that refusal to comply would lead to a damaging customs barrier

---

[43] J. B. Dooher, 'Tyrone Nationalism and the Question of Partition 1910–25' (M.Phil. Thesis, University of Ulster, 1986), 357.

[44] Middlemas, *Thomas Jones Diary*, 137.

[45] Cabinet Conclusions, 4 Nov. 1921, PRONI CAB4/26/19.

[46] Lady Craig's diary, 5 Nov. 1921, PRONI D1415/8/38.

along the border and economic dislocation. It would appear that Lloyd George was hoping to bribe the Ulster unionists into an all-Ireland settlement if he could not intimidate them into one. As one writer has noted, this letter 'shocked and embittered Craig and his colleagues, whose considered reply on the following day, larded with loyalty but with scarcely concealed indignation, firmly rejected an all-Ireland parliament'.[47] Craig was angered by this development, having genuinely believed that the British Government was determined to implement the Government of Ireland Act. Indeed, as late as September he had written to Spender that the situation 'will gradually be unravelled, and my confidence is quite unshaken in Mr Lloyd George's good intentions'.[48]

In rejecting Lloyd George's terms, Craig refused to meet either the Sinn Fein delegation or the British Cabinet, and demanded Dominion status for Northern Ireland. This, he was convinced, would resolve the financial and tariff problems 'which Lloyd George claimed would result from the existence of two unequal governments in Ireland'.[49] It would also have strengthened the Ulster unionist position by giving Northern Ireland greater legislative independence and a more financially advantageous status. However, the London government was infuriated with Craig's proposals, Thomas Jones noting in his diary that Arthur Griffith (who was leading the Sinn Fein delegation in London, as de Valera had opted to remain in Ireland during the negotiations) was 'pleased to see that the cloven hoof of Ulster's sordidness had shown itself in their willingness to forgo representation at Westminster for the sake of a lower income tax'.[50] At a British Cabinet conference on 11 November, Austen Chamberlain, Chancellor of the Exchequer, predicted that the demands by the unionists for Dominion status would cause 'a great revulsion of feeling against Ulster. Hitherto they had always desired to be full members of the UK. They now actually ask for Dominion status. This will come as a shock to those accustomed to receive their passionate assurances of union.'[51]

Indeed, the position being adopted by the Ulster unionists made them intensely unpopular in Great Britain. Tension in Northern Ireland was increased by an orchestrated British press campaign against the Ulster unionists, who were depicted as a stumbling-block to a settlement. The shower of unfavourable press comment intensified as the English press lectured Ulster on how she 'must sacrifice herself in the

---

[47] Harkness, *Northern Ireland*, 11.
[48] Craig to Spender, 2 Sept. 1921, Spender Papers, PRONI D1295/5/18.
[49] M. Laffan, *The Partition of Ireland 1911–1925* (Dundalk, 1983), 85.
[50] Middlemas, *Thomas Jones Diary*, 163.   [51] Ibid.

interests of peace and the Empire or be guilty of the greatest political crime in history'.[52] Newspapers such as the *Daily Express*, which had previously supported the Ulster unionists, now poured scorn on them. No doubt this switch in editorial policy was due to the attitude of the London government, given that many of the most powerful newspapers were strong government supporters. Indeed, no previous 'British government had established such close relations with successful newspapers of large circulation' as had Lloyd George's.[53] The great uncertainty about the constitutional future of Northern Ireland raised grass-roots unionist fears to fever pitch, and set off a fresh round of violence which soon became self-perpetuating.

As public disorders escalated, Cabinet conferences of Northern Ireland ministers were held in Belfast on 23 and 24 November to discuss what additional security measures could be taken. The conferences called for more troops to be deployed, for the number of armoured cars to be increased, and for a vigorous search for firearms to be conducted.[54] Craig crossed to London again and, despite the intense pressure to compromise, he stood firm (indeed, on 17 November he had restated his total opposition to Irish unity and once again called for Dominion status to be granted to Northern Ireland). His meeting on 25 November with Lloyd George in London came to nothing, although he did extract a pledge that Northern Ireland's rights would not be compromised against her will.[55] By skilful political manœuvring, which appeared to show that he had secured the existence of Northern Ireland, Craig retained the confidence of the bulk of Ulster unionists, and his restraining influence undoubtedly saved much bloodshed. Isolated and abandoned by her former friends, Ulster unionism had stood against all the pressures of the London government and related press opinion. Craig more than ever appeared to symbolize the spirit of resistance, and to many unionists he was the embodiment of Ulster. His official biographer, St John Ervine, has noted: 'His countrymen believed . . . that Craig was, under God, chosen to perform a task that must have baffled, if not defeated, any other person.'[56]

Nevertheless, the rumour that in the event of Northern Ireland's

---

[52] Buckland, *Northern Ireland*, 38. For further details of British press hostility, see D. G. Boyce, *Englishmen and Irish Troubles: British Public Opinion and the Making of Irish Policy 1918–22* (London, 1972), 161–3.

[53] C. E. Callwell, *Field-Marshal Sir Henry Wilson: His Life and Diaries* (London, 1927), 296.

[54] Cabinet Conclusions, 23 Nov. 1921, PRONI CAB4/27/20.

[55] J. M. Curran, *The Birth of the Irish Free State 1921–1923* (Birmingham, Ala., 1980), 101.

[56] St John Ervine, *Craigavon: Ulsterman* (Aberdeen, 1949), 4.

refusing to come under the authority of an all-Ireland parliament, a
Boundary Commission would be formed to reduce the territory terrified
unionists along the border. One prominent border loyalist called for
unionists to rally to the support of Northern Ireland, and declared:
'Not an Inch of this country will ever be surrendered!'[57] Scenting danger
from their 'hereditary' enemies, and suspecting betrayal by their former
friends, Ulster unionists were falling back behind the ramparts to prepare
for the siege. If unionists in Ulster were accused of once again adopting
a siege mentality, then they could rightly claim that here was an example of the besieged not lacking in besiegers. Ulster unionists believed that they were fighting a battle against a traditional threat, of
which Sinn Fein and the IRA were only the latest violent manifestation.
While a settlement with Sinn Fein and the establishment of an all-
Ireland parliament might be in the international interests of the British
Empire (at least according to the views of a section of the British
establishment), such an outcome alarmed Ulster unionists. They
genuinely feared that their absorption into an all-Ireland parliament,
dominated by Roman Catholic Irish nationalists, would offer no guarantee to safeguard their interests, and that Dublin rule would threaten
their very identity. As dislike of the English increased among the Ulster
unionists, so support grew for a Northern Ireland Dominion in which
they felt they would be 'in a better position than if we still hang on to
the Imperial Parliament to be harassed and snubbed by the Imperial
Parliament's friends of rebels and murderers'.[58]

Realizing that he could not coax Northern Ireland into an all-Ireland
settlement, and that Ulster unionism had withstood all the moral
pressure he had applied, Lloyd George decided to reach an accommodation with Craig. Coercion of Ulster was not practical, as it was
clear to Lloyd George that the unionists would have actively opposed
his government—Northern Ireland was rife with rumours of new
preparations for armed resistance. In addition, Lloyd George, dependent
upon the support of Conservatives to sustain his coalition government,
did not wish to push the Ulster unionists too far in case he provoked
a backlash among their remaining friends on the Tory back-benches.
In particular, Lloyd George was apprehensive as to how Bonar Law, the
former Conservative leader and still a staunch pro-Ulster supporter,
would react should the government move against Craig. Bonar Law,
who had stepped down from active politics owing to ill health, had
been out of the country when the truce was agreed with Sinn Fein.

[57] Cecil Lowry, Enniskillen, to Craig, 17 Nov. 1921, PRONI PM1/42.
[58] Col. Fred Crawford to Craig, 7 Nov. 1921, Crawford Papers, PRONI D640/7/14.

However, as his biographer Robert Blake has pointed out, there is no evidence that he disapproved of the truce; indeed, he 'seems to have welcomed the prospect, which now appeared on the horizon, of peace in Ireland'.[59] But to Bonar Law peace in Ireland did not mean peace at any price. He had no intention of allowing Northern Ireland's interests to be compromised, nor would he facilitate Lloyd George's coercion of the Ulster unionists. Back in London, with his health restored and once again taking an active part in politics, Bonar Law was a serious concern for Lloyd George and his coalition Tories, who feared that if he moved against the government, he might carry a majority of the Conservative Party with him.

Even without Bonar Law actively adopting a hostile attitude to the Lloyd George Cabinet, there were already rumblings from Conservative 'diehards' who opposed talks with Sinn Fein. On 31 October what amounted to a parliamentary vote of censure on the government for negotiating with Sinn Fein was moved by Colonel Gretton. Some forty-three MPs voted against the government, but most interestingly, the Ulster Unionist MPs did not vote with the dissident Conservatives. The Ulster Unionist Parliamentary Party at Westminster had agreed in consultation with Craig that, if Lloyd George gave them a definite pledge about the transfer of powers to the Government of Northern Ireland, they should not take part in the debate and would not vote against the coalition government.[60] This showed the essential differences between the Ulster Unionists and the die-hard Conservatives. Although united as allies in the fight against Sinn Fein, their opposition to Irish republicanism was for different reasons. To the die-hard Conservatives, Sinn Fein was a threat to the integrity of the empire which should therefore be defeated, and talks should play no part in the government strategy. While the Ulster Unionists always used imperialistic language to explain their opposition to Sinn Fein, especially on the mainland, their main concern was for the survival of the Ulster unionist people. This is reflected in their desire to safeguard their position by securing the transfer of services to Northern Ireland while not objecting to the London government dealing with Sinn Fein about the rest of Ireland.

Seeking to assuage growing Conservative hostility to his negotiations with Sinn Fein, Lloyd George agreed on 5 November to transfer services to Northern Ireland. He thus succeeded not only in winning the co-operation of the Ulster Unionists who consequently did not attack him, but also in reducing the number of Conservative dissidents. The Conservative Party appears on the Irish issue to have been composed of three major groups. One group, committed to the coalition, supported talks with Sinn Fein, while another group—the imperialist die-hards—totally opposed such talks. The third group, though prepared to go along with talks provided an imperial Dominion loyal to the Crown was established in Southern Ireland, was not prepared to tolerate any coercion of the Ulster unionists. It was the confidence of this third group which Lloyd George had to retain if he wished to preserve the support of the Conservative Party for his coalition. By announcing that services would be transferred, Lloyd George managed to isolate the Conservative die-hards. An attempt was then made by the die-hards to persuade the Conservative Party in the country to reject the government's strategy. A party convention of 1,800 representatives was held in Liverpool on 17 November where Colonel Gretton once again moved a vote of censure on the government's negotiations with Sinn Fein. However, a compromise motion—endorsing a settlement—was adopted, though the vote reflected not a commitment to government policies but rather a strong desire 'not to split the Tory party. But the price of unity was a settlement that clearly safeguarded Crown, Empire, defence and Ulster.'[61] It was against such a backdrop of political intrigue that control of the Northern Ireland services was partly transferred to Craig's government on 22 November 1921.

Some six months after the Northern Ireland General Election, the Northern Ireland government at last had responsibility for some, if not yet all, of its services. For those who choose to regard the establishment of Northern Ireland as a creation of British imperialism, the events of October and November 1921 must prove something of a problem. It was the Ulster unionists who pressed for the assumption of self-government, while it was the British establishment, in its efforts to reach a settlement with Sinn Fein, which endeavoured to prevent the consolidation of Northern Ireland. Some Marxist writers have recognized that 'in the long run British imperialism would itself prefer a form of territorial completion [in Ireland]. The real objections to unification came not from Britain but from local Protestants.'[62] As Lloyd George continued his struggle to reach a settlement with Sinn Fein, the Ulster unionist leadership were conscious of a delicate political situation requiring them to be careful in all they said and did. With the transfer of services to Northern Ireland secured, the unionists were able

---

[61] Curran, *Birth of the Irish Free State*, 106.
[62] P. Bew, P. Gibbon, and H. Patterson, *The State in Northern Ireland 1921–72* (Manchester, 1979), 29.

to demonstrate what they saw as their loyalty to the empire—which had always been an important, albeit secondary, part of their political philosophy—by doing nothing to undermine the negotiations. Despite the efforts of Lloyd George to push Craig towards accepting subordination to an all-Ireland parliament in Dublin, the Ulster unionist leader showed remarkable restraint.

Forced to concede the transfer of services, and faced with the reality of a Northern Ireland that was a self-governing entity, Lloyd George still attempted to preserve some semblance of Irish unity to placate the Sinn Fein negotiators. Even if a separate parliament existed in Belfast, provided that it could be persuaded to transfer its allegiance from Westminster to Dublin, Lloyd George could declare that the unity of Ireland was intact. Although unable to force the Ulster unionists to accept the sovereignty of a Dublin parliament or to agree to changes in the border of Northern Ireland, Lloyd George spectacularly managed to reach a settlement with Sinn Fein on 6 December 1921. The settlement—which was given the title 'Articles of Agreement for a Treaty between Great Britain and Ireland', but was commonly called the 'treaty'—gave virtual independence to Ireland, with Dominion status similar to that of Canada.[63] While in theory the treaty embraced all of Ireland, it also recognized the existence of Northern Ireland and provision was made for it to opt out of the Irish Free State—as the new Irish Dominion was to be called—if it so wished. If the Parliament of Northern Ireland opted out, as everyone expected it would, Article 12 of the treaty provided for a Boundary Commission 'with powers to modify the partition line—although to what extent was left undefined'.[64] At a meeting of the British Cabinet on the morning after the treaty was signed, Lloyd George stated that if Northern Ireland opted to remain within the United Kingdom, then 'she must be prepared to share the burdens and responsibilities of the United Kingdom for better or worse'.[65]

Although there were to be deep and bitter divisions within Sinn Fein about the treaty's acceptance of allegiance to the British Crown, there was a 'virtual consensus that the treaty provided a means for making the Northern Ireland state unviable'.[66] It was Sinn Fein's general euphoria over the treaty which alarmed Ulster unionists. Nationalists within Northern Ireland believed that the 'boundary

---

[63] Articles of Agreement for a Treaty between Great Britain and Ireland, Cmd. 1560, 1921, Sess. II, i, 75.

[64] A. C. Hepburn, *The Conflict of Nationality in Modern Ireland* (London, 1980), 119.

[65] British Cabinet Conclusions, 6 Dec. 1921, PRO(L) CAB23/27 90(21).

[66] Laffan, *Partition of Ireland*, 87.

commission, by removing vast tracts of territory from the jurisdiction of the Belfast government . . . would effectively end partition and provide for the reunification of the country'.[67] On 9 December the *Belfast Newsletter*, a strongly Ulster unionist newspaper, denounced the treaty as a betrayal and a disgrace intended to force Ulster into the Free State. The objections of Ulster unionists were threefold:

to the principle of the treaty, which theoretically included Northern Ireland in the Free State with the option of leaving; to the financial provisions which were thought likely to lead to high taxation and a tariff border, all to the detriment of Northern Ireland; and above all else, to the proposed Boundary Commission to look again at the North's territorial limits.[68]

Craig, initially 'very suspicious of the Boundary clause and financial arrangements' of the treaty, was somewhat mollified by the assurances he received from Lloyd George on 9 December that only 'mere rectifications' of the boundary were envisaged.[69] However, the outrage of the Ulster unionists against the treaty remained unabated, as was shown by the many letters Craig received expressing fury at its terms.[70] Writing to the Ulster Unionist Chief Whip, Captain Herbert Dixon MP, Craig expressed his fear that if Lloyd George persisted with the Boundary Commission it could lead to great violence and 'possibly to a declaration of independence by Northern Ireland'.[71]

The bitterness of the Ulster unionists at what they regarded as a betrayal of their interests was not confined to the grass-roots. Lilian Spender, wife of the Secretary to the Northern Ireland Cabinet, noted in her diary that the week since the publication of the treaty had been 'the most depressing I have ever known over here. Up to the last I don't think we ever really believed England would do this thing—would reward murder, treachery, treason, crime of all kinds, & penalise loyalty.'[72] Referring to Sir James Craig's having lost his remnant of faith in Lloyd George, she wondered 'why it lingered so long'. In his speech to the Northern Ireland House of Commons on the treaty, which was received with cheers, Craig carefully attempted to balance anger with reason.[73] He stated the view that, as Northern Ireland had not been a party to the treaty, she would not be bound by its terms. Anxious to relieve tension in Belfast, he declared that the steps taken

[67] Dooher, 'Tyrone Nationalism', 390.

[68] D. Kennedy, *The Widening Gulf: Northern Attitudes to the Independent Irish State 1919–49* (Belfast, 1988), 69.

[69] Lady Craig's diary, 7 and 9 Dec. 1921, PRONI D1415/8/38.

[70] See correspondence in PRONI PM1/50 (parts 1 and 2) and PM1/51 (parts 1 and 2).

[71] Craig to Captain Herbert Dixon MP, 15 Dec. 1921, PRONI PM1/50 (part 2).

[72] Lilian Spender's diary, 16 Dec. 1921, PRONI D1633/2/25.

[73] See *Parl. Deb.* (House of Commons), i, 12 Dec. 1921, cols. 542–6.

by Ulster unionists must be 'constitutional steps'. It would appear that he was eager to dispel the mood of separatist Ulster nationalism which was evident at this stage among the Ulster unionist people,[74] and which could have led to Northern Ireland unilaterally declaring her independence. He reminded MPs that they must not depart from 'the pledge that we are only anxious to remain part and parcel of Great Britain and of the Empire'.

Despite the efforts of Craig to convince the Ulster unionists that their position was secure so long as they did nothing to damage their cause, many doubts remained. Spender stated that he wished the Ulster unionists could set up a separate Dominion, as 'one would feel safer if one were less dependent on Westminster'.[75] Although Craig had talked in November of granting Northern Ireland Dominion status as an option, he did not pursue this as an objective and, indeed, as mentioned above, employed his energies in preventing the Ulster unionists from seeking independence. There is no doubt that he believed that for the Ulster unionists to declare independence unilaterally would have been a disaster in political, economic, and military terms. Nevertheless, the experience of the pressures brought against Northern Ireland during the London negotiations with Sinn Fein and the subsequent treaty 'reinforced Ulster unionism's distrust of British politicians and its determination to build strong and hold firmly its own safeguards against future perfidy'.[76] Although Craig sought no extension of the constitutional powers he had under the devolved government system, he renewed his determination to consolidate Northern Ireland by strengthening his government and administration. Acutely aware of the highly charged political atmosphere in Northern Ireland, with the potential for grave public disorder, he preferred to play down the possible threat of the Boundary Commission. That he was able to concentrate on building up the new administration in Northern Ireland was due to the fact that no effort was made at this stage to activate the boundary clauses. However, the genie of the Boundary Commission, having been released from the bottle by the British Government, became a spectre which, in a couple of years, returned to haunt the Craig government. Meanwhile, on 14 December Craig sent his government's formal reply to Lloyd George rejecting the proposed Boundary Commission and accusing the British Government of breach of faith.

[74] e.g. Crawford referred in his diary to the need to 'establish an Ulster Free State. Everyone I have met since the terms [of the treaty have] been known that I have spoken to says this must happen. Some of the most loyal men I know have said they will never drink the King's health again.' 8 Dec. 1921, PRONI D640/11.

[75] Spender to Lt.-Col. Singleton DSO, Surafend, Palestine, 29 Dec. 1921, PRONI PM1/51 (part 2 of 2). [76] Harkness, *Northern Ireland*, 11.

Once forced to concede the transfer of services, Lloyd George had allowed the British administration to act swiftly to arrange for the transfer. On 9 November, only four days after Lloyd George had agreed to Craig's request for the transfer, the King made two Orders in Council under Section 69 of the Government of Ireland Act, 1920, to enable the transfer to take place. The transfer of powers to Northern Ireland proceeded in the absence of a government in Southern Ireland, as Craig had urged for some months that it should. The London government now found it politically acceptable to empower the Lord-Lieutenant of Ireland to nominate the representative of Southern Ireland to the Civil Service Committee in the absence of any government. As the establishment of the Irish Free State was to render impossible any representation on the Civil Service Commission from what was to have been Southern Ireland, the constitution of the committee was altered by statute. The Order in Council[77] had not only provided for this, but it also gave the Lord-Lieutenant authority to appoint persons on behalf of Southern Ireland to the Joint Exchequer Board.

The Order in Council set 22 November 1921 as the appointed day on which those financial provisions of the 1920 Act not yet implemented would come into operation. Law and order and the administration of justice were also to be transferred on 22 November, while local government, housing, old-age pensions, road transport, and public health were to be transferred on 1 December. All other Irish services, apart from education, were to be transferred on 1 January 1922, and education was then to follow on 1 February. The Orders also provided for the transfer of those Irish officers employed in the administration of those services which had been transferred. On 10 November, the day after the Orders in Council were made, Sir John Anderson wrote to the secretaries of each Irish government department, directing them to prepare lists of those officers automatically becoming officers of the Government of Northern Ireland[78] and those who wished to be considered for transfer to Northern Ireland. Anderson also suggested that departments might select some officers for temporary service in Northern Ireland whom they might intend to recommend to the Civil Service Committee for ultimate retention in Southern Ireland.

As the Irish administration had not taken up the suggestion of the Ulster unionists to prepare, in anticipation of the transfer of services,

---

[77] 'The Government of Northern Ireland (Temporary Constitution of Joint Exchequer Board and Civil Service Committee) Order, 1921', in *Belfast Gazette*, 18 Nov. 1921.

[78] Under the provisions of Section 59(1) of the Government of Ireland Act, 1920, any Irish officers who on the appointed day were administering Irish services which came entirely within the jurisdiction of the new government, automatically became officers of that government.

lists of those civil servants who wished to transfer to Northern Ireland, there was likely to be a delay between the appointed day and the allocation of officers. During this period the salaries of those officers whose allocation had not yet been decided were to be paid by the United Kingdom Government and charged to a suspense account. As each officer was finally allocated, he was to be deemed to have been an officer of the government to which he was allocated as from the appointed day, and his salary from that day was to be recovered from the government concerned.[79] The staff in the office of the Assistant Under-Secretary in Belfast, who had proved to be so important in the preliminary planning and preparation of the new administration in Northern Ireland, were absorbed by the new Civil Service with the transfer of services on 22 November. Sir Ernest Clark relinquished his post as Assistant Under-Secretary and was appointed Permanent Secretary to the Ministry of Finance and Head of the Civil Service in Northern Ireland.

Clark, who had, as already noted, made extensive preparations to ensure that there was adequate accommodation for the staff of the new Civil Service, increased his efforts in response to the immediate transfer of services. He had continued to liaise with the Permanent Secretaries to ascertain the accommodation needs of their respective departments, and by mid-December he anticipated that accommodation would be needed for a total staff of some 800 persons. The leasing or purchase of premises provided the necessary accommodation, though the matter remained a problem with office space always at a premium. That accommodation, albeit barely adequate, was available to enable the transfer of services to proceed was entirely due to the hard work of Clark and his staff. They had made preparations in advance to resolve the accommodation problem, including even identifying suitable offices for possible use, and had also made strong and frequent representations to the Office of Works to ensure that it took the necessary action.

Meanwhile measures continued to complete the administrative legislation process enabling the transfer of services to take place. The adaptation of enactments made by a series of Orders in Council under Section 69 of the Government of Ireland Act, 1920—to maintain the smooth administration of services once they were transferred—was made on 21 November. However, the administrative problems to be overcome were enormous and at times forced the Northern Ireland government to slow down or postpone the assumption of responsibility for certain

---

[79] Anderson to the Secretary of each Irish government department, 24 Oct. 1921, Cabinet Secretarial, PRONI CAB5/5.

functions. The transfer of National Health Insurance is a good example of some of the difficulties which the new government experienced. The National Health Insurance Joint Committee had appointed a committee under the chairmanship of Sir Alfred Watson, the Imperial government's actuary, to report upon the steps necessary to arrange for the transfer of the National Health Insurance. The committee of six members, including J. A. Dale, Permanent Secretary to the Northern Ireland Ministry of Labour, presented its report by 7 December 1921. It recognized that since its appointment the position had been profoundly altered by the treaty.

There were some 750,000 insured persons resident in Ireland, of whom 276,000 were in Northern Ireland and, as the report noted, great numbers of persons were resident in both Northern Ireland and Southern Ireland or were members of societies whose head offices were located in Great Britain or the legislative area of Ireland other than that in which they resided. The committee felt that attention had to be given by the approved societies to the allocation of the benefits drawn according to the actual residence of the members at the time when benefit was claimed. As two-ninths of the cost of benefits were to be charged upon the exchequer in the area in which the person was resident, exact accounting was essential. Thus payments made to persons 'resident (or deemed to be resident) in Northern Ireland will be drawn from the National Health Insurance Fund for Northern Ireland'.[80]

The committee in their report recommended that a new National Health Insurance Fund for Northern Ireland be opened on 1 January 1922 and that the Joint Committee should administer the Irish National Health Insurance Fund up to 31 December. The Joint Committee, it was suggested, should apportion any funds in hand on the basis of the relative numbers of insured persons in Southern Ireland and Northern Ireland respectively. The committee was conscious that uniformity in the administration of National Health Insurance was essential, but it was acknowledged that this was only possible 'so long as the several Parliaments concerned proceed on identical lines in regard to those fundamental matters in which uniformity is essential'.[81] The administration of National Health Insurance in Northern Ireland was to be transferred to Craig's government on 1 January 1922 by virtue of the Order in Council of 9 November 1921. However, amid growing

[80] 'Report of the Departmental Committee on the Application of the Act to National Health Insurance', 4, Provisional Govt. of Ireland Cabinet Committees Papers, PRONI HO5 CIM604/1/6.
[81] Ibid. 22.

administrative problems about the division of the Insurance Fund and difficulties in establishing the mechanism to make payments, the transfer was postponed until 1 March 1922 by a new Order in Council dated 22 December 1921.

Following the formation of the Joint Exchequer Board, Clark attended a meeting in London on 2 December on behalf of the Northern Ireland government. It approved the provisional Regulations to enable advances to be made to the Exchequer of Northern Ireland in respect of the Irish residuary share of reserved taxes. There was considerable discussion at the meeting as to how to calculate the revenue and expenditure for the period from the transfer of services on 22 November until the end of the financial year. The London Treasury wanted the calculations made on the basis of a proportional amount of the figure for the total year, while the Northern Ireland government favoured calculations on the basis of the actual revenue received and the estimated actual expenses. There was a considerable difference between the Estimates prepared by the London Treasury and by the Northern Ireland government, and the former were obliged to acknowledge a mistake in their calculations.[82] Milne Barbour, the Northern Ireland Financial Secretary, presented on 1 December Supplementary Estimates of £1,961,333 to cover the costs of services transferred to Northern Ireland.

The formation of a Provisional Government by Sinn Fein for what was to become the Irish Free State was a source of concern to the Government of Northern Ireland. The Ulster unionists were aware of the hostility of Sinn Fein to the existence of Northern Ireland and were worried that it would obstruct the consolidation of the Belfast administration. Craig was anxious that the apportionment of existing government property and assets between Northern Ireland and Southern Ireland (as proposed by Paragraph 69(f) of the Government of Ireland Act) should go ahead before the formation of a Provisional Government in Dublin. He judged that it would be 'most inexpedient' to allow any assets to pass into the possession of the Provisional Government. Writing to Sir Hamar Greenwood on 22 December, Craig also expressed his concern about the possibility of services being transferred to the Provisional Government before the appointed days fixed for the transfer of services to Northern Ireland. He wanted to avoid any Northern Ireland services being administered by the Sinn Fein Provisional Government. Realizing the political repercussions which such a situation could have in Northern Ireland, Greenwood replied that if services had

---

[82] Clark to Rt. Hon. Hugh Pollock MP, 5 Dec. 1921, PRONI CAB5/5.

not already been transferred to Northern Ireland, steps would be taken to prevent responsibility for them being handed over to the Provisional Government.[83] While the Provisional Government thus did not gain control over any services in Northern Ireland, it was nevertheless still able to exercise considerable influence on, and create difficulties for, the development of the Northern Ireland government.

Although the Provisional Government was composed of relatively moderate Sinn Fein members—in contrast to the more doctrinaire republicans who had rejected the treaty—it was from its inception hostile to Northern Ireland. One of its first actions was to issue a proclamation on 17 January 1922 suspending transfers of civil servants from Dublin to Northern Ireland. At a meeting of the Provisional Government, held on 20 January, it was agreed that no civil servant could be transferred to Northern Ireland without the direct approval of the relevant Dublin minister, an approval which no minister was inclined to grant.[84] Anticipating that the Provisional Government might attempt to interfere with the transfer of civil servants to Northern Ireland, Clark had acted to have the Civil Service Committee allocate all those prepared to serve in Belfast.[85] Some 120 civil servants, already allocated to the Civil Service of Northern Ireland, did not receive their formal notification to enable the transfer to go ahead.

Clark proposed that the Civil Service Committee should proceed to issue letters of notification for those officers who had been allocated prior to the Provisional Government's proclamation of 17 January. The committee rejected his proposal and decided, in deference to the Sinn Fein administration in Dublin, to discontinue its meetings. Clark was incensed and informed the Civil Service Committee that it might be necessary for Northern Ireland under these circumstances 'to engage its staff on its own responsibility, throwing on to the Imperial Government any responsibility for the pensioning of men who might ultimately be transferred'.[86] The Civil Service Committee was eventually re-formed in May 1922, but only to allocate officially the remaining volunteers (who by then were already in Belfast). Meanwhile the Government of Northern Ireland, anxious that the obstructionist policy of the Provisional Government should not impede the consolidation of Northern Ireland, endeavoured to carry on by the appointment of temporary officers.

Administrative problems were compounded by the obstacles raised

[83] Greenwood to Craig, 28 Dec. 1921, PRONI CAB5/5.

[84] Minutes of Provisional Government, 20 Jan. 1922, State Paper Office of Ireland, NAI G1/1.

[85] Clark to Pollock, 18 Jan. 1922, PRONI CAB5/5.　　　　[86] Ibid.

by the Sinn Fein government, and the National Health Insurance once again provides a good example of the difficulties which their obstructionist policy caused. Not only did the Provisional Government refuse to allow the transfer of staff from the Irish Insurance Commission, but it also prevented the transfer to the Belfast government of health-insurance records relating to Northern Ireland. The absence of the necessary insurance documents was, as the Secretary of the Northern Ireland Ministry of Labour commented, a source of 'great embarrassment'.[87] Nevertheless, the Northern Ireland government struggled on as best it could and, in an effort to overcome the serious problems caused by the lack of experienced staff, obtained five trained officers on loan from the Imperial Ministry of Health. These English officers were then replaced in due course by Ulster people trained by the English-men before their return to London.

The Government of Northern Ireland made strong representations to the London government in the hope that it could force the Provisional Government to transfer the needed staff and records. Lionel Curtis, secretary to the Provisional Government of Ireland Committee of the Imperial Cabinet, wrote on behalf of Winston Churchill (who was chairman of the committee) to Andrew Cope at the Irish Office in Dublin, urging him to persuade the Provisional Government to transfer staff and records to Belfast. Should the Provisional Government refuse to co-operate, Curtis added, the Imperial government would proceed to act independently and 'make such arrangements with the Northern Government as in the circumstances seem to them best'.[88] However, although the Provisional Government did not co-operate, the assistance actually given by the Imperial government to the Northern Ireland government was limited to supplying on loan experienced insurance officers capable of administering the Northern Ireland fund.

It would appear that the Imperial government did not want to take any action to help Northern Ireland which might upset the Irish nationalists and thus undermine the position of the Provisional Government. As the split in Sinn Fein, caused by the refusal of a substantial minority to accept Dominion status, deepened and became more bitter, so the London government saw the need to strengthen the hand of the pro-treaty faction. The easiest way for the government in London to help the Provisional Government was to appear indifferent to the fate of the Government of Northern Ireland. Once again the wishes of the

[87] Mr J. A. Dale to Spender, 11 May 1922, Cabinet Secretarial, PRONI CAB9A/1/1.

[88] Lionel Curtis to Andrew Cope, 11 Feb. 1922, Provisional Govt. of Ireland Cabinet Committee Papers, PRONI MIC545.

Ulster unionists were to be sacrificed to accommodate the needs of the overall imperial strategy. Writing to Sir James Masterton-Smith, Permanent Secretary of the Colonial Office, Wilfrid Spender stated bluntly that: 'Mr Cope is so afraid of hurting the susceptibilities of the Provisional Government that he is quite prepared to overlook the obligations of the Imperial Authorities in seeing that Northern Ireland is not handicapped by the establishment of the Irish Free State.'[89]

The difficulties created for the Government of Northern Ireland by the lack of civil servants were largely offset by recruiting and appointing local people on a temporary basis and by securing the loan of experienced officers from the British Civil Service. However, the refusal of the Provisional Government to transfer records relating to the administration of Northern Ireland services proved a more difficult obstacle for Craig's government to overcome. The Provisional Government retained the Northern Ireland records of the Commissioners of National Education, the Commissioners of Intermediate Education, the Registrar General, the Irish Land Commission, and the Office of Public Works. Cope complained to the Provisional Government that it was 'essential' that these records be transferred without delay to Northern Ireland. Nevertheless, in some cases, it was not until 1924 that the Government of Northern Ireland secured the transfer of its records.[90] The Northern Ireland government did manage in 1922 to obtain those records considered vital to enable it to preserve the administration of its services. However, such records—those of the Land Purchase Collection Branch, for example—were only transferred when the attitude of the Provisional Government softened as a result of the pact signed in March 1922 by Craig and Collins, Chairman of the Provisional Government. Even then, the records were barely received by the Land Purchase Collection Branch in time to enable it to issue 80,000 new Receivable Orders for the gale day collections of rents.

Despite the enormous administrative problems in setting up and sustaining the new Civil Service, problems aggravated by the obstructionist tactics of the Irish Free State, there was no breakdown in the public administration. The education system was sustained and teachers were paid as normal, pensions and other benefits were processed without delay, while the infrastructure of society was properly maintained. Indeed, not only had self-government been planned and established in Northern Ireland, but with the assumption by Craig's government of administrative responsibility, self-government was effectively consolidated.

[89] Spender to Sir James Masterton-Smith, 17 May 1922, PRONI CAB9A/1/1.
[90] For details, see 'Transfer of Documents to Northern Ireland', NAI S3 111.

No doubt the successful birth of Northern Ireland was due to the iron will of the Ulster unionist government and the resolute leadership of Sir James Craig. However, it is questionable whether his Cabinet could have been so effective in its struggle against political opponents and administrative saboteurs without the dedicated support of its civil servants. Indeed, the creation of the Civil Service was one of the government's main achievements and was in itself an enduring symbol of the success of the establishment of Northern Ireland. Speaking at the first annual dinner of the new Civil Service, Sir Ernest Clark praised his staff in all Northern Ireland departments for their hard work and sense of professionalism, and declared that the 'Government of Ulster is the child of its people, and if the Ministers and their Parliamentary Secretaries are its Godfathers and Godmothers, we are certainly its nurses'.[91]

Yet in 1921 no one could have predicted with confidence the success of the Northern Ireland Civil Service, nor indeed could anyone have been confident of the survival of Northern Ireland itself. Looking back to that period, Clark felt that no one could 'repress a shudder, as well as utter a sigh of relief, if he ponders upon the abyss into which Ulster might now have fallen had she not been wisely and strongly governed'.[92] The role of the Northern Ireland Civil Service in the establishment and consolidation of self-government in Northern Ireland was invaluable. However, no matter how competent administrators might be, and no matter how resourceful they might be in overcoming administrative obstacles, by themselves they cannot survive against terrorist subversion. The IRA offensive in 1922 was designed to overthrow Northern Ireland by making it totally ungovernable. Northern Ireland could only survive if she had the security forces to oppose the IRA, and above all the political will to deploy them as part of what today would be called a strong counter-insurgency programme. In the event, Sir James Craig was to demonstrate his recognition of the fact that if Northern Ireland was to survive, she had to be not only wisely but also strongly governed.

[91] Manuscript of speech delivered by Clark at the first annual dinner of the Northern Ireland Civil Service, *c.*1924, Clark Papers, PRONI D1022/2/21.
[92] Ibid.

5

Defending Self-Government

Achieving responsibility for law and order was a major objective for the fledgeling Government of Northern Ireland, particularly given the deteriorating security situation. The truce between the Crown forces and the IRA insisted upon by Sinn Fein as a preliminary to negotiations came into operation on 11 July 1921. Applying the truce in Northern Ireland without London's consulting the Craig administration highlighted the latter's lack of control over security matters. With the Special Constabulary virtually demobilized, the force which 'the Unionists had lobbied so hard to get established had been almost neutralised overnight'.[1] The IRA did not stand down its men during the truce but rather took the opportunity to consolidate its position. Following an attack by IRA gunmen on the police in Belfast on 14 July, full-scale rioting (accompanied by widespread sniping) broke out, resulting in twenty deaths and some 200 wounded.[2] Further serious outbreaks of trouble on 20, 30, and 31 August left seventeen dead and ninety-one wounded. The Government of Northern Ireland could only lobby the military authorities and the British Government for the deployment of additional troops in the hope of preventing further disorder.

As the Government of Northern Ireland floundered in its efforts to persuade the British Government to adopt a tougher law-and-order stance, its popularity plummeted and its control over its grass-roots supporters weakened. Although Sir Richard Dawson Bates had as yet no administrative responsibility for security, in the eyes of the general public he had liability for it. In a memorandum issued to the Cabinet he warned of widespread anxiety among loyalists because of 'the aggression of Sinn Fein and the lack of defensive measures being taken up by the Authorities. This has found vent, amongst other things, in the formation of Provisional Committees, and the organisation of armed loyalists to supply protection which they consider is withheld by the Authorities.'[3]

---

[1] M. Farrell, *Arming the Protestants: The Formation of the Ulster Special Constabulary and the Royal Ulster Constabulary 1920–27* (London, 1983), 62.

[2] Cabinet Conclusions, 15 July 1921, PRONI CAB4/9/1.

[3] Memo to the Northern Ireland Cabinet from Sir Richard Dawson Bates, 10 Sept. 1921, Private Office, PRONI HA20/A/1/2.

Bates's report was not hysterical exaggeration, for in the 'Weekly Survey of the State of Ireland', a secret memorandum prepared by the Chief Secretary of Ireland for the British Cabinet, it was stated that 'the number of breaches of the truce shows an increase which is somewhat disquieting', and that in Belfast 'an atmosphere of unrest still prevails and a general feeling of nervousness is apparent'.[4] IRA records reveal that it was training men during the truce and that one member was accidently shot dead by another during 'brigade manœuvres'.[5] The IRA's training within Northern Ireland with guns was unlikely to calm the fears of the unionist people. Nor was the Northern Ireland government likely to be reassured by the knowledge that the truce 'allowed the IRA to appear in areas hitherto under government control'.[6] Without the operational deployment of the Special Constabulary, the unionists felt particularly vulnerable. Colonel Wickham, divisional police commissioner, had told Spender, Secretary to the Northern Ireland Cabinet, that only by the mobilization of the Specials could the unionist population 'be restrained from taking the law into their own hands, and from putting a stop forcibly to such [IRA] proceedings'.[7]

In many ways the Ulster unionists found themselves in a position similar to that of August 1920 when, with a deteriorating political and security situation, communal tension had inevitably risen. Like then, so in July 1921 control of grass-roots unionists was once again slipping away from the unionist leadership, as intensifying loyalist fears of the republican menace combined with their feeling of vulnerability. Craig attempted to calm the fears of the unionist people, not only urging restraint but also taking practical steps in an effort to prevent rioting and other disorders. He requested that extra troops be deployed in Belfast and had discussions with senior police and military officers to advise them about a more effective security policy. Anxious to prevent further outbreaks of violence, he urged the British Government to take 'vigorous steps to protect lives and property'.[8] His Cabinet was increasingly worried that, in the event of a breakdown in the proposed talks between Sinn Fein and the London government, the IRA would launch a terrorist offensive against Northern Ireland. It was, therefore,

---

[4] 'Weekly Survey of the State of Ireland', 16 Sept. 1921, Cabinet Memoranda, PRO(L) CAB24/128.

[5] A report from the 3rd IRA Northern Division to IRA GHQ, c.Aug. 1921, Mulcahy Papers, UCDAD P7/A/II/23.

[6] J. B. Dooher, 'Tyrone Nationalism and the Question of Partition 1910–25' (M.Phil. Thesis, University of Ulster, 1986), 365.

[7] Col. Wickham to Col. Wilfrid Spender, 9 Aug. 1921, PRONI CAB4/14/6.

[8] Rt. Hon. Sir James Craig to Rt. Hon. Sir Hamar Greenwood MP, 22 Sept. 1921, PRO(L) CAB24/128 (CP3369).

suggested that a senior army officer be appointed by the War Office as military adviser to the Government of Northern Ireland, to assist in drawing up plans 'to meet contingencies if the "Truce" breaks down'.[9]

However, just as the London government had been reluctant to transfer power to the Northern Ireland government in case Sinn Fein be offended and the proposed talks placed in jeopardy, it was equally reluctant to take any security measures which might appear belligerent to Sinn Fein. The extent to which security policy in Northern Ireland was subordinated to the attempts by the British Government to reach a settlement with Sinn Fein is illustrated by the former's refusal to open new police barracks during the truce.[10] In contrast to the strict adherence to the truce by the British Government, the IRA adopted a selective approach which allowed it to strengthen its position. The organization of training camps was an attempt by the IRA not merely to hold its organizational structure together during the truce, but also to prepare its men for a new post-truce offensive. Writing to the IRA Chief of Staff, the Officer Commanding the 3rd IRA (Northern) Division stated that he believed hostilities in Northern Ireland would have a great bearing on the whole situation. Accordingly, he was 'making preparations to intensify the fight throughout the Division and . . . I am confident that with some extra arms &c the whole Division can take the field after the truce'.[11]

The Government of Northern Ireland assumed responsibility for law and order on 22 November 1921, at a time when the truce was becoming even more meaningless as public disorders escalated. Indeed, in the period 19–25 November twenty-seven people were murdered and ninety-two injured in Belfast alone.[12] In practice, would Craig's government be any more effective than the British had been in attempting to restore law and order? Although responsibility for law and order was transferred on 22 November, the handover did not become fully operative until after the British Government signed the treaty with Sinn Fein on 6 December. Even then the situation remained somewhat complex. While the Royal Irish Constabulary operating in Northern Ireland was placed under the control of the Northern Ireland government, the force itself was not transferred. Under the Government of Ireland Act it had been envisaged that the RIC would continue as a

---

[9] Craig to Rt. Hon. Sir Worthington-Evans MP, 1 Dec. 1921, PRONI HA20/A/1/2.

[10] See correspondence between Clark and Anderson in Treasury Division Papers, PRONI FIN18/1/382.

[11] OC 3rd IRA Northern Division to IRA Chief of Staff, Dublin, 16 Aug. 1921, UCDAD P7/A/II/23.

[12] Sir Arthur Hezlet, *The 'B' Specials: A History of the Ulster Special Constabulary* (London, 1972), 49.

single force but be divided for operational purposes and handed over to the new administrations in Belfast and Dublin. During the negotiations with Sinn Fein it became clear that the RIC had no future, at least in Southern Ireland. As the British Government decided that disband-ment of the RIC 'would necessarily apply to those members of the force . . . serving in Northern Ireland',[13] the Northern Ireland govern-ment would be left without a police force. Before the government could tackle its law-and-order problems it had to create an effective police-force capable of implementing its policies.

The Irish Chief Secretary, Sir Hamar Greenwood, hoped that Craig would do all in his power to secure for the new Northern Ireland force the greatest possible number of suitable recruits from the ranks of the existing Royal Irish Constabulary. A number of RIC men, particularly those who had Ulster associations or sympathies, were keen to serve in the new Northern Ireland police-force. One RIC County Inspector wrote to Craig that they hoped to bring to the new force the 'discipline and traditions which won for it [the RIC] the respect and admiration of the civilised world, until it was betrayed and stabbed to death'.[14] Westminster passed without delay the Constabulary (Ireland) Act, 1922, which made provision for the disbandment of the RIC. The RIC in Southern Ireland was disbanded on 31 March 1922, but in Northern Ireland this was delayed until 31 May to smooth the transition to the new force. The Northern Ireland government was to pay the pensions of some 2,000 disbanded RIC men. However, if they were re-engaged in the new police-force, payment of pension would be suspended dur-ing service.[15]

Bates appointed a departmental committee under the chairmanship of Mr Lloyd Campbell MP to examine the existing police organization in Northern Ireland and to consider the changes necessary to establish a new force under the command of the Government of Northern Ire-land. The committee, formally appointed on 31 January 1922, comprised MPs, councillors, the RIC Belfast Divisional Commander, Charles Wickham, and the Chief Constable of Glasgow, with T. W. Bunting of the Ministry of Home Affairs acting as secretary. In an attempt to have a balanced committee Bates endeavoured to appoint two Roman Catholics, and he also invited members of the public to submit their views on police organization for consideration by the committee.[16] The

[13] Greenwood to Craig, 20 Dec. 1921, PRONI FIN18/4/168.

[14] Vere Gregory, Londonderry, to Craig, 31 Dec. 1921, Cabinet Secretariat, PRONI CAB6/33.

[15] See 'Disbandment of RIC', PRONI CAB6/33.

[16] Bates to Sir R. N. Anderson MP, 18 Jan. 1922, PRONI HA5/104.

committee worked unremittingly to fulfil its important task and by 31 March it had produced an Interim Report.

This proposed that the new police-force be called the Ulster Constabulary and that the King be requested to grant permission to use the prefix 'Royal'. The report recommended a total force of all ranks not exceeding 3,000. The existing RIC strength in Northern Ireland was 2,817, and the small increase was to allow for headquarters and administrative staff, hitherto based in Dublin. One-third of the new force, it was suggested, should be Roman Catholic drawn from the RIC and/or the Special Constabulary.[17] If sufficient men were not available to meet this target of 1,000 Roman Catholics, then the committee envisaged that Roman Catholic civilians should be recruited. The remainder of the force was to be recruited from the Protestant population, and up to 1,000 men were to be recruited from the RIC and Special Constabulary. Thus provision was made for up to 2,000 of the new force's proposed strength of 3,000 to be drawn from existing regular or special constabulary. Conscious of the need to establish the Royal Ulster Constabulary from the date of disbandment of the RIC (31 May 1922), the Government of Northern Ireland promptly passed the Constabulary (Northern Ireland) Act, 1922. The Act also clarified the position of the Special Constabulary, making it an integral part of the RUC under the command of the RUC Inspector-General. Henceforth the Special Constabulary was known as the Ulster Special Constabulary (USC).

It was some months before the RUC became operationally effective against the IRA, and indeed by the midsummer of 1922 only 1,000 recruits had been taken on. Although there were eight battalions of the regular army stationed in Northern Ireland, these remained under the command of the British Government. Thus in the interim period from November 1921, when they accepted responsibility for law and order, the Northern Ireland government had to rely upon the USC as its main counter-insurgency force. The Special Constabulary as transferred to Craig's government in November 1921 had comprised 3,453 'A' Specials, 15,944 'B' Specials, and 1,084 'C' Specials. However, of the 3,453 men in the 'A' Specials, only 2,466 were deployed on operational duties, with the remainder either engaged in clerical work or undergoing training in camp.[18] The Northern Ireland Cabinet quickly acted to strengthen the force by recruiting an additional 700 'A' Specials

---

[17] *Interim Report of the Committee on Police Reorganisation in Northern Ireland*, Cmd. 1 (Belfast: HMSO, 1922).

[18] Craig to the Chancellor of the Exchequer, 8 Nov. 1921, Cabinet Secretariat, PRONI CAB9A/4/1.

and 5,000 'B' Specials. It also discussed raising an additional 3,000 'A' Specials should there be a complete breakdown in the truce.[19] Although the buildup of the USC placed a heavy burden on the Northern Ireland exchequer, Craig was convinced that it was vital expenditure. He claimed that no government could survive which did not fulfil its elementary duty of protecting life and property, and declared that 'he would rather incur bankruptcy than fail in this respect'.[20]

A product of the treaty between the British Government and Sinn Fein was an amnesty for prisoners arrested for offences committed before the truce. With Dail Eireann's ratification of the treaty, the British Government went ahead with its plan as agreed during the negotiations and released IRA internees on 14 January. IRA activities in Northern Ireland, which had never really ceased, now received a new impetus. Many of the released IRA men went to Belfast, and IRA snipers began operations there which rapidly led to rioting and further bloodshed.[21] Soon the cycle of violence had once again become self-perpetuating. However, in addition to the widespread sectarian disorders (which mainly consisted of attacks by Protestants on Roman Catholics), there was now the problem of IRA incursions across the border. The Northern Ireland government attempted to restore law and order by improving its intelligence-gathering activities; it took over financial and operational control of the police Crime Special Branch. A Belfast-based Special Constabulary provided less opportunity for penetration by IRA spies. Craig's government also supported the tough measures adopted by the military to stamp out sniping by gunmen. The Belfast military commander, Major-General Cameron, proposed to destroy derelict buildings used by snipers, and in the case of occupied buildings he planned to arrest all male inhabitants and close the house where he deemed it necessary. Although actions by the military were carried out by the authority of the Restoration of Order in Ireland Act, the Northern Ireland government accepted financial liability for any compensation claims.[22]

In an effort to solve Northern Ireland's growing security problem by conciliation rather than confrontation, Craig sought a meeting with Collins. This took place in London on 24 January 1922 and resulted in a five-point peace agreement. However, it appears to have been based on a mutual misunderstanding and the full extent of the leaders' disagreement was publicly revealed when they met in Dublin on

---

[19] Cabinet Conclusions, 1 Dec. 1921, PRONI CAB4/28/4.
[20] Cabinet Conclusions, 28 Nov. 1921, PRONI CAB4/27/11.
[21] St John Ervine, *Craigavon: Ulsterman* (Aberdeen, 1949), 467.
[22] Spender to Maj.-Gen. Cameron, 9 Jan. 1922, PRONI CAB6/36.

2 February. Their meeting ended in total breakdown and within days IRA raids across the border into Northern Ireland had begun again.[23]

Following reorganization, training, and consolidation during the truce, the IRA in Northern Ireland was in a relatively strong position. The 3rd (Northern) Division, which comprised three brigades, had 1,222 members. The Belfast IRA Brigade was commanded by Roger McCorley, and he alone had 632 men available to engage in acts of terrorism.[24] The IRA was thus able to launch a sustained series of attacks in Belfast, and it proved to be a major source of worry and trouble to Craig's government over the coming months. However, it was along the border with the Irish Free State that IRA attacks were concentrated in early February 1922. On the night of 7/8 February, the IRA made a number of cross-border raids and kidnapped forty-two local loyalists in Fermanagh and Tyrone, including the High Sheriff of Fermanagh. The kidnappings caused uproar in Northern Ireland and tension along the border reached fever pitch. The sense of outrage felt by Ulster unionists was increased by a statement from Eoin O'Duffy, now Chief of Staff of the IRA, who appeared to justify the kidnappings by stating that 'it was not surprising that there should have been "spontaneous and determined action in Ulster" '.[25] What was seen as the soft line taken by both the London government and press on the kidnappings added to unionist fears and anger. By contrast, the unionist newspapers made strident calls for the restoration of the pre-truce security arrangements. Craig himself 'attributed the incident to Britain's lack of courage and the demobilisation of the special constabulary'.[26]

Some additional troops were moved into Fermanagh and, for the first time since the truce, the 'B' Specials were mobilized. Reinforcements of 'A' Specials were sent by train from their depot in Newtownards to Enniskillen. This train journey involved crossing into Free State territory and changing trains at Clones, County Monaghan, but for one detachment the journey went badly wrong. Within minutes of arriving at Clones station, the USC detachment was involved in a gun battle with the IRA. The precise circumstances of the incident remain unclear and it may well be the case that, during moments of high tension and with a confused flurry of events, shooting had accidentally broken out. While conflicting allegations would be made at the inquiry held by the British Government as to who started the shooting, there was no

[23] M. Laffan, *The Partition of Ireland 1911–1925* (Dundalk, 1983), 91.

[24] Manpower report on the 3rd Northern IRA Division, UCDAD P7/A/II/23.

[25] D. Kennedy, *The Widening Gulf: Northern Attitudes to the Independent Irish State 1919–49* (Belfast, 1988), 74.

[26] B. Barton, *Brookeborough: The Making of a Prime Minister* (Belfast, 1988), 46.

disputing the result.[27] Although the IRA commandant was killed, the worst casualties were suffered by the Special Constabulary. Five men were killed, nine were wounded, and five others taken prisoner by the IRA. The effect of the incident upon loyalists was immediate. When the blood-stained train reached Lisbellaw, County Fermanagh, loyalists were so incensed that they drove Roman Catholics suspected of being Sinn Feiners from their homes. Loyalists regarded the 'Clones Incident' as an IRA 'ambush' and 'massacre', and their press reported it as such.[28] The Clones incident sparked off a new wave of bitter inter-communal violence in Belfast: from 12 to 16 February there was a serious outbreak of rioting, shooting, and bomb-throwing in which thirty-one people were killed.

Concerned at the violence in Belfast, the Northern Ireland government considered proclaiming martial law. However, the Cabinet, unwilling to adopt what it regarded as panic measures, instead opted to press for a greater deployment of troops to prevent further disorder.[29] Craig believed that the violence was a direct result of the IRA's determination to stir up trouble and thus discredit the Northern Ireland government. The Fermanagh County Commandant of the USC, Sir Basil Brooke, deeply concerned at the deteriorating situation along the border, visited Craig in Belfast. A week later, accompanied by his wife, Craig began a morale-boosting border tour, as he told his daughter, to 'buck up the Specials'.[30] Starting from Newry, he travelled 382 miles in three days and visited several police barracks, where he commended the men for their courage and delivered speeches in towns and villages on the way. In Fermanagh he visited some of the kidnapped loyalists (now released), and appealed to the loyalist people for 'strict discipline and restraint'.[31]

Meanwhile, in addition to increasing the USC establishment, Craig also sought the deployment of further troops along the border. General Cameron believed that twelve battalions of troops in Northern Ireland were sufficient to cope with the situation, but Craig wanted 'two additional battalions who would be able to be used for restoring public confidence by showing troops in [a] threatened locality'.[32] Although Churchill suspended the evacuation of British troops from the Irish Free State, he declined Craig's request to deploy troops on the Free

[27] For details of the inquiry, see 'The Clones Inquiry', PRONI FIN18/1/681.
[28] Kennedy, *Widening Gulf*, 78.
[29] Cabinet Conclusions, 16 Feb. 1922, PRONI CAB4/33/11.
[30] St John Ervine, *Craigavon*, 472.   [31] Barton, *Brookeborough*, 47.
[32] Craig to Rt. Hon. Winston Churchill MP, 13 Feb. 1922, Provisional Govt. of Ireland Cabinet Committee Papers, PRONI H05 CIM604/1/3.

State side of the border so as to prevent possible IRA raids. Churchill clearly did not wish to take any action which could undermine Collins's Provisional Government, it being in the British interest to prop it up against the powerful anti-treaty faction. He warned Craig that 'violent measures would do more harm than good and might entail the resignation of the Irish Provisional Government, thus creating chaos and leaving the extremists in control'.[33]

Churchill also told Craig that the 'actual watching of the frontier must be undertaken by police, the troops acting in aid of the civil power'.[34] Realizing that it could not depend upon the British Government to make troops readily available to defend them from IRA attacks, the Northern Ireland government took further steps to build up its own forces. Craig requisitioned 30 Fords, 100 Lancias, 100 Crossley tenders, 3 armoured Rolls-Royce, 4 three-ton lorries, 100 Lewis guns, 50 Vickers, and 25 wireless sets. The British Government felt that Craig's request was excessive and feared that he might be preparing an expedition against the Free State to rescue kidnapped loyalists still held on that side of the border. Churchill passed on to General Cameron Craig's request for arms and armoured cars, seeking advice as to what Northern Ireland would need for 'defensive purposes'.[35] Meanwhile, however, at a meeting of the Provisional Government of Ireland Committee on 20 February, Churchill supported an application from Collins for the issue to the Provisional Government of 1,000 rifles and three or four armoured cars. He was prepared to accept Collins's word that they would not be used along the border.

In the mean time the Ulster Unionist MPs at Westminster lobbied on behalf of Craig's government.[36] Their representations on the law-and-order crisis struck a chord with many Conservatives concerned at events in Ireland. At a time when the coalition government was showing signs of splintering, Churchill could not afford to ignore such stirrings on the Conservative back-benches. This, no doubt, explains the pressure he applied in private on the Provisional Government to secure the release of the kidnapped loyalists.[37] These efforts eventually proved successful and all were released by April. Churchill also agreed to send another three battalions of troops and promised a further six battalions if necessary.

In a memorandum to Lloyd George, Tom Jones, the Assistant

---

[33] Churchill to Craig, 13 Feb. 1922, PRONI HO5 CIM604/1/3.
[34] Churchill to Craig, 14 Feb. 1922, Cabinet Secretariat, PRONI CAB11/1.
[35] Churchill to Craig, PRONI HO5 CIM604/1/3.
[36] Craig to Charles Craig MP, 13 Feb. 1922, ibid.
[37] For details, see telegrams between Churchill and Collins in PRONI CAB11/1.

Secretary to the British Cabinet, expressed his disquiet at the direction of government policy in relation to Northern Ireland. He felt that in supporting the USC it was 'cloaking a military force under the guise of a police force', and thus was 'departing from the spirit of the bargain with the South'.[38] However, Northern Ireland's need for a militarized police force arose from the threat of IRA hostilities from Southern Ireland. The Northern Ireland government was dealing not with a few renegade units, but with active opposition from the entire IRA. IRA plans to disrupt Northern Ireland reveal that the terrorist attacks were not the work of local IRA hotheads operating without the authority or approval of their headquarters in Dublin. In any general offensive against Northern Ireland, the IRA 4th (Northern) Division (covering Belfast, Antrim, and Down) was to have the pivotal role. IRA General Headquarters—under the control of the pro-treatyites—promised that 'the driving power would be supplied from the South . . . because in this way Belfast can be brought to the brink of ruin'.[39]

The wave of IRA attacks in February 1922 resulted, as a member of the IRA boasted, in 'shooting a number of Northern Government Officials and Police; capturing a few barracks and destroying several thousands of pounds worth of Northern Government property'.[40] The pro-treaty IRA Chief of Staff, Eoin O'Duffy, organized the attacks with the authority of Michael Collins and his Minister of Defence, Richard Mulcahy. At a meeting in London with ministers of the British and Northern Ireland governments, Collins, in 'a truculently boastful mood, made no attempt to deny responsibility for outrages in the North and even claimed absolute control over the IRA'.[41]

To combat the IRA threat, Craig continued with the steady buildup of his own security forces. By 8 March his government had agreed

to raise 20 new mobile platoons of 'A' Specials, plus another 300 'A' Specials to train the 'B' force, bringing the 'A' force total to 5,800 men. It aimed to recruit another 2,000 'B' Specials, bringing their total to 22,000, and to make a serious effort to develop the 'C' force.[42]

Meanwhile Wickham repeated the request for 150 machine-guns and 264 motor cars and lorries, and now also asked for an additional 10,000 rifles for the 'B' and 'C' forces. The Ministry of Finance estimated that

---

[38] K. Middlemas (ed.), *Thomas Jones Whitehall Diary: Ireland 1918–1925* (London, 1971), 194.

[39] IRA GHQ directive to 4th Northern Division, UCDAD P7/A/II/47.

[40] Memo: 'The position of 2nd Northern Division in 1922', 8 Apr. 1925, Thomas Johnson Papers, NLI MS 17,143.

[41] P. Buckland, *James Craig* (Dublin, 1980), 76.

[42] Farrell, *Arming the Protestants*, 95.

the new cost for the Special Constabulary would be £1,829,000, or almost £1 million in excess of the British Government grant.[43] In February 1922 Craig invited Field Marshal Sir Henry Wilson, the recently retired Chief of the Imperial General Staff (and from 21 February Ulster Unionist MP for North Down at Westminster), to advise on security.

Wilson presented his plans on 17 March at a conference held at the Ministry of Home Affairs. His recommendations did not depart from previous Northern Ireland government policy but rather suggested a strengthening of the existing forces. In particular, he called for the appointment of an additional 3,000 'A' Specials. Although Sir Henry has often been viewed as a unionist hothead, he in fact presented a very reasoned analysis of the situation. He felt that 'it was essential to secure the confidence of all law-abiding people in the ability of the government to govern' by adopting stern measures.[44] However, he also believed that the police-forces should be composed of citizens 'irrespective of class or creed', and that 'encouragement should be given to Catholics to join equally with the other religions'.

Wilson also counselled caution regarding the proposal to flog those persons caught carrying firearms. He felt that to 'adopt flogging prematurely might alienate English public opinion, and it was better to wait until public opinion in England was on [Northern Ireland's] . . . side'. The Northern Ireland Cabinet realized that Sir Henry's recommendations 'would involve considerable additional expenditure, but it was agreed unanimously that it was necessary to see the present crisis through no matter what the cost'.[45] Wilson also proposed the appointment of a senior army officer, Major-General Arthur Solly-Flood, as military adviser and commander of all Northern Ireland police-forces, both regular and special. Churchill cleared the way for the Northern Ireland government to obtain the services of Solly-Flood, an Anglo-Irish officer, and six other army officers on the active list.[46]

It has been stated that with the appointment of Solly-Flood, the 'line between police and military in the North's forces was wearing very thin'.[47] However, Craig believed that securing the services of a few army officers of standing would improve the organization and discipline of the USC. This, he hoped, would make it more acceptable to

[43] Memo about Special Constabulary expenditure, 8 Mar. 1922, Private Office, PRONI FIN30/FC/9.
[44] Minutes of a conference held at the Ministry of Home Affairs, 17 Mar. 1922, PRONI HA20/A/1/8.
[45] Cabinet Conclusions, 27 Mar. 1922, PRONI CAB4/37/4.
[46] Craig to Maj.-Gen. Solly-Flood, 30 Mar. 1922, PRONI FIN18/2/234.
[47] Farrell, *Arming the Protestants*, 98.

the Roman Catholic minority, given that 'Michael Collins seemed to look upon the military as more or less impartial, whilst he appears to be prejudiced against our existing Constabulary officers'.[48] Craig's acting in a rather militaristic manner was a response to an increasingly warlike situation. As Patrick Buckland has observed: 'By the middle of March the north and south were to all intents and purposes openly at war.'[49]

Despite having been reinforced along the border, USC forces were obliged, under increasing IRA attacks, to fall back in March 1922 upon more defensive positions. They abandoned the Old Fort at Belleek, County Fermanagh, which overlooked the town but which was actually in the Irish Free State. Along the border, most minor roads were blocked by the Special Constabulary to prevent IRA flying columns crossing into Northern Ireland, and the major roads were patrolled by Specials. In Fermanagh all but seven roads were blocked, and those left open were heavily guarded. To restrict further the movement of subversives, the USC also blew up various bridges at strategic points along the border.[50]

Apart from the border unionists, the other group of unionists which felt particularly threatened by IRA violence was 'the Protestant working class of Belfast, inclined by history towards sectarianism, and very much in the front-line as regards IRA activity'.[51] Inter-communal tension rose, bringing with it renewed outbreaks of violence. Republican writers tend to regard the violence as part of an anti-Roman Catholic pogrom orchestrated by the Northern Ireland government. Referring to attacks on Roman Catholics, it is claimed that: 'the intoxicated and bloodthirsty [loyalist] mob, led on by armed Specials and supplied with bombs, would rush the narrow streets, howling and looting, burning and murdering as they went.'[52]

However, it can be argued that attempts to portray the violence in Belfast as part of a deliberate policy to exterminate Roman Catholics are a simplistic approach taking little account of IRA activity in Northern Ireland or of Protestant casualties. Of the 236 people killed in Northern Ireland between December 1921 and the end of May 1922, 147 were Roman Catholics and 89 either Protestants or members of the security forces.[53] Of those wounded during the same period, 166

---

[48] Craig to Churchill, 3 Apr. 1922, Cabinet Secretariat, PRONI CAB98/47/2.

[49] P. Buckland, *Ulster Unionism and the Origins of Northern Ireland 1886 to 1922* (Dublin, 1973), 154.

[50] Memo by Joseph Johnston: 'Report on Visit to Swanlinbar and Clones', 12 July 1923, NAI S3 161.

[51] Kennedy, *Widening Gulf*, 94.

[52] D. Macardle, *The Irish Republic* (London, 1937), 619.

[53] P. Buckland, *A History of Northern Ireland* (Dublin, 1981), 46.

were Roman Catholics and 180 were Protestants or members of the
security forces.

The casualty figures clearly indicate a high level of IRA activity and
while the fact remains that Protestant attacks on Roman Catholics did
take place, it is important to differentiate between the attitude of the
Northern Ireland government and the actions of some of its grass-roots
supporters. While a minority of working-class unionists might engage
in spontaneous rioting or in sniper attacks against the Roman Catholic
areas, they received no support from Craig's government. Indeed, Craig
consistently denounced attacks against Roman Catholics, and unionist
newspapers in their reporting of such incidents also roundly condemned
them. However, unionists believed that the blame for creating the
overall state of lawlessness rested with the IRA men, who were thus
'responsible for all the violent deaths, whether they are perpetrated by
themselves, or provoked by them'.[54]

The USC—at this stage in 1922 the main force employed by the
Northern Ireland government for maintaining law and order—has been
accused of carrying the main responsibility for the violence. It has been
claimed that instead of 'trying to curb violence, the Specials often
incited it, with the aim of cowing or expelling subversive elements'.[55]
It is true that the 'B' Specials on occasions contributed to the tension
and violence in Belfast, but it can be argued that they were reacting
to, rather than creating, a situation which was clearly born of the IRA
outrages and inter-communal rioting. In addition, the sometimes unacceptable behaviour of USC members had more to do with lack of
training and discipline than with a spirit of government-supported
partisanship. Indeed, Craig complained to London that the failure to
provide adequate numbers of troops to defend the border meant that
he had to deploy the best members of the Special Constabulary along
that frontier.[56] Consequently, he had to use the less effective, and also
less disciplined, members in Belfast.

The fact remains that in the face of great provocation, including the
murder of their friends and comrades, the vast majority of the members
of the USC displayed surprising restraint. Despite the shortcomings
of relatively few of its members, the force did make a significant contribution to the restoration of law and order. For example, by protecting Roman Catholic-owned public houses and spirit groceries from

---

[54] *Belfast Newsletter*, 1 June 1922.
[55] J. M. Curran, *The Birth of the Irish Free State 1921–1923* (Birmingham, Ala., 1980),
176.
[56] St John Ervine, *Craigavon*, 207.

Protestant mobs,[57] the 'B' Specials not only prevented public disorder but also demonstrated a commitment to impartial policing.

Nevertheless, the controversy surrounding the murder of members of the McMahon family casts a long shadow over the USC. On the night of 23/4 March 1922 men wearing Special Constabulary uniforms burst into the homes of a Roman Catholic family in Belfast and killed the father, three sons, and an employee who worked in their bar, while two other sons were wounded. It was believed that the attack was a reprisal for the murders of two special constables in Belfast on 22 March, and it is claimed that 'the killers seem to have made no effort to disguise the fact that they were members of the police or Specials'.[58] Unfortunately no evidence is offered to substantiate this view that the killers were in reality members of the security forces. Admittedly the fact that they wore police uniforms does suggest this, but surplus police uniforms were on sale in several shops in Belfast. William Grant, an Ulster Unionist MP, pointed out the danger that subversive elements might purchase the uniforms and impersonate police officers to perpetrate terrorist attacks.[59]

Disguised as police officers, terrorists could move relatively freely through Belfast during the curfew. While we shall never know for certain if the murderers of the McMahon family were members of the police, it is beyond question that the attackers were Protestants. The public assumption at the time was that 'B' Specials were involved, and there was widespread outrage among nationalists in both Northern Ireland and the Free State.[60] Craig's government unreservedly condemned the McMahon murders and made every effort to trace the culprits, even offering a reward of £1,000 for information leading to their arrest. In an effort to end the cycle of rioting and sniping, which frequently resulted in further deaths, Bates authorized each County Commandant to mobilize the Special Constabulary as a preventive measure.[61]

Although the McMahon murders were particularly savage, it was not long before fresh atrocities were being committed, this time by Roman Catholics. On 31 March a bomb was thrown into the house of a Protestant family called Donnelly. Two children were killed, while the father and two other members of the family were wounded. On

---

[57] R. Harrison, Ministry of Home Affairs, to G. C. Duggan, Ministry of Finance, 23 Feb. 1922, PRONI FIN18/1/578.

[58] Farrell, *Arming the Protestants*, 100.

[59] *Parl. Deb.* (House of Commons), ii, 18 May 1922, col. 557.

[60] Minutes of Provisional Government of Ireland Cabinet Committee, 24 Mar. 1922, PRONI HO5 CIM604/1/3.

[61] Samuel Watt to Sir Ernest Clark, 27 Mar. 1922, PRONI FIN18/1/578.

19 June an IRA gang from Dundalk attacked and burned four Protestant homes near Newry, and 'six of their occupants [were] shot dead in the roadway as the families were lined up'.[62] However, it was the McMahon murders which received most publicity—no doubt because of the tragic circumstances in which almost all the male members of an entire family were wiped out, and the apparent involvement of the security forces—and the British Government felt compelled to 'formally request' Craig to visit London.

The British Government had planned to invite Craig and Collins to London for talks after parliament had passed the Irish Treaty Bill. However, the deterioration in law and order in Belfast, and more particularly the outrage expressed after the McMahon murders, forced them to convene the meeting without delay.[63] Craig crossed to London on 28 March 1922 and his negotiations with Collins resulted in a new peace pact signed two days later. The pact was intended to 'cure unrest and disorder in Northern Ireland by creating Catholic confidence in the government and securing Catholic co-operation in the maintenance of law and order',[64] and in return the IRA were to cease their activities.

Despite the enthusiasm with which the British press greeted the pact, it had little real effect on the situation in Northern Ireland where violence continued unabated. The statistical survey prepared by the Northern Ireland Ministry of Home Affairs, which recorded all violent outrages, does not indicate a significant reduction in incidents committed after the pact.[65] Indeed, the Northern Ireland government had to maintain a high level of USC mobilization, with 350 men mobilized in Belfast alone, in an attempt to preserve some semblance of law and order. After the signing of the pact the IRA General Headquarters had ordered units in Northern Ireland on to the defensive, but that did not last for long. Many young IRA members on the anti-treaty side repudiated the pact, and Collins himself was impatient for it to produce results. When agreement with Craig on the boundary question was not forthcoming, instead of trying to restrain the IRA, Collins 'encouraged both its factions to step up their campaign against the north'.[66] No doubt he also believed that the resumption of full-scale hostilities by the IRA

---

[62] Kennedy, *Widening Gulf*, 77.

[63] Minutes of Provisional Government of Ireland Cabinet Committee, 24 Mar. 1922, PRONI HO5 CIM604/1/3.

[64] P. Buckland, *The Factory of Grievances: Devolved Government in Northern Ireland 1921–39* (Dublin, 1979), 202.

[65] See graph prepared by Ministry of Home Affairs recording violent outrages in PRONI CAB6/11.

[66] Curran, *Birth of the Irish Free State*, 178.

in Northern Ireland would act as a protection for the Roman Catholic minority. It was a false assumption, as it was the fear and anger generated by IRA attacks which had stirred Protestants into action against Roman Catholics. Nevertheless, at a series of meetings in mid-April of the commanders of the five IRA northern divisions, it was decided, 'with the agreement of the pro-treaty GHQ, to resume operations in the six counties'.[67]

At a meeting on 5 May convened by O'Duffy, a new IRA offensive against Northern Ireland was discussed and, although Collins was not directly involved, it is 'certain his associates would not have embarked on such a dangerous enterprise without his blessing'.[68] All factions of the IRA co-operated in the planning, and to strengthen their forces in Northern Ireland it was agreed to send additional men and guns north. These preparations included the swapping of British-supplied arms with the anti-treaty units who, in return, provided arms for use in Northern Ireland.[69] It appears that the IRA had planned to launch its new terror offensive in early May but had to postpone the attacks because the Northern Ireland government became aware of them. From the time the Northern Ireland government assumed responsibility for intelligence gathering, it had steadily built up an effective intelligence organization. Indeed, IRA documents captured by the authorities confirmed that a new offensive against Northern Ireland was being organized with the approval of its Dublin headquarters.[70]

Conscious all along of the potential danger of renewed IRA attacks, the Northern Ireland government had taken steps to improve its defences against a possible terrorist offensive. In addition to seeking the early establishment of its new regular police-force and the strengthening of its Special Constabulary, the Northern Ireland government had introduced the Civil Authorities (Special Powers) Act (NI), 1922. The Bill had been introduced in parliament on 15 March and become law on 7 April 1922. It authorized the civil authority to 'take all such steps and issue all such orders as may be necessary for preserving the peace and maintaining order'.[71] The Act adapted the powers formerly exercised by the military under the Restoration of Order in Ireland Act, 1920, and delegated powers to the Minister of Home Affairs to make regulations for the maintenance of public order (a schedule

---

[67] Farrell, *Arming the Protestants*, 127.
[68] Curran, *Birth of the Irish Free State*, 178.
[69] Macardle, *The Irish Republic*, 899.
[70] Cabinet Conclusions, 12 May 1922, CAB4/41/19.
[71] [12 & 13 Geo. 5] Civil Authorities (Special Powers) Act (Northern Ireland), 1922, Sect. 1 (1).

attached to the Act listed some thirty-five regulations). When drafting
this schedule, the Northern Ireland Cabinet had consulted the RIC
Divisional Commissioner so as to ensure that all necessary counter-
insurgency measures had been included. Following the peace pact with
Michael Collins, the Northern Ireland Cabinet had considered whether
it should proceed with the Special Powers Bill.[72] Although it agreed to
do so, it was decided not to implement at that stage the regulations
contained in it.

IRA violence increased during May 1922, an attack on the Belfast
police headquarters at Musgrave Street in the early hours of 18 May
heralding the general offensive against Northern Ireland. Assisted by a
sympathizer who opened the back door of the barracks, twenty-one
IRA members entered the headquarters in an attempt to seize a large
quantity of arms and drive off with them in a police armoured car.
Although they overpowered police in the guard-room and arms-room,
the alarm was raised by another sentry and a guard on the first floor
opened fire on the IRA with a machine-gun. While unable to capture
any weapons, the IRA attackers managed to escape, leaving behind
them one constable dead and a special constable wounded.[73]

Also in May the IRA launched an incendiary campaign, burning
down the homes and business premises of unionists. Among the man-
sions destroyed by the IRA was Shane's Castle, the ancestral home of
the father of the Speaker of the Northern Ireland Commons, Sir Hugh
O'Neill. Claims for compensation arising from malicious injuries totalled
a staggering £794,678 in May and £760,018 in June, compared with
£252,578 for April.[74] Parallel to the burnings, there was a rise in intimidation, bombing, and murder. In the month of May alone, ninety
murders were committed in Belfast—though not all by the IRA—and
as Bates complained, not one person was brought to justice. Unionists
were convinced that the IRA was simply attempting to make the task
of government impossible and thus prevent the consolidation of
Northern Ireland.

Some believe that the decision by the IRA commanders not to
involve the southern-based IRA divisions straddling the border was
part of a plan 'to give the impression that it [the offensive] was an
indigenous reaction by the Northern minority against their oppression
by the Northern government'.[75] However, it is equally possible that

---

[72] Cabinet Conclusions, 1 Apr. 1922, PRONI CAB4/38/17.
[73] Report from OC 3rd IRA (Northern) Division, to IRA Chief of Staff, 19 May
1922, UCDAD P7a/173.
[74] Graph showing claims for compensation because of malicious injuries suffered, PRONI
FIN18/4/40.
[75] Farrell, *Arming the Protestants*, 128.

the measures taken by the Northern Ireland government to secure the border were so effective as to deter large-scale cross-border raids. The IRA may, therefore, have been obliged to concentrate its activities in Belfast, relying mainly upon the 2nd and 3rd Northern Divisions, which were entirely within Northern Ireland, to carry out the attacks. In Belfast the violence reached a peak in the second and third weeks of May 1922. There were some 606 violent incidents in Northern Ireland during May, 100 more than in April.[76] Fourteen murders, including that of an Ulster Unionist MP, W. J. Twaddell, were perpetrated in the weekend of 20/21 May alone. Speaking in parliament, Sir James Craig referred to Twaddell's murder as the culmination of the attacks on the loyalist community, but declared: 'if those who committed this dastardly outrage thought it would for a moment weaken the functions of this Parliament or the steadfast courage of the people of Ulster they never made a greater error.'[77]

Although the Government of Northern Ireland had hitherto been reluctant to adopt security measures which might appear provocative to the Dublin government,[78] it now acted decisively. Following a Cabinet meeting to authorize a clamp-down, Bates invoked his powers under the Civil Authorities (Special Powers) Act. On 22 May the IRA and related organizations were proscribed and internment of terrorist suspects introduced.[79] The police, 'both regular and special, arrested 500 people within twenty-four hours of the proclamation and those arrested were interned in a wooden hulk, the *Argenta*, a prison ship anchored in Belfast Lough'.[80] The prison ship had previously been acquired by the Military Adviser in anticipation of the introduction of internment. Authority was given to the security forces—where they considered it necessary—to close any road, lane, alley, or bridge without publishing or giving notice. Another regulation provided that, should any property be used for unlawful purposes, it would be blocked up. This was aimed at ending the unrestricted use by IRA snipers of buildings in Belfast. Recognizing that alcohol was a contributory factor in rioting, the Northern Ireland government curbed the opening-hours of public houses. Since 13 May Belfast had been subject to a curfew between the hours of 9 p.m. and 7 a.m. and from 1 June the rest of

[76] From a graph illustrating claims for criminal injuries against local authorities in Northern Ireland during 1922, PRONI FIN18/4/40.

[77] *Parl. Deb.* (House of Commons), ii, 23 May 1922, col. 593.

[78] Despite the request of their Military Adviser that the IRA be proscribed, the Northern Ireland Cabinet at a meeting on 16 May 1922 declined to do so: Cabinet Conclusions, PRONI CAB4/42/16.

[79] *Belfast Gazette*, 26 May 1922, No. 46.

[80] Buckland, *A History of Northern Ireland*, 46.

Northern Ireland was placed under curfew between 11 p.m. and 5 a.m., a curfew which was rigorously enforced. The movement of individuals was further restricted by a later regulation allowing the government to exclude a person from certain areas.

The Civil Authorities (Special Powers) Act had extended the use of flogging as a 'special punishment', and it was now increasingly used. Anxious to prevent IRA attacks on government buildings and avoid the destruction of records whose loss would disrupt the administration of public services, the government established a night-watchman service. Meanwhile, eager to protect commercial buildings and factories from IRA incendiary attack but unable to deploy police to guard them, the government agreed to a suggestion by Solly-Flood that shotguns be issued to civilian watchmen. However, the issue of shotguns was only permitted following an undertaking from the employer that the weapons would be properly safeguarded and entrusted to responsible persons of good character.[81] These shotguns were later safely recalled by the government once the emergency had passed.

Although the Northern Ireland Cabinet had decided against military courts,[82] it acknowledged the importance of bringing people quickly to justice in order to demonstrate the effectiveness of the judicial system. Two additional resident magistrates were appointed to help deal with the numerous cases requiring attention. In addition to saturation patrols along roads to prevent movement by terrorists,[83] the Special Constabulary conducted patrols by motor boat in Lough Erne to help secure the border with the Free State. Within Northern Ireland itself, the security forces also stepped up the number of searches for arms, ammunition, and subversives. The Northern Ireland government was able to undertake such a wide range of security operations because it could draw upon the large manpower reserves of the 'B' Specials. In May and June, during the height of the violence, the government mobilized a very large number of 'B' Specials for full-time duty. In Belfast alone some 778 men were mobilized; in County Down, 820; and 1,060 in County Fermanagh.[84] The mobilized 'B' Specials were used to reinforce platoons on operational duty, to guard barracks, factories, bridges, and private houses, and for escort duties to protect public

    [81] Watt to Clark, 23 June 1922, PRONI FIN18/2/64.
    [82] Cabinet Conclusions, 20 May 1922, PRONI CAB4/43/9.
    [83] Speaking in parliament, an Ulster Unionist MP, D. G. Shillington, stated that travelling between Armagh and Belfast on a 'miserably dirty night', he had been stopped by fifteen different patrols of 'B' Specials: *Parl. Deb.* (House of Commons), ii, 23 May 1922, col. 617.
    [84] W. A. Hamill, Ministry of Home Affairs, to Ministry of Finance, 16 June and 20 July 1922, PRONI FIN18/1/578.

figures. Meanwhile, Craig's government had also pressed the British Government for more troops; it agreed to an additional five battalions, making a total of twenty-two. The murder of Twaddell and the upsurge in violence spurred the British Government into granting arms and equipment on loan to the USC, having previously refused Craig's request for them.[85]

Despite the series of government measures against the terrorists, the IRA continued its attacks and, while the campaign was to prove limited, it was none the less intense. The violence was so severe that many feared the Northern Ireland administration was in danger of being overwhelmed as the country collapsed into anarchy. However, as the counter-insurgency measures implemented by Craig's government began to take effect, the IRA was forced back on to the defensive and the level of violence began to fall. Indeed, the Commander of the 3rd IRA (Northern) Division confessed to his headquarters that the Northern Ireland government had 'beaten the IRA completely in Antrim and Down'. Reporting on the situation in Belfast, he acknowledged that the IRA were 'daily losing ground and the tactics the Enemy are now adopting is having the desired effect. If they succeed everywhere as they are succeeding in Belfast, it will not be long till the Northern government will have complete recognition from the population of the six counties.'[86]

Although the Government of Northern Ireland did succeed in overcoming the IRA offensive, in May 1922 its eventual success appeared far from certain. Craig's Cabinet was deeply worried and, speaking in parliament, Craig called for more recruits to the USC. Despite already having 5,500 'A' Specials and 19,000 'B' Specials in arms, he feared that 'the time may come when the whole of Ulster may have to be mobilised'.[87] It would appear that the electoral pact between Collins and de Valera, announced on 20 May, was regarded by Ulster Unionists as an overture to a concerted attack on Northern Ireland. Craig believed the Collins–de Valera pact signalled that the time had passed when he was under an obligation to seek a compromise solution on the boundary question. Indeed, he was determined not to work with the Boundary Commission under any circumstances, and declared: 'we will hear no more about a Commission coming to decide whether our boundaries shall be so and so. What we have now we hold, and we will hold against all combinations.'[88]

[85] Lord Curzon to Craig, 24 May 1922, Cabinet Secretariat, PRONI CAB11/2.
[86] OC 3rd IRA (Northern) Division to IRA GHQ, 27 July 1922, UCDAD P7/B/II/ 77.   [87] *Parl. Deb.* (House of Commons), ii, 23 May 1922, col. 605.
[88] Ibid., col. 598.

Behind Craig's confident public utterances was a fear that Northern Ireland might be invaded from the Irish Free State. This fear of invasion is reflected in the preparations of the Government of Northern Ireland to further strengthen and expand the constabulary forces. Approaching Churchill, Craig 'requested the immediate dispatch of 23,000 rifles, 15,000 bayonets, 242 Lewis guns, 50 Vicker guns, and a large supply of mortars, grenades, uniforms and tents'.[89] The preparations were intended to counter a very real threat. So real was the possibility of invasion that Major-General Cameron—commanding the troops in the Ulster District—told Craig that 'resisting invasion from the Free State . . . especially since the Collins–de Valera agreement is the most important and the most suitable work for troops'.[90] It is against this background that the Northern Ireland government reacted to events in Belleek and Pettigo.

The predominantly Roman Catholic village of Belleek is located in a triangle of County Fermanagh cut off by the River Erne on one side and County Donegal on the other. The only roads connecting the 'triangle' with the rest of Northern Ireland ran through Free State territory for a few hundred yards near Pettigo, a mainly Protestant village which, although just inside the Irish Free State, had a few of its outlying houses in Fermanagh. Free State forces loyal to Collins occupied Pettigo and an old fort just outside Belleek. On the Northern Ireland side, Craig's government had to rely upon its constabulary forces to protect the area as there were no troops in the vicinity of the 'triangle'.[91] Tension in the area was mounting and a full-scale crisis broke when a group of anti-treaty IRA men invaded the 'triangle' and seized a number of local unionists. The Free State forces made no effort to prevent their activities.

Sir Basil Brooke, the USC County Commandant, assembled a composite force of sixty-four 'A' and 'B' Specials which crossed by water and occupied Magherameena Castle in an effort to defend Northern Ireland against the IRA attacks. Two special constables were killed and reinforcements, sent by road, were driven back, abandoning a Lancia armoured car and three Crossley tenders. Under IRA attack and with reinforcements unable to break through, Brooke's force was compelled to evacuate its exposed position by boat.[92]

By 30 May there were no Northern Ireland forces left in the 'triangle' and local loyalists had fled from the IRA, who now openly patrolled

---

[89] Farrell, *Arming the Protestants*, 130.

[90] Appendix 'A' to Cabinet Conclusions, 23 May 1922, PRONI CAB4/44/24.

[91] Memo from Chief of Imperial General Staff, 9 June 1922, PRONI HO5 CIM604/1/11.   [92] Barton, *Brookeborough*, 50.

Belleek in the captured armoured car. Loyalist Ulster was outraged and its press reported that, following the 'Invasion of Ulster', thousands of 'Protestants were fleeing into Enniskillen from the occupied villages and the triangle of territory between them and the border'.[93] Solly-Flood informed Craig that, as the constabulary forces lacked the weapons for open battle, he opposed their deployment on a large scale to clear the 'triangle'. Craig thereupon telegraphed Churchill to take immediate military action in case the IRA seized further Northern Ireland territory and the loyalist people 'feeling outraged may take matters into their own hands'.[94]

On 30 May two army officers, a police officer, and a few regular soldiers in two armoured cars were sent to the Pettigo area in an attempt to restore confidence among the inhabitants. However, they themselves were fired on while still in Northern Ireland and were forced to withdraw. Major-General Cameron informed Craig that it would be unfair to ask troops to clear the villages and hold the area unless they could protect their flank by occupying the Ballyshannon–Bundoran area in the Free State.[95] A meeting of the Northern Ireland Cabinet on 31 May agreed that Craig and Lord Londonderry should cross to London and make Churchill fully aware of how serious the situation was. In addition to the threat which Craig believed the incursion posed to Northern Ireland, he was acutely aware that it had raised communal tensions and fears to fever pitch. He realized that unless the government was able to demonstrate its ability and willingness to defend the people against IRA aggression, the incursion was likely to precipitate widespread inter-communal violence. Churchill agreed to take a tough line and General Macready was ordered to clear the area and informed that, if necessary, his troops could pursue hostile IRA units across the border.

Troops, supported by artillery dispatched from Enniskillen, re-took the village of Pettigo on 4 June, although some Northern Ireland territory remained under the occupation of the Free State forces. One special constable, who was acting as a driver for the military, was killed during the operation, as were seven IRA men, and fifteen IRA prisoners were taken.[96] Collins protested at the military action and Lloyd George became alarmed that Churchill's measures could lead to a major clash and political rupture between London and Dublin. He attempted

[93] Kennedy, *Widening Gulf*, 50.
[94] Craig to Churchill, 30 May 1922, PRONI CAB4/46/3.
[95] Maj.-Gen. A. R. Cameron, Comdr., Ulster District, to Craig, 30 May 1922, PRONI CAB4/46/3.
[96] Report by GHQ, Ireland, 10 June 1922, PRONI HO5 CIM604/1/11.

to persuade Churchill against using troops to dislodge the IRA from Belleek, but Churchill threatened to resign if Lloyd George continued to interfere.[97] Macready—no friend of Ulster unionism—claimed that Collins's complaint was full of inaccuracies. Indeed, he believed that there was no reason 'why an armoured car should not have proceeded a mile and a half into the Free State Territory and fire[d] on the retreating IRA, as the latter had fired continually on the British troops until successfully driven from their position'.[98]

Before the military launched their operation against Belleek, Churchill warned Collins that if British troops were fired at, they had 'full discretion either to bombard or occupy the Fort or any other points from which fire is brought to bear upon the British Forces'.[99] On 8 June troops advanced on Belleek and came under fire, whereupon they shelled the old fort in the Free State which was the barracks of the pro-treaty troops, who then retreated. Local unionists were to claim that the Free State forces had made 'common cause' with the republicans during the incursion and the beginning of the trouble was attributed 'to a failure of discipline among the local Free State troops'.[100] British troops occupied the fort and remained there until 25 August 1924. The occupation of the Belleek fort enabled troops to keep open the road from Enniskillen and Garrison into the 'triangle' at Belleek.[101] A neutral zone under British military command was established for a couple of miles on either side of the border. The Irish Provisional Government accepted in due course the creation of the neutral zone, and the 'triangle' area was thereafter fairly quiet. A major crisis had thus passed.

Some commentators have considered the scale of Churchill's response 'disproportionate, even faintly ludicrous'.[102] The IRA occupation of Belleek and Pettigo is often regarded as 'amusing or faintly ridiculous. But to the Unionists in 1922 they were deadly serious assaults on the territorial integrity of Northern Ireland, especially significant in the light of possible boundary revision.'[103] A British civil servant, Stephen Tallents, reported that the IRA occupation:

reduced the local Unionists to a state of nerves, comparable only, so far as my experience goes to the panic among the better class inhabitants of villages which the Bolsheviks have once held and threaten to revisit. They say and some at least of them, I am sure, believe that the Republicans and their local

---

[97] Farrell, *Arming the Protestants*, 133.   [98] GHQ, PRONI HO5 CIM604/1/11.
[99] Churchill to Collins, 6 June 1922, NAI S1 235.
[100] S. G. Tallents to Sir James Masterton-Smith in a report about Belleek and Pettigo, 13 Nov. 1922, Colonial Office Irish Papers, PRO(L) CO 739/1.
[101] Report by Col. M. Dunphy to GHQ Dublin, 14 Aug. 1924, NAI S1 235.
[102] Farrell, *Arming the Protestants*, 134.   [103] Kennedy, *Widening Gulf*, 73.

enemies are only waiting for the withdrawal of the British troops to enter the village and massacre them.[104]

Churchill later wrote that the military action he authorized was a means of reassuring Ulster unionists that whatever else happened, 'the integrity of their territory would be protected'.[105]

Churchill believed that the Free State government now realized that a line had been drawn over which it could not step. Although the blame for the incursion has traditionally been ascribed to the republican elements in the IRA, the contemporary military reports of the Free State forces indicate that there were no irregulars in the area.[106] If these statements are true, then the responsibility for the whole affair rests with Collins's own forces. This would confirm the views expressed to Tallents—as mentioned earlier—that the problems arose because of a breakdown in discipline among the Free State troops.

Despite the firm action taken by Churchill in response to the IRA incursion in Fermanagh, Craig still did not feel that he could wholly rely on support from the British Government. Indeed, many Ulster unionists regarded the British Government as not merely indifferent to the security needs of Northern Ireland but actually sympathetic to the Irish Provisional Government. The efforts of the British Government to restrain the Northern Ireland government in its counter-insurgency programme were greatly resented by unionists, and one Ulster writer declared: 'There are times when English shallowness is very hard to "thole" [endure], and there were many moments in 1922 when Ulstermen loathed the English almost as much as they were loathed by Republicans.'[107]

Lloyd George had opposed the use of British troops along the Northern Ireland border in any conflict with the IRA except 'on an issue like the Constitution itself, which would unite opinion in the Empire'.[108] Although some might regard Lloyd George's position as only tactical, it appeared that he and some of his close advisers were biased in favour of the Provisional Government. However, the murder in London on 22 June 1922 of Field Marshal Sir Henry Wilson by two Irish republicans dramatically changed attitudes to Dublin. The impact of Wilson's murder was profound, and in Britain the politicians responsible for the treaty were immediately placed on the defensive. It was widely felt that the Provisional Government was morally responsible for the murder

---

[104] Tallents's report to Masterton-Smith, 13 Nov. 1922, PRO(L) CO 739/1.
[105] W. S. Churchill, *The Aftermath: A Sequel to the World Crisis* (London, 1941), 336.
[106] In his report to GHQ, Col. Comdt. Hogan claimed that at 'no time were there any Irregulars stationed in or in the immediate vicinity of Pettigo'. 7 June 1922, NAI S1 235.
[107] St John Ervine, *Craigavon*, 402.   [108] Middlemas, *Thomas Jones Diary*, 211.

because of its failure to suppress the anti-treaty forces, 'and it was felt that the British Cabinet by condoning such a state of affairs bore some responsibility too'.[109]

It was rumoured that Bonar Law threatened to lead a die-hard Conservative parliamentary revolt against Lloyd George's coalition unless it insisted upon immediate restoration of law and order in Ireland. It was with its future under political threat that the British Government exerted pressure on Collins to 'deal with the military threat presented by the occupation of the Four Courts' in Dublin by anti-treaty IRA.[110] Churchill had planned, if need be, to use British troops in Dublin to dislodge the irregulars from the Four Courts, but his action was anticipated by Collins. After a three-day bombardment, on 30 June the anti-treaty IRA units were compelled to surrender to Collins. Thus began an open civil war between the pro-treaty and anti-treaty sections of Sinn Fein, which lasted several months. The civil war, fought by both sides with great ferocity, created deep divisions within Irish society, and it was to be two generations before the scars began to heal.[111]

Wilson's murder had forced the British Government to act firmly against the Provisional Government, and in doing so it had appeared to stand shoulder to shoulder with the Government of Northern Ireland. However, while such action might provide public reassurance for grass-roots unionists that the British Government was going to stand by Northern Ireland, Craig's Cabinet remained conscious of the differences between London and Belfast. Although Craig had forwarded to Churchill captured IRA documents which clearly proved that the terrorist campaign in Northern Ireland was organized by the faction of the IRA loyal to Collins,[112] the British Government remained unwilling to break with Dublin. Indeed, it might be argued that the action taken by the British Government in response to the murder of Sir Henry Wilson was the minimum it could have taken in the circumstances.

No doubt for the benefit of political opinion in London, Churchill had warned the Dublin government that, unless law and order were immediately restored, the British Government would regard the treaty as having been violated. But, anxious to prop up the pro-treaty faction

---

[109] R. Blake, *The Unknown Prime Minister: The Life and Times of Andrew Bonar Law 1858–1923* (London, 1955), 440.

[110] Middlemas, *Thomas Jones Diary*, 213.

[111] For an account of the civil war, see R. Fanning, *Independent Ireland* (Dublin, 1983), 15–22.

[112] Craig to Churchill, 28 June 1922, PRONI CAB6/89.

in Dublin, the British Government did not actually take any steps which would have undermined the authority of the Provisional Government. It was clearly in Britain's imperial interests to ensure that an overtly hostile republican government did not gain power in Dublin. While there might be problems with a government led by Collins, it was preferable to one led by de Valera. The Lloyd George coalition thus chose to continue to turn a 'Nelson's eye' to the security needs of Northern Ireland. Consequently, Craig's complaints, supported by documentary evidence, that Collins's government was 'very gravely implicated' in murders and incendiarism in Northern Ireland, were largely ignored by the British Government.

In common with his fellow Ulster unionists Craig displayed a siege mentality, for he, like them, was a victim of an all-too-real modern-day siege, combining psychological political pressures with physical violence. Not only did Craig share in the siege of his people but he also experienced the personal effects of being besieged. His home at Cabin Hill, Knock, on the outskirts of Belfast, was heavily fortified with sandbags and barbed-wire entanglements and had a guard squad to protect it against IRA attack. With his move into his official residence at Stormont Castle, the security precautions were even more tight and he had a guard squad of thirty men.[113] Nevertheless, the IRA launched an attack, albeit unsuccessful, on Craig's residence and also attacked the homes of four other ministers. Whatever Craig may have felt about the danger to his life, he did not allow that to interfere with the discharge of his duties. He displayed a personal courage which undoubtedly bolstered the morale of the unionist people and so strengthened their resolve to resist the IRA.[114]

The outbreak of civil war in Southern Ireland further reduced the IRA threat against Northern Ireland, since not 'only did cross-border attacks collapse suddenly as the IRA factions abandoned their cooperation but also the northern IRA men moved south to join the fray'.[115] Nevertheless, it would be incorrect to assume that the defeat of the IRA campaign in Northern Ireland was due to the outbreak of the civil war. Prior to the start of hostilities with the fighting at the Four Courts, the IRA campaign had already proved a dismal failure. The IRA offensive flagged and then failed owing to the resistance of

---

[113] 'Barrack Furniture for Police Guard at Stormont Castle', PRONI FIN18/1/886.

[114] e.g. he insisted upon accompanying the funeral procession of murdered Ulster Unionist MP, William Twaddell, along its entire route, despite the great risk of IRA sniper attack. See PRONI CAB6/68 for details.

[115] Laffan, *Partition of Ireland*, 97.

the USC armed with the formidable powers of the Special Powers Act. The IRA Officer Commanding the 3rd Northern Division, in a report to his General Headquarters, conceded that the effective deployment of the Special Constabulary had forced him to disband IRA flying columns in counties Antrim and Down within two weeks of the offensive's launch.[116] Demoralization among his men had completed the work of the Special Constabulary, the 2nd and 3rd Brigades ceasing to be military organizations.

The 3rd Northern Division attempted to concentrate its energies on Belfast, but once again the Government of Northern Ireland managed to outmanoeuvre the IRA. Many of the Roman Catholic population, war-weary and anxious for peace, supplied the Northern Ireland government with information, and as the Officer Commanding observed:

several of our [arms] dumps have been captured within the last few weeks . . . in many of these raids company and battalion papers have been found with the result that many officers and men are forced to go on the run . . . They found it difficult to get accommodation with people now . . . The Enemy are continually raiding and arresting; the heavy sentences and particularly the floggings make the civilians very loth to hide 'wanted men' or arms.[117]

The IRA offensive in the western part of Northern Ireland, carried out by the 2nd Northern Division, also failed and the USC, drawing upon its large reserve of manpower, was able to launch a counter-offensive.[118] The 4th Northern Division had clashed with the security forces in County Armagh, but by the end of June law and order was also restored in this area, with IRA activities practically petering out.

The forces of the Government of Northern Ireland had broken the IRA terror offensive. The outbreak of the civil war was only the final blow against a failed campaign. As one contemporary writer has observed, with the outbreak of the civil war, the IRA gunmen drifted increasingly to Southern Ireland.[119] IRA officers of the Northern divisions met Collins, Mulcahy, and other members of the GHQ staff in Dublin on 9 July to discuss the situation in Northern Ireland and it was agreed that the campaign should be called off. At a further meeting on 1 August, Eoin O'Duffy, the IRA Chief of Staff, proposed a reorganization of both divisions and brigades to make the northern area

---

[116] Memo from OC 3rd IRA Northern Division to IRA GHQ, Dublin, 27 July 1922, UCDAD P7/B/II/77.

[117] Ibid.

[118] Report by the Acting Comdt., 2nd Northern Division, to IRA Chief of Staff, GHQ, Dublin, 26 June 1922, and letter from OC 2nd Northern Division, to Director of Organization, GHQ, Dublin, 10 July 1922, ibid.

[119] W. A. Philips, *The Revolution in Ireland 1906–23* (London, 1926), 271.

coterminous with Northern Ireland.[120] He also set up a separate command for the Northern Ireland area, with a military policy of avoiding
any conflict with the Special Constabulary or the British army. The
IRA offensive against Northern Ireland, effectively ended in June by
the USC, was now officially halted.

Although the Government of Northern Ireland had survived the
IRA assault, its methods in dealing with the assailant have been strongly
criticized. Indeed, it has been said that if 'there is one field which
exemplifies the specific characteristics of state formation in Northern
Ireland it is that of security, that is, the constitution of the repressive
state apparatuses'.[121] It has been claimed that 'the fundamental legal
rights of all citizens against arbitrary arrest and imprisonment were
effectively annulled by the provisions of the Civil Authorities (Special
Powers) Act of 1922'.[122] However, the introduction of the Special Powers
Act had been forced upon the Government of Northern Ireland by the
army's reluctance to use its powers under the Restoration of Order
(Ireland) Act. Indeed, it was the military who, through the British
Government, had urged Craig to introduce his own legislation for the
maintenance of law and order.[123]

Craig's government was hesitant in taking full advantage of the
powers available to it. Indeed, so anxious was it not to appear to British
public opinion to be acting in a belligerent manner, that it declined to
accept the recommendations of military advisers to introduce internment as a preventive measure against the predicted IRA offensive.[124]
Only when Northern Ireland was engulfed in IRA violence and society
appeared to be rapidly descending into a state of complete lawlessness
did the unionist government invoke its powers and act decisively. Existing legislation had proved ineffective, and the failure to bring anyone
to justice for the murders committed in May demonstrated the inad-
equacy of routine methods. Unless the government could show that
the judicial system was capable of protecting the people, it was likely
to lose the confidence of its grass-roots supporters who, on the basis
of past evidence, could be expected to take the law into their own
hands, accelerating the slide into anarchy. Even then, the Northern

---

[120] Memo from IRA Chief of Staff to C.-in-C., 31 July 1922, UCDAD P7/B/II/77.

[121] P. Bew, P. Gibbon, and H. Patterson, *The State in Northern Ireland 1921–72*
(Manchester, 1979), 57.

[122] K. Boyle, T. Hadden, and P. Hillyard, *Law and State: The Case of Northern Ireland*
(London, 1975), 7.

[123] Memo, 'Report of the Adjutant General's Committee', presented to the Provisional Government of Ireland Cabinet Committee, 22 Dec. 1921, PRONI HO5 CIM604/
1/4.

[124] Cabinet Conclusions, 19 Apr. 1922, PRONI CAB4/40/45.

Ireland government used the wide powers provided by the Act in a restrained and rational manner, and law enforcement was not as Draconian as some critics assert.

The Special Powers Act has been condemned for granting unlimited power to the Government of Northern Ireland.[125] It would be altogether fairer and closer to reality to judge the Northern Ireland government not by the powers it sought but by the way the powers were exercised. For example, although the government established special non-jury courts to try terrorists, it did not empower these courts to impose the death penalty (as the police and military would have preferred).[126] In contrast, the various Public Safety Acts passed by the Irish Free State parliament not only allowed for the introduction of internment and the use of flogging, but also provided for the establishment of military courts with the power to execute prisoners.[127]

When the anti-treaty IRA murdered a member of the Dail and wounded another, the Irish Cabinet agreed that four republicans then in prison should be executed without trial as a deterrent against further assassinations of elected representatives. As Professor Tom Wilson observes, one 'can readily envisage the horrified reaction there would have been . . . and the outrage that would have been provoked if the hard-pressed Ulster Government had done so'.[128] However, the words of Kevin O'Higgins, the Irish minister responsible for law and order, when justifying the executions, could equally have been used by the Northern Ireland government to defend its own actions against the IRA:

The whole question as to whether it is to be a Nation governed by constitutional principles, or whether it is to be a mob dictated to by an armed minority was at stake. There is a point beyond which we could not coax or compromise. The point came at which it became necessary to strike to save the life of the nation. And only then we struck.[129]

The Ulster Special Constabulary, the main weapon in Northern Ireland's counter-insurgency arsenal, has generally attracted unfavourable comment as to its composition and the attitude of its members. It has been denounced for being exclusively Protestant, and accused of indiscipline and bias. However, a much more damaging allegation is that the USC engaged

---

[125] National Council for Civil Liberties, *Report of a Commission of Inquiry Appointed to Examine the Purpose and Effect of the Civil Authorities (Special Powers) Acts (Northern Ireland) 1922 and 1933* (London, 1936), 8.

[126] Buckland, *Factory of Grievances*, 201.

[127] T. de Vere White, *Kevin O'Higgins* (London, 1948), 121–4.

[128] T. Wilson, *Ulster: Conflict and Consent* (Oxford, 1989), 63.

[129] De Vere White, *Kevin O'Higgins*, 125.

in a significant number of reprisal killings as well as widespread petty and not so petty harassment of Catholics. The evidence also indicates that many of their officers knew what was going on and, if they did not actually encourage it, did not do anything to prevent it. The Northern government showed no concern to discipline its forces and stamp out reprisals and seemed oblivious to the effect this must have on the Catholic population.[130]

It is difficult to dispel a myth, and the truth about the USC is shrouded in myths. To the nationalist community the Specials were not agents of law enforcement but political opponents who, motivated by partisan spite, willingly carried out a policy of repression against them. However mistaken these perceptions might have been, the reality was that as a minority community within Northern Ireland which had suffered disproportionately from sectarian violence, the nationalists genuinely believed themselves to be under an additional threat from the Specials. Partly in reaction to the sustained allegations of nationalists and partly in appreciation of the contribution by the USC to the restoration of public order, the loyalists also created a myth about the force. In this myth the Specials were regarded as being above reproach, and every member was personally endowed with the highest and most noble of motives. Criticism of the USC was equated with disloyalty and seen as proof of hostility to Northern Ireland itself. One myth depicted the Specials as demons; the other viewed them as angels—the truth is probably somewhere in between.

While undoubtedly gross excesses were carried out by some members of the USC, there is no evidence to substantiate the allegation that there existed a policy of harassing the Roman Catholic population. Members of the force were subject to a disciplinary code and those who breached it were punished. For example, a group of Specials who had looted a public house and exchanged gunfire with the regular police were court-martialled, dismissed from the force, and given terms of imprisonment.[131] Nevertheless, it has been suggested that because the USC was almost exclusively Protestant in composition it 'could have only a limited value as a police force'.[132] However, the decision by the British Government to disband the RIC, coupled with its reluctance to use the army in Northern Ireland, meant that Craig had no alternative but to rely on the USC.

Though mainly Protestant, it does not automatically follow that the USC was sectarian in the sense of being largely composed of bigots or showing sectarian bias in its collective attitudes and activities. Many

---

[130] Farrell, *Arming the Protestants*, 166.

[131] P. Shea, *Voices and the Sound of Drums: An Irish Autobiography* (Belfast, 1981), 63.

[132] Buckland, *A History of Northern Ireland*, 41.

officers in the force, such as Sir Basil Brooke, Fermanagh County Commandant, were loyalist in outlook, but there is no evidence to indicate that they allowed their personal political attitudes to affect their behaviour. Indeed, one senior British civil servant, Stephen Tallents, judged that Brooke acted without party bias, while Clark described him to Sir John Anderson as 'an eminently level-headed, active and moderate man'.[133]

As regards the serious allegation that the USC engaged in reprisals against Roman Catholics, Craig's government never adopted the policy pursued by the British Government in Southern Ireland against the IRA of 'authorized reprisals'. Farrell cites the killing on 23 June 1922 of three Roman Catholic youths in Cushendall, County Antrim, as the best-documented case of reprisals by the USC. It was claimed that 'a party of "A" Specials had driven into the predominantly Catholic village and immediately opened fire on a crowd of people in the street, then dragged a couple of youths up an alleyway and shot them'.[134] The attack was depicted by local nationalists as retaliation for the murder on the previous day of Sir Henry Wilson and for recent IRA action in the area. The findings of two separate inquiries established by the British and Northern Ireland governments appeared to contradict one another regarding the legality, or otherwise, of the behaviour of the USC patrol.[135]

The judgment of Sir Denis Henry, the Roman Catholic Lord Chief Justice of Northern Ireland, delivered in the cases brought for compensation by the families of those killed or injured in the Cushendall shootings, exonerated the USC patrol. In open court, the witnesses for the plaintiffs were cross-examined under oath and there was 'an extraordinary conflict of testimony'.[136] Admitting the statements made by the military officers who had accompanied the detachment of special constables, and whose evidence corroborated that of the 'A' Specials, the Lord Chief Justice accepted that the security forces had been fired on. Rejecting the claims for compensation, he found that the deaths arose out of unlawful assembly.

The success of the USC as the main agency of Craig's government in establishing control throughout Northern Ireland no doubt helps to

[133] Clark to Sir John Anderson, 28 Sept. 1920, Clark Papers, PRONI D1022/2/9.

[134] Farrell, *Arming the Protestants*, 390.

[135] Churchill to Craig, 12 Oct. 1922, PRO(L) CAB27/216 and J. F. Gelston, RUC Deputy Inspector-General, to Bates, 20 Nov. 1922, and J. R. Moorhead, Northern Ireland Chief Crown Solicitor, to Bates, 22 Nov. 1922, Cabinet Secretariat, PRONI CAB8B/11.

[136] 'Judgment of the Rt. Hon. Sir Denis Henry, Bart. Lord Chief Justice, 1 November 1923, High Court of Justice in Northern Ireland, King's Bench Division', PRONI CAB8B/11.

explain its unpopularity with nationalists. Given that the separation of Northern Ireland was bitterly opposed by the nationalist population, their resentment against those perceived to be the main guardians of the new state was understandable. A small number of outrages committed by certain elements in the force against a recalcitrant minority undoubtedly added to that unpopularity. However, those outrages were of a localized and unauthorized nature, and were not part of a comprehensive policy of sectarian repression. Indeed, one of the Special Constabulary officers in County Fermanagh, much hated by nationalists for his tough approach, was a Captain Dunne who was a Roman Catholic from County Kerry.[137]

The tough response of the Northern Ireland government to IRA violence has been unfavourably contrasted with its circumspect approach to loyalist violence. It would appear that fear of 'alienating Protestant opinion sometimes deterred those responsible for the maintenance of law and order from making decisions that were known to be just and proper, as was indicated by the special treatment accorded to the Ulster Protestant Association (UPA)'.[138] The UPA, which had about fifty hard-core members mainly centred in East Belfast, attracted, according to a police report, the 'lowest and least desirable of the Protestant hooligan element',[139] and engaged in a number of sectarian murders in Belfast.[140] Although the police had long known about the group, they lacked definite information until March 1922 when they received a 'tip-off' about the location of arms and ammunition. The police then took immediate action, but only secured the conviction of one person, who was sentenced to eleven months' hard labour. While there has been criticism of the government for not always taking prompt steps against loyalist law-breakers, when they were apprehended (and provided there was sufficient evidence), the law did take its full course.

Unfortunately the Government of Northern Ireland accepted the recommendations of its Military Adviser, General Solly-Flood, who wished to tame the UPA by enrolling some of its members in the Special Constabulary and in the newly created secret service.[141] The

---

[137] 'Report on Visits to Swanlinbar and Clones' by Joseph Johnston, 12 July 1923, NAI S3 161.

[138] Buckland, *Factory of Grievances*, 216.

[139] District Inspector R. R. Spears to Minister of Home Affairs, 7 Jan. 1923, PRONI T2258.

[140] The UPA was originally formed in the autumn of 1920 as a defence organization to protect Protestant interests against IRA attacks. However, by 1922 it had degenerated into a criminal organization responsible for several sectarian attacks, including on various occasions the murder of innocent Roman Catholics.

[141] Farrell, *Arming the Protestants*, 144.

Ulster Unionist Chief Whip, Captain Herbert Dixon, an MP for East Belfast, acted as the intermediary with the UPA in early June in an attempt to end the violence. However, by the beginning of September the UPA had resumed its murderous activities and continued them throughout the month. Unable to negotiate an end to the violence, the Northern Ireland government decided, following a conference at the Ministry of Home Affairs, to take resolute action against the UPA. It was agreed that a loyalist area in East Belfast should be cordoned off and thoroughly searched, during which operation curfew regulations were to be enforced and those Protestants suspected of being involved in violence interned.

In the event the government appears to have wavered, since this tough action was not taken, but following the murder on 5 October 1922 of a Roman Catholic woman on the Newtownards Road, the authorities moved to intern four UPA members.[142] The UPA continued its vicious bombing and shooting during October and November, and on 5 November there was a tougher clamp-down. By the end of 1922 several loyalists had been jailed for firearms offences, while a dozen others were interned, and by February 1923 the UPA was completely broken up. As Buckland has observed: 'there is no denying that this could have been achieved earlier and lives saved had the government been willing to use its powers as fully against loyalists as it [did] against nationalists.'[143]

By the summer of 1922 Northern Ireland, which had been handed over to Craig's government in a deplorable and disorderly condition, was enjoying comparative peace. Without doubt, the 'assertion of the government's authority was the most significant achievement during the first twelve months of Northern Ireland's existence'.[144] The complete fragmentation of the IRA and the ensuing Irish civil war, which raged on for several months, meant that Northern Ireland did not face the threat of a new terror offensive. The death of Collins and the more conciliatory attitude adopted towards Northern Ireland by the Irish Free State under the leadership of Cosgrave led to a fundamental shift in its policy, with military or terrorist action no longer considered a viable option.

With the restoration of law and order and the gradual return of normality over the next couple of years, there were indications that the Northern Ireland government was 'anxious to act responsibly and

---

[142] Ibid. 178.   [143] Buckland, *Factory of Grievances*, 218.
[144] Wilson, *Conflict and Consent*, 48.

on behalf of the whole community'.[145] However, the violence of the IRA's efforts to strangle Northern Ireland at birth had left deep psychological and physical scars upon the unionist population. The attacks upon Northern Ireland reawakened and reinforced the Ulster unionist siege mentality, while the tough response of Craig's government to these attacks confirmed the nationalists' initial rejection of the state. Northern Ireland had survived, but at a price: 'community relations were almost irreparably harmed. Protestants/unionists and Catholics/nationalists looked upon each other with suspicion. Both had had their victims and both had their grievances.'[146]

However, it is questionable whether community relations in Northern Ireland were shattered by the terrorism and communal violence in 1920–2. It might be more accurate to say that it was the fragile peace which existed between two hostile communities that was shattered, since community relations had not previously been harmonious. It can indeed be argued that the violence surrounding the establishment of Northern Ireland was a manifestation rather than a cause of poor community relations. This conflict between two hereditary enemies would no doubt help to explain the intensity of the violence and the problem of attempting to heal the wounds. While one may speculate about the origins of the violence, there is no dispute about its intensity, and for Northern Ireland to have survived such violence was remarkable: an achievement made possible by the resolution and skill of the Government of Northern Ireland supported, in no small measure, by the USC.

[145] Buckland, *A History of Northern Ireland*, 56.
[146] Buckland, *Ulster Unionism*, 176.

6

Financing Self-Government

The Northern Ireland Cabinet had to grapple with various administrative problems as it endeavoured to establish the new government. Although these problems had been exacerbated by the obstructionist tactics of the Irish Free State, the government succeeded in consolidating its authority and in shaping Northern Ireland as a viable entity. With the implementation of a tough counter-insurgency programme and the defeat of the IRA terrorist offensive in 1922, Northern Ireland appeared to have secured its existence. Doubts, however, remained in the minds of many people about the ability of Northern Ireland to avoid a budget deficit and national bankruptcy. Even at the height of the IRA campaign in 1922, the funding of the Ulster Special Constabulary appeared to pose an almost greater problem than the acts of terrorism themselves.

The financial threat to Northern Ireland's existence concerned her capacity, or otherwise, to fund public services. In a memorandum to his Cabinet colleagues prepared immediately after the transfer of power, Hugh Pollock, the Northern Ireland Minister of Finance, stated his view 'that the Northern [Ireland] Government will not pay its way on the present basis of taxation and expenditure. In the case of a Government starting without a balance in hand, this leads very soon to the actual practical difficulty of cash.'[1] It was predicted that the inability to maintain a balanced budget would overwhelm Northern Ireland and that financial pressures would end the separate administration. Indeed, some seem to have feared that the country would share the fate of Newfoundland a decade later and go 'openly on the dole'.[2] Half-bankrupt and economically hard pressed, Newfoundland was obliged to abandon dominion status and accept 'a status like that of a Crown Colony, with imperial loans to keep out the cold'.[3] It was later absorbed as a province by the Dominion of Canada.

---

[1] Memo from Rt. Hon. Hugh Pollock MP and Milne Barbour MP about 'Financial Position of Northern Ireland', 25 Nov. 1921, Treasury Division Papers, PRONI FIN18/1/383.
[2] P. Buckland, *The Factory of Grievances: Devolved Government in Northern Ireland 1921–39* (Dublin, 1979), 102.
[3] S. Leacock, *Our British Empire* (London, 1941), 173.

Although Newfoundland did not abandon her separate administration until 1931, there were those in 1921 who expected that such a fate might overtake Northern Ireland. The *Irish News* believed that the financial provisions of the 1920 Act could only be favourably readjusted by a new all-Ireland settlement. It declared that the Northern Ireland parliament was incompatible 'with a national settlement involving national control over finance'.[4] The Ulster unionists, conscious that the Northern Ireland parliament was a bulwark against their absorption into the Irish Free State, were determined to retain their separate administration. The Cabinet realized that good financial management was essential both on monetary and political grounds. Having adequate revenue to meet necessary expenditure was regarded, not merely as a budgetary exercise, but as vital to the existence of the nation. Pollock's warnings suggested that Northern Ireland might not be a financially viable entity, and that the government could 'be involved in commitments which we shall be unable to meet'.[5]

The ability of the Ulster unionists to control their political destiny by safeguarding their financial position was crippled by the severely restrictive provisions of the 1920 Act, in which most kinds of major taxation were matters 'reserved' to the parliament at Westminster. Those taxes to be transferred to the devolved parliament were few and unimportant: they consisted, in the main, of motor-vehicle and stamp duties, death duties, and a few minor excise duties. Most of the revenue came from the reserved taxes, the chief of these being taxes on income, customs duties, and most of the excise duties. All of these taxes were imposed and collected at uniform rates throughout the United Kingdom. The amount of this revenue to be allocated to the Northern Ireland parliament was to be calculated and agreed by the Joint Exchequer Board, consisting of a chairman appointed by the Crown, one member from the Treasury in London, and one from the new Ministry of Finance in Belfast. However, from Northern Ireland's share of this revenue were deducted, first, the cost of reserved services (for example, the Supreme Court), and second, the contribution to be made by Northern Ireland for imperial services (such as defence or diplomatic representation).[6] The financial relationship between Belfast and London was from the outset a complex one and of the seventy-six articles and nine schedules comprising the 1920 Act, some fourteen articles dealt with financial provisions.[7]

[4] *Irish News*, 27 June 1921.
[5] Memo from Pollock, 25 Nov. 1921, PRONI FIN18/1/383.
[6] Government of Ireland Act, 1920, Sects. 22 and 23.
[7] D. Harkness, *Northern Ireland Since 1920* (Dublin, 1983), 4.

The United Kingdom Government was anxious that members of the Joint Exchequer Board be nominated at the earliest possible date, and on 2 September 1921 Sir James Craig reported that Lord Colwyn had accepted the chairmanship of the board.[8] Although the work of the board was delayed by the negotiations between the London government and Sinn Fein, Sir Ernest Clark was soon to emerge as Northern Ireland's representative, while O. E. Niemeyer, Deputy Controller of Finance, served on behalf of the London Treasury. It was from money apportioned to Northern Ireland by the Joint Exchequer Board that the transferred services were to be mainly funded. This expenditure was divided between the consolidated fund services and the supply services. The consolidated fund services consisted principally of certain permanent charges on the Treasury, while expenditure on supply services 'was authorized annually by parliament on the basis of estimates prepared towards the end of each calendar year by the different administrative departments and subsequently approved by the Ministry of Finance'.[9]

The Government of Ireland Act had calculated that the imperial contribution from the two Irish governments for each of the first two years after the Appointed Day should be £18,000,000. Northern Ireland was to pay some £8,000,000, which represented 0.77 per cent of United Kingdom total expenditure on imperial services such as the armed forces, the Foreign Office, and the Customs Service.[10] In a White Paper published in May 1920 the London government had predicted that, after paying for transferred services, the Government of Northern Ireland would have a surplus of £1,500,000 with which to develop services.[11] However, the optimism of these estimates, based upon the financial year 1920/1, proved to be misplaced given the economic down-turn, and there was a dramatic fall in revenue from reserved taxation. Although there had been considerable retrenchment by the United Kingdom in its expenditure on the armed forces with a consequent reduction in Ulster's contribution to imperial services, there was still a serious problem with the Northern Ireland budget. Writing to Craig on 30 August 1921, Pollock declared that the Estimates having been prepared, it was clear that with reduced revenue and increased expenditure on transferred services there was no surplus. He stated that: 'expenditure has been so increased that not only is there no adequate

[8] Rt. Hon. Sir James Craig MP to Rt. Hon. Hugh Pollock MP, 2 Sept. 1921, Cabinet Secretariat, PRONI CAB6/1.

[9] Buckland, *Factory of Grievances*, 84.

[10] Memo: 'Outline of Financial Position', c.Jan. 1922, PRONI CAB6/1.

[11] Government of Ireland Bill: Further Memorandum on Financial Provisions, 1920, UK Cmd. 707.

provision for the services incidental to setting up a new Government and no surplus out of which they can be met, but there is an actual estimated deficit on the account.'[12]

Pollock recognized that the only way to improve the budget was to reduce the Northern Ireland contribution to imperial services, but he acknowledged that this had been set for two years by the 1920 Act. However, even then the new figure for Northern Ireland's imperial contribution was dependent upon the 'taxable capacity' of Ireland, and no account was taken of increased expenditure on transferred services. Pollock pointed out that expenditure on education and labour services had increased by an alarming £563,000—alarming because the estimate in the White Paper for total expenditure in Northern Ireland on transferred and reserved services was only £6.3 million. In a memorandum prepared by Clark for Pollock, it was stated that the

question to be determined is what interpretation should be placed upon the words 'relative taxable capacity', used in Sections 23(3) and 23(4) of the Act. There is no definition of this term . . . it looks as if there is introduced into the midst of an Act of Parliament, dealing with measures of extraordinary importance, a technical expression, which not one man in a thousand can explain or define unaided.[13]

Sir James Craig's view was that the additional costs should be borne by the British Government and should not fall, as he put it, upon the shoulders of Northern Ireland. The British Government showed no sign of accepting any additional financial liability for Northern Ireland. As Clark realized, if the Northern Ireland government was to survive it was 'necessary to provide a sufficient revenue to balance expenditure, and also to provide credits for its necessary capital expenditure'.[14]

Clark attended the first meeting of the Joint Exchequer Board in London on 2 December 1921, and made representations on behalf of the Northern Ireland government to have some of the financial provisions of the 1920 Act amended. He identified three major questions which required immediate attention: the date at which the Joint Exchequer Board could consider the fairness of Northern Ireland's contribution to the Imperial Exchequer; the actual basis of the contribution; and whether police charges might be regarded as military expenditure under the 6th Schedule of the Act, and the costs thus fall to the Imperial Exchequer. However, the London Treasury insisted upon a

[12] Pollock to Craig, 30 Aug. 1921, PRONI CAB6/1.
[13] Memo: 'Taxable Capacity', c.Aug. 1921, Cabinet Secretariat, PRONI CAB5/5.
[14] Memo: 'Financial needs of the Northern Ireland Government', 2 Feb. [1921], PRONI CAB5/5.

strict interpretation of the existing legislation and Clark was forced to concede that, unless the 1920 Act was amended by parliament, the Joint Exchequer Board could not consider the points he raised.[15]

During the parliamentary passage in 1920 of the Government of Ireland Bill, the Ulster Unionist Party—which was to form the Government of Northern Ireland—had realized that the financial provisions of the measure could well prove inadequate. A Finance Sub-Committee had been established by the Standing Committee of the Ulster Unionist Council to consider the financial clauses of the 1920 Bill. Hugh Pollock, in a draft report to fellow members of the Sub-Committee, suggested that Ireland pay an imperial contribution of £5,000,000 (instead of the proposed £18,000,000).[16] However, as has been pointed out, the 'Ulster Unionists had eventually become reconciled to the imperial government's proposals because of public and private assurances that the new Irish parliaments would be treated not only with justice but also with generosity'.[17] Indeed, as Pollock told Craig, it was only because of such assurances from British ministers that the Ulster Unionist Party had facilitated the passage of the 1920 Act without criticism of the financial clauses.[18]

While the Ulster Unionist Finance Sub-Committee had believed that the figures of the imperial government in the finance White Paper were unrealistic, not even it could have envisaged the dramatic fall in revenue. In the financial year 1922/3 Northern Ireland had a revenue yield of £13.8 million, while the projected figure in 1920/1 had been £16.5 million.[19] Although partition may have aggravated her economic problems, the main reason for her industrial decline was a post-war depression which badly hit her staple industries of agriculture, linen, and shipbuilding and swelled the numbers of unemployed persons.[20] The decline in revenue and increase in expenditure made it all the more pressing for the Northern Ireland government to secure a revision of the 1920 financial provisions, or at least obtain the promised generous interpretation. The refusal of the London Treasury at the meeting of the Joint Exchequer Board to allow a consideration of the points raised by Clark dismayed the Northern Ireland government.

---

[15] Clark to Pollock, 3 Dec. 1921, PRONI CAB5/5.
[16] See minutes of the Ulster Unionist Council Finance Sub-Committee, 4 Mar.–19 Oct. 1920, Ulster Unionist Council Papers, PRONI D1327/15/4.
[17] Buckland, *Factory of Grievances*, 82.
[18] Pollock to Craig, 8 May 1922, Private Office, PRONI FIN30/FC/9.
[19] R. J. Lawrence, *The Government of Northern Ireland: Public Finance and Public Services 1921–1964* (Oxford, 1965), 42.
[20] F. S. L. Lyons, *Ireland Since the Famine* (London, 1973), 710.

Perhaps foolishly, they had expected that 'the assurance given on behalf of the British Government would be honoured'.[21] However, Pollock had warned his Cabinet colleagues that, although there was an expectation that the United Kingdom Government would meet the costs of the Special Constabulary on the grounds that this force was raised in lieu of a military presence, there was 'a danger of the Northern [Ireland] Government being lulled into a false sense of security on this most important financial question by what are merely expressions of favourable opinion'.[22]

Initially the British Government had borne the cost of equipping and maintaining the Special Constabulary, but as it was defined as an Irish service under the terms of the Government of Ireland Act, financial liability for the force shifted to Northern Ireland with the transfer of services.[23] Pollock had quickly identified the funding of the Special Constabulary as an intolerable burden on the Northern Ireland ex-chequer. At a meeting of the Northern Ireland Cabinet on 23 August 1921, he told his colleagues that, as the Special Constabulary had been raised to take the place of a military force, it was 'obvious . . . that these charges [for it] should be made against Imperial funds'.[24] Craig strongly believed that the imperial government should pay for the Special Constabulary as it was a force which, while controlled by the Northern Ireland government, was performing an imperial service. The Treasury in London took the view that Craig's government was attempting to 'sponge off the British taxpayer', and objected to spending money on 'a transferred service [over] which it had no control'.[25]

The scale of the problem was indicated by the Estimates prepared by the Ministry of Home Affairs, revealing that £489,697 would be required to finance the Special Constabulary for the remaining four months of the financial year, during which the Government of North-ern Ireland would be responsible for the service.[26] Although Craig managed to persuade Austen Chamberlain, the Chancellor of the Exchequer, to grant-aid the Special Constabulary, the agreement was only reached on an *ad-hoc* basis, and even then there were differences of opinion as to what had been agreed. The imperial Treasury later attempted to suggest that the understanding had been that London would support the force for only the current financial year. Northern Ireland meanwhile claimed that it had been agreed that 'all expenses

[21] Lawrence, *Government of Northern Ireland*, 42.
[22] Memo from Pollock, 25 Nov. 1921, PRONI FIN18/1/383.   [23] Ibid.
[24] Cabinet Conclusions, 23 Aug. 1921, PRONI CAB4/15/13.
[25] P. Buckland, *A History of Northern Ireland* (Dublin, 1981), 43.
[26] Samuel Watt to Clark, 30 Nov. 1921, PRONI FIN18/1/474.

in connection with the Special Constabulary, just be regarded as military expenditure', and should thus fall to London.[27]

Craig succeeded where Clark had failed because he was able to bypass the Treasury officials with whom Clark grappled on the Joint Exchequer Board and deal directly with their political masters. Not only was he able to operate on a political plane, but the arguments he employed to obtain imperial funding for the Special Constabulary were of a political as distinct from a financial nature. Conscious that the imperial government was keen to disengage administratively from Ireland, north and south, Craig hinted that his government would have to resign if it did not receive the necessary money.[28] As the London government was anxious to avoid reopening the whole Irish question, his argument proved extremely effective. He was also able to plead that the existence of the Special Constabulary relieved the London government of the 'necessity to keep large numbers of troops in the six counties'.[29] Given that the imperial government had to deal with various trouble-spots in the empire and was faced with a shortage of troops, Craig's argument made military sense.

Some imperial officials considered, however, that the Northern Ireland government was acting *ultra vires* in trying to build up what was in effect a military organization with British money. Northern Ireland's defence was that, while the Special Constabulary performed tasks of a military nature (such as searching for arms), it was essentially a police-force under the command of the civil authorities.[30] Nevertheless, to avoid legal difficulties which might endanger British funding, Craig told a Cabinet committee that the Special Constabulary had to be left 'on a purely police basis as the Government of Ireland Act prohibits the Northern government from [raising] military forces'.[31] Niemeyer insisted that if it was a police-force, then the Northern Ireland government was obliged to pay for it. Craig's government made the counter-claim that the expenses of the Special Constabulary were of

a quasi-military nature which cannot be regarded as chargeable upon the revenue available for ordinary civil purposes in Ulster, and that it is of such a nature that it should be met out of Ulster's contribution for military purposes. The cost is incurred in connection with the protection of a part of the Empire under particular circumstances, and is similar in general character to the cost thrown

[27] Wilfrid Spender to Clark, 11 Jan. 1922, Spender Papers, PRONI D1295/23A.
[28] Craig to Rt. Hon. Stanley Baldwin MP, 28 Nov. 1922, ibid.
[29] M. Farrell, *Arming the Protestants: The Formation of the Ulster Special Constabulary and the Royal Ulster Constabulary 1920–27* (London, 1983), 85.
[30] Memo: 'Special Constabulary', c.Feb. 1922, PRONI CAB5/5.
[31] Minutes of Cabinet committee on USC, 15 May 1922, PRONI FIN18/1/487.

upon the Metropolitan police by their special duties, towards which the Treasury contributes a special grant of £100,000 a year.[32]

The kernel of Northern Ireland's argument was that the situation which necessitated the existence of the Ulster Special Constabulary was created (or at least aggravated) by the policies of the London government, and that the latter should therefore bear financial responsibility. Craig did promise, however, that it would be possible to 'reduce the Special Constabulary charges very materially, as soon as there is a clear indication on the part of Southern Ireland that it desires peace'.[33]

Craig had made full use of his contacts at Westminster to further Northern Ireland's interests and secure financial support. However, the Treasury officials, and Niemeyer in particular, 'disliked Craig's informal methods of conducting business and his demand that the imperial government should spend millions of pounds on the Special Constabulary, over which it had no control'.[34] Appalled by Craig's demands for *ad-hoc* payment from the British Treasury, he was startled by detailed proposals presented by Craig in November 1922 for a revision of the financial relations between the governments in Belfast and London, exclaiming that the figures would be 'incredible if they were not in black and white'.[35]

One nationalist commentator has argued that the British Government willingly financed the Ulster Special Constabulary and thus showed its close relationship with the Ulster unionists. All the evidence suggests, however, that any funding which the Northern Ireland government obtained from London was secured only in the face of stiff opposition from elements of the British establishment. Yet some believe that successive British governments favoured the unionist government in Northern Ireland by financing its police-forces despite as a consequence irrevocably alienating the nationalist minority from the state.[36] However, any financial support from the British Government for the USC was given only after consideration of broader British interests and with particular reference to relations with the Irish Free State. Even Michael Farrell has conceded that British policy 'chopped and changed with the exigencies of Britain's relations with the South'.[37] Far from being close allies of the British Government, the Ulster unionists heartily reciprocated London's resentment and suspicion, and 'believed that

---

[32] Memo: 'Special Constabulary', PRONI CAB5/5.
[33] Spender to Clark, 11 Jan. 1922, PRONI D1295/23A.
[34] Buckland, *Factory of Grievances*, 90.
[35] O. E. Niemeyer to Baldwin, 20 Nov. 1922, Treasury Establishment Series, PRO(L) T160/150/5314/1.
[36] Farrell, *Arming the Protestants*, p. vi.   [37] Ibid. 281.

Westminster was far too responsive to the lying propaganda of the South'.[38]

Any grants won by the Northern Ireland government from the British Government were on a purely *ad-hoc* basis. Each request for funding was individually considered by London and had to be fought for by Northern Ireland. Although the Northern Ireland government attempted to devise a development plan for its security forces, it had no guarantee that it would have the financial ability to sustain their activities. The government's very existence continued to be a hand-to-mouth affair, and financing the USC a nightmare. The seriousness of the problem is evident from the frequency of its discussion by Craig's Cabinet[39]—indeed, it received more discussion in Cabinet than law and order itself. Craig objected to an uncertainty surrounding future funding which obviously prevented his government from formulating long-term policies. However, he was unable to persuade the London government to provide an assurance of financial security. He remarked to Spender that 'Churchill is particularly sticky about only meeting us in regard to three months at a time, I rather imagine with a view to keeping the whip handle over us in regard to other matters'.[40]

The Northern Ireland government judged that, given the uncertainty of the political situation, it would be necessary to retain a large force of the USC in the financial year 1922/3. Craig believed that the uncertainty had been aggravated by the British Government's decision to appoint a Boundary Commission, and regarded this as another reason why London should finance the Special Constabulary. At a meeting with the Chancellor on 9 February 1922 he managed to obtain a grant of £850,000 for the USC (equal to half of the then-current expenditure).[41] However, as the projected expenditure of the USC continued to rise, Clark warned that, viewed 'solely from the financial standpoint, the proper course is to reduce the provisional Estimate to the sum guaranteed by the British Exchequer'.[42]

The increasing IRA threat to the stability, if not indeed to the very existence, of Northern Ireland obliged Craig's government to strengthen its security forces considerably. In the interests of state security, financial considerations were to a large extent overruled. The Ministry of Finance pointed out that the estimated cost of the enlarged USC was £1,829,000,

---

[38] P. Buckland, *James Craig* (Dublin, 1980), 74.

[39] See Cabinet Conclusions, PRONI CAB4/35, 41, 48, 50, 51, 53, 58, 60, 65, 70, 71, 89, 103, 115, 134, 140, and 155.

[40] Craig to Spender, 18 July 1922, PRONI FIN30/FC/9.

[41] Clark to Spender, 22 Feb. 1922, Cabinet Secretariat, PRONI CAB6/1.

[42] Clark to Watt, 13 Mar. 1922, PRONI FIN18/1/514.

almost £1 million more than the British Government was prepared to pay.[43] On 10 March Craig met Churchill and the Secretary of State for War, Sir Laming Worthington-Evans, who agreed to supply all the arms, vehicles, and wireless sets required by the Special Constabulary. This helped reduce the Northern Ireland government's share of its cost. Nevertheless, as the rapidly deteriorating security situation required the further expansion of the security forces, so the cost dramatically increased. A scheme proposed by Major-General Solly-Flood, the Military Adviser to Craig's government, envisaged a much larger USC equipped with 750 motor vehicles and fourteen motor boats for use on lakes and coastal waters.[44] It was estimated that Solly-Flood's scheme would increase the Special Constabulary cost to £4,600,000, and at meetings with the Chancellor on 6 and 9 May 1922, Craig pressed the British Government to accept responsibility for the extra cost. Sir Robert Horne, the Chancellor, would not give any undertaking, and later in a letter to Craig declared: 'I think it only fair to point out that my Budget programme as announced to the House of Commons makes no kind of provision for extras of this sort and from many points of view it is exceedingly difficult to defend further grants in the House.'[45]

Horne was prepared to ask parliament to increase the 1922/3 grant to such a sum as might be necessary to make good the difference between the Northern Ireland residuary share of revenue as ultimately ascertained and the £1,250,000 actually received. However, he made this offer on condition that the Northern Ireland government would not raise any questions about the basis on which Northern Ireland's reserved taxes, or deductions from them for 1921/2, were calculated. Craig apparently accepted Horne's advice that he should keep a very severe curb on Solly-Flood who, like other experts, wanted a force completely equipped for every contingency, however remote. Pledges from Churchill that another five battalions of regular troops would be made available for the defence of Northern Ireland sufficiently reassured Craig to allow him quietly to drop Solly-Flood's scheme. Craig had been invited to address the British Cabinet in May 1922 to explain the necessity for London to contribute towards payment of the USC. He managed to secure London's agreement to pay for the Special Constabulary as

---

[43] Memo about Special Constabulary expenditure, 8 Mar. 1922, PRONI FIN30/FC/9.

[44] The Cabinet Conclusions of 12 May 1922 reveal that Solly-Flood proposed 'a defensive force amounting to 8,290 "A" Specials and 63,000 "B" and "C" Specials, for whom he required a training staff of 200 officers and a large number of other ranks'. PRONI CAB4/41/19.

[45] Rt. Hon. R. S. Horne MP to Craig, 10 May 1922, PRONI FIN18/1/862.

then constituted for at least another three months.[46] Apart from the financial objections made by London to the rather grandiose scheme proposed by Solly-Flood, Craig had realized that the changes suggested would have so altered the status of the USC as to make it 'an almost purely military force'.[47]

The Northern Ireland government was acutely conscious of the financial privileges which the Irish Free State appeared to gain under the Anglo-Irish Treaty, in sharp contrast to its own lack of powers. Craig's Cabinet believed that the

administration reserved to the Imperial Government in regard to Northern Ireland cannot be carried out, as contemplated by the Government of Ireland Act, in connection with the similar services for Southern Ireland, because the latter are now within the sole competence of a Dominion Government in the Free State.[48]

The Northern Ireland government very cleverly linked the issue of the British Government's partly funding the Special Constabulary with that of the financial concessions gained by the Irish Free State. Craig's tactic was simple but very successful. He argued that Northern Ireland would make no complaints about the Irish Free State, nor claim equally favourable treatment, provided that the British Government financially supported the USC.[49] This strategy helped persuade the British Government to give grant-aid to the Special Constabulary in order to avoid a major political row over the Free State which could have damaged further the crumbling coalition, but it was in some ways a short-term victory. Northern Ireland did receive the necessary financial support from London, but only through *ad-hoc* grants. In the long term Northern Ireland remained dependent for financial support upon the political goodwill of London. Such a situation was acceptable while it was in London's interests to give assistance to Northern Ireland, but the Belfast government would be extremely vulnerable in the event of a hostile administration taking office in London.

By associating financial support for the USC with the question of the Irish Free State, Craig unintentionally but inescapably made a formal link between the two issues in the eyes of London. The funding was seen as more than just a financial matter, and London had to

---

[46] Cabinet Conclusions, 19 June 1922, PRONI CAB4/48/21.

[47] Farrell, *Arming the Protestants*, 122.

[48] Memo: 'Northern Ireland's Constitution Under the Treaty', c.Jan. 1922, PRONI CAB5/5.

[49] Memo: 'Proposals put forward by the Government of Northern Ireland for supplementing the Treaty arranged between the British Government and the Provisional Government of the Irish Free State', c.Jan. 1922, PRONI CAB5/5.

consider how its actions would affect relations with the Irish Free State. The British Government's anxiety to foster the fortunes of the pro-treaty faction of Sinn Fein constituting the Provisional Government made it very susceptible to complaints from the latter that, by financing the USC, it was increasing the Provisional Government's difficulties. Michael Collins, the Chairman of the Provisional Government, told Churchill that if London persisted in financing the Specials then the very existence of the Anglo-Irish Treaty would be gravely threatened. It was following such representations that Churchill had summoned Craig and Collins to London for talks, in the belief that if political agreement between Dublin and Belfast brought peace there would be no need for London to fund the Special Constabulary. The outcome of the talks was the second Craig–Collins Pact of 30 March 1922, seeking, among other things, to increase Roman Catholic participation in the USC. There is no doubt that Collins's promises of peace would have persuaded the British Government to cut their contribution to the Special Constabulary and forced Craig to reduce its size. However, the breakdown of the pact and the new IRA terrorist offensive against Northern Ireland in May 1922 demonstrated beyond all doubt that there was still a need for a strong defensive force. In such circumstances, Craig could continue to rely upon London's financial assistance.

The defeat of the IRA offensive in 1922 and the gradual return in 1923 to normal conditions enabled the government to reduce the Estimates from £9,784,041 for 1922/3 to £8,270,000 for 1923/4.[50] The USC was one of the services cut back. Nevertheless, the Craig Cabinet still required a grant from London of £1,500,000, and although, after some haggling, the money was eventually obtained, Neville Chamberlain, then Chancellor of the Exchequer, complained to Craig that it was 'very disconcerting to find that you are counting upon a further contribution from the Exchequer'.[51] To reduce Special Constabulary expenditure and balance the Northern Ireland budget, various economies were made. Pollock had always been keen to ensure that the USC did not squander Northern Ireland's scarce public money. Indeed, at the height of the IRA attacks he had criticized the Special Constabulary for incurring expenditure considered by him extravagant. Craig defended the force, arguing that in the exceptional circumstances of the country it was not possible for it to be 'as economical as they would be expected

---

[50] 'Memorandum by the Financial Secretary to the Ministry of Finance about the Estimates 1923–4', Cabinet Secretariat, PRONI CAB8J/1.

[51] Rt. Hon. Neville Chamberlain MP to Craig, 4 Oct. 1923, Cabinet Secretariat, PRONI CAB9A/4/1.

to be if there were time for preparation of proper estimates'.[52] Pollock was convinced that if Northern Ireland was to secure financial assistance from London, he had to be able to assure the Chancellor of the Exchequer that he would exercise the 'closest financial scrutiny and supervision' to ensure expenditure was kept to the absolute minimum.[53]

Pollock did maintain a strict control on expenditure and was always eager that, where possible, savings should be made. However, the Ministry of Finance was not merely concerned with restricting expenditure but also sought, as the security situation improved, to make major cuts in Special Constabulary expenditure. To meet a reduction of £300,000 in the cost of the force, the Cabinet agreed to cut the pay of all mobilized 'A', 'B', and 'C1' Special Constables from 10 shillings to 7 shillings per day; to reduce the 'B' Special annual bonus from £10 to £5 per year; and to reduce the number of police and mobilized special constables from 15,400 to 6,000.[54] The reductions in pay and allowances were so much resented by the serving members of the USC that some officers and men in the C1 Force threatened to go on strike.[55] The strike was planned to coincide with the visit of Lord Derby, the British Secretary of State for War, at a time when the Northern Ireland government could least afford any disruption. While standing firm on the major issue of pay, Craig authorized Bates to make concessions to the rank and file on minor points, thus dividing the men from the dissident officers and averting the strike. Pollock had opposed any concessions, as he believed that 'utmost economy' in all branches of the Special Constabulary was essential if a satisfactory financial statement was to be produced at the end of the year.

Craig was aware, however, that in cutting expenditure on the USC he had to consider political as well as financial factors. Along with the Inspector-General of the RUC, Craig was somewhat apprehensive about making drastic reductions in the Special Constabulary until the situation in the Irish Free State was wholly normal. In addition, they were aware that if, as had been proposed, the full reduction were made in the border counties, then 'there may be started a feeling of uncertainty and disquietude which will have its reflex action and promote unrest'.[56] Craig accordingly slowed down, and in some cases even postponed, the reductions in the USC. However, as the cost of the force exceeded the

[52] Cabinet Conclusions, 19 June 1922, PRONI CAB4/48/21.
[53] Pollock to Craig, 8 May 1922, PRONI FIN30/FC/9.
[54] Cabinet Conclusions, 9 Aug. 1922, PRONI CAB4/51/15.
[55] Rt. Hon. Sir Richard Dawson Bates MP to Spender, 18 Sept. 1923, PRONI CAB8G/23.
[56] Craig to Rt. Hon. Winston Churchill MP, 12 Sept. 1922, PRONI FIN30/FC/9.

Vote, it was necessary for the government to present Supplementary Estimates.

The first Labour government in Britain, led by Ramsay MacDonald, took office as a minority administration on 22 January 1924. This development alarmed some Ulster unionists owing to Labour's perceived sympathies with Irish nationalism; and unionist worries were increased by nationalist speculation that the Labour government was unlikely to contribute to the cost of the Specials. The Northern Ireland government was concerned that the pledge from the outgoing Conservative Chancellor, Neville Chamberlain, of a grant of £1,000,000 might even be in jeopardy. The new Labour Chancellor, Philip Snowden, indicated to Craig in a letter of 18 February 1924 that he could not justify to Westminster the grant for USC expenditure. Craig was indignant, especially since he had met MacDonald on 1 February and had been led to believe that the grant would be forthcoming. On 20 February he wrote to Snowden that he hoped the Chancellor would honour the promise made by his predecessor and confirmed by MacDonald. Craig also complained directly to MacDonald, who replied in a friendly manner that 'in all our negotiations we must both be actuated by a spirit of mutual goodwill'.[57] However, he did not give any firm promise of the £1,000,000.

The Northern Ireland government, increasingly apprehensive about the attitude of the Labour administration, began to plan major reductions in the USC to avoid a heavy deficit. A special Cabinet conference was held on 4 March 1924 attended by Pollock, Bates, Spender, Samuel Watt (the Home Affairs Permanent Secretary), and Colonel Wickham (the RUC Inspector-General) to discuss reductions. It was agreed to disband the 'C1' force in the country districts and to reduce the pay and allowances of all serving special constables. However, at a full Cabinet meeting on 7 March Craig opposed cutting pay as he thought that would cause more trouble than the financial savings were worth. Instead, he suggested that 'there might be a considerable saving in the B Constabulary by transferring to a B1 reserve a considerable portion of the men, especially in the quieter districts where there was no longer the same necessity for patrolling'.[58] The fact that the Northern Ireland government was contemplating such a drastic scaling-down of the USC, particularly at a time when the Boundary Commission appeared to pose a threat to the country, indicates how seriously it regarded the problem that would arise should London fail to grant the £1,000,000.

[57] Rt. Hon. Ramsay MacDonald MP to Craig, 22 Feb. 1924, PRONI FIN18/4/655.
[58] Cabinet Conclusions, 7 Mar. 1924, PRONI CAB4/104/15.

Craig had wanted to maintain the Special Constabulary as a force under the control of his government, 'as a deterrent against large transfers of territory to the South'.[59] But it was precisely because of the boundary question that Labour was reluctant to give any financial support to the USC. After a conversation with Sir John Anderson (now at the Home Office), Clark predicted that whatever 'was done this year . . . it was most unlikely that a Labour Government would put forward a Vote for further money for Special Constabulary for Northern Ireland next year, or so long as the question of the Boundary remained in its present form'.[60]

Northern Ireland's fears and suspicions that London was using financial blackmail to secure political conformity were confirmed at a meeting on 11 April between Pollock and Labour ministers, when the question of the Special Constabulary grant was explicitly linked to the Northern Ireland government's attitude to the boundary. Pollock endeavoured to explain to Snowden the need for the £1,000,000, but Clark noted that it was 'evident from the beginning that we had a very unsympathetic listener'.[61] The Colonial Secretary, J. H. Thomas MP, later joined the meeting and, while he was prepared to support Northern Ireland's claim, he would do so only conditionally. Thomas introduced the boundary question into the discussions and urged Northern Ireland to adopt a more conciliatory attitude towards the Boundary Commission.

Despite the pressing need for the grant, Craig's government did not capitulate to London's demands. At a meeting of the Northern Ireland Cabinet on 5 and 7 May 1924, the invitation from the British Government to appoint a representative to the Boundary Commission was thoroughly discussed, and the Northern Ireland government resolved to refuse the invitation. Nevertheless, Craig had to admit that it would be impossible to carry on without the grants. He hoped that he would have an opportunity to raise the financial position of Northern Ireland with the government in London and 'press for a final settlement of all outstanding questions'.[62] Yet Labour continued to withhold the grant, and when they fell from power in October 1924 no final decision had been made, though 'Snowden later claimed that no grants would have been paid had they remained in office'.[63]

The newly elected Conservative government was less hostile than

[59] Farrell, *Arming the Protestants*, 217.
[60] Minute about the Special Constabulary by Clark, 26 Mar. 1924, PRONI FIN18/4/655.
[61] 'Notes of interview in the Chancellor of the Exchequer's Room, House of Commons', by Clark, 11 Apr. 1924, PRONI CAB4/109/1.
[62] Cabinet Conclusions, 19 May 1924, PRONI CAB4/115/12.
[63] Farrell, *Arming the Protestants*, 233.

the Labour administration and, within a few weeks of taking office as Chancellor, Churchill had agreed to pay £1,250,000 for the Specials.[64] The army mutiny in the Irish Free State had alarmed Craig's government, which noted that among those 'now appointed to the highest positions in the Free State Army are men—for the most part very young men—who are notorious for their hostility to Northern Ireland'.[65] Consequently Craig halted the proposed economy measures for the USC, thus leaving the necessary funding above the £1,000,000 grant initially requested.

The Boundary Agreement entered into on 3 December 1925 by the governments of Northern Ireland, the Irish Free State, and the United Kingdom heralded a new era of peaceful coexistence. The removal of a territorial threat to Northern Ireland also removed the need for a large defence force in the form of the USC. The British Government agreed to a further, but final, grant to the Special Constabulary of £1,200,000 to cover the costs of disbanding the force, which it insisted should be done without delay. London also undertook to write off payment of £700,000 for arms and equipment supplied to the force in 1922. Northern Ireland could not afford to maintain the force from its own financial resources, so at a meeting on 7 December 1925 Craig's Cabinet accepted the British terms and agreed to the speedy disbandment. Speaking in parliament on 9 December Craig announced that the 'A' and 'C1' forces would be disbanded, while the 'B' Specials would be retained. As the 'B' Special Constabulary relied for its operational manpower on its unpaid part-time members, the Northern Ireland government could afford to meet the limited expenses incurred. Craig's announcement brought strong criticism from the Independent Unionist MPs and caused 'shock and dismay to the A Constables provoking many to a resistance approaching mutiny'.[66]

The government handled the issue firmly and coolly and managed successfully to avert a crisis. Craig informed parliament that the Special Constabulary had cost £7,420,000, of which some £6,780,000 had been met by grants from the British Government.[67] Although it was a 'matter of unspeakable regret' to Craig to have to part with the full-time Special Constabulary, he reminded MPs that policy had to be 'measured by the means at our disposal'. It was painful to dismiss men

[64] Niemeyer to Clark, 24 Nov. 1924, PRONI FIN18/5/46.
[65] Lord Londonderry to Rt. Hon. Arthur Henderson MP, Home Secretary, 26 Mar. 1924, PRONI FIN18/4/655.
[66] Harkness, *Northern Ireland*, 41.
[67] *Parl. Deb.* (House of Commons), vi, 9 Dec. 1925, col. 1859.

who 'never faltered in their devotion to duty and never hesitated to face danger',[68] but the Northern Ireland government was aware that if the 'A' and 'C1' forces were not disbanded, the state would face bankruptcy. Craig's government duly took the only course open.

The difficulties which the government experienced in funding the USC illustrated the financial inadequacies of the 1920 Act. If Northern Ireland was to be spared what John Andrews called 'repeated begging expeditions' to London, there was need of a formal revision of the financial provisions in the Act.[69] As has already been noted, as soon as the Joint Exchequer Board was constituted in 1921, Pollock had instructed Clark to raise the issue of Northern Ireland's imperial contribution, questioning its fairness and the basis of calculation.[70] As also mentioned earlier, the London Treasury would not shift from a strict and, from Northern Ireland's point of view, punitive interpretation of the Act, and showed no inclination to secure a comprehensive financial settlement by agreeing to a radical revision of the 1920 financial provisions. The alarming slump in Northern Ireland's revenue, coupled with the burden of increased costs for her services, was in itself sufficient grounds to seek amendment to the financial aspects of the Act. However, the agreement between the British Government and Sinn Fein which led to the establishment of the Irish Free State made a financial revision between London and Belfast an absolute necessity.

In the Government of Ireland Act, 1920, the sections dealing with Northern Ireland were set out in the larger context relating to the rest of Ireland. Indeed, as Professor Calvert has pointed out, the 1920 Act 'was designed to provide for what it was hoped would be a transitional government in a temporarily partitioned Ireland and, ultimately, for government for the whole of Ireland'.[71] The political architects in London had planned two wings upon which they 'meant to balance certain central features to lend prospective unity to the design', but with the Anglo-Irish Treaty 'the southern wing was cut away, bringing down with it the central structure'.[72] Northern Ireland thus found itself operating under an Act designed for a radically different situation, and indeed 'in the extraordinary position of trying to function under a fragment of a constitution'.[73] The treaty was legislatively formalized by the Irish Free State Constitution Act, 1922 (which received the royal

---

[68] Ibid.   [69] Buckland, *Factory of Grievances*, 86.

[70] Clark to Pollock, 3 Dec. 1921, PRONI CAB5/5.

[71] H. Calvert, *Constitutional Law in Northern Ireland: A Study in Regional Government* (London and Belfast, 1968), 41.

[72] A. S. Quekett, *The Constitution of Northern Ireland*, 3 vols. (Belfast, 1928–46), vol. ii, p. v.

[73] J. A. Oliver, *Working at Stormont* (Dublin, 1978), 23.

assent on 5 December 1922) and Northern Ireland immediately opted out as provided by Article 12. The consequences of the ratification and of Northern Ireland's withdrawal were dealt with by the Irish Free State (Consequential Provisions) Act, 1922. Although this Act contained some administrative and procedural changes to the financial provisions of the 1920 Act, there was no radical reform.[74] Not only was no improvement made in Northern Ireland's financial base by amendment of the method of calculating her imperial contribution, but Craig's government had to accept the additional blow of the Irish Free State's appearing to enjoy financial advantages over it.

During the negotiations in 1921 between the British Government and Sinn Fein, Craig had felt certain that in the event of a settlement Southern Ireland would not be granted financial terms more favourable than those of Northern Ireland.[75] Subsequent events proved his financial, and indeed his political, confidence in the British Government to have been misplaced. Northern Ireland did not delay in seeking financial conditions as good as those granted to the Irish Free State. Although Craig had accepted London's funding of the USC in lieu of a formal revision of Northern Ireland's financial powers, Clark hoped that this would be only an interim arrangement. He believed that there had to be a comprehensive settlement of financial relations; indeed, he was convinced that a radical amendment of the method for calculating the imperial contribution was the most vital issue to be resolved by Northern Ireland. Pending a fundamental revision, he proposed that Northern Ireland should endeavour to extract whatever financial concessions she could from the British Government. Among the objectives that Craig should pursue, he suggested that 'if the Irish Free State established its claim that Ireland has been overtaxed in the past, the Northern Government shall be allowed a proportionate diminution of its contribution equivalent to the interest upon its share of such over-taxation'.[76]

Craig met Austen Chamberlain, the Chancellor of the Exchequer, on 2 and 3 March 1922 and, although he encountered a frosty response to Northern Ireland's claim to a share in any settlement for over-taxation, he did gain the other points which Clark had suggested. The Chancellor undertook to ask Westminster to provide £1,500,000 as a contribution towards the settlement of the claims for malicious injuries

---

[74] For details, see 'First Schedule: Modification of the Government of Ireland Act, 1920', of the Irish Free State (Consequential Provisions) Act, 1922 (Session 2), in Quekett, *Constitution*, ii. 221–9.

[75] Cabinet Conclusions, 19 Sept. 1921, PRONI CAB4/22/24.

[76] Memo on Northern Ireland's financial requirements prepared by Clark, 22 Feb. 1922, PRONI CAB6/1.

in Northern Ireland up to 14 January 1922. It was also agreed that, should the Irish Free State set up a protective tariff against the United Kingdom, the Northern Ireland border was to be regarded as the British customs frontier. The cost of maintaining such a customs frontier was to be shared between London and Belfast on the basis of a ratio of respective revenues from customs and excise. The British Government accepted that Northern Ireland should not receive less favourable treatment than Southern Ireland in regard to the completion of the scheme for Irish land purchase. The cost of a Crown representative for Northern Ireland (should there be a need for a separate representative from the one serving the Irish Free State) was not to exceed the charge borne by Northern Ireland under Section 37(3) of the Government of Ireland Act, 1920. Any additional costs in the administration of reserved services as a result of the establishment of the Irish Free State were to be taken into consideration by the Joint Exchequer Board when apportioning the cost of such services. Perhaps most significantly, the British Government consented to the referral of Northern Ireland's imperial contribution for 1922/3 and 1923/4 to the Joint Exchequer Board. The Board was to examine the contribution in the light of the 1922/3 budget estimates, and report 'whether any modification should properly be made in the present statutory sum, and, if so, what steps will be necessary to give effect to their recommendation'.[77]

The British Government's acknowledgement that any increased expenditure on reserved services attributable to the establishment of the Irish Free State should be considered by the Joint Exchequer Board was embodied in the Irish Free State (Consequential Provisions) Act, 1922. Concerned at the rising costs of reserved services following the separation of Southern Ireland from the United Kingdom,[78] Clark wrote on 10 September 1923 to the Treasury in London that: 'the cost of reserved services . . . should be regarded as Imperial expenditure towards which Northern Ireland in common with Great Britain should only be called upon to contribute rateably having regard to her relative taxable capacity.'[79] He added that, assuming the Treasury concurred with this view, Pollock would have the matter submitted for the ratification of the Joint Exchequer Board at the next meeting. Although Niemeyer

[77] 'Heads of Working Arrangements in regard to Northern Ireland supplementing the Treaty with the Irish Free State', 6 Mar. 1922, PRONI CAB4/35/15.

[78] In a memo forwarded to Upcott at the Treasury on 19 Jan. 1924, Clark listed those services which he felt would cost more to administer. These included superannuation; customs and excise; inland revenue; Post Office; RIC; Registry of Deeds; diseases of animals, and fisheries; Land Purchase Commission; Supreme Court; and Office of Works: Joint Exchequer Board, PRONI FIN26/2/88.

[79] Clark to Niemeyer, 10 Sept. 1923, PRONI FIN26/2/88.

agreed with Clark's proposal, it was a 'left-handed acceptance'. Under the Treasury scheme, instead of all additional expenditure on reserved services being regarded *in toto* as imperial expenditure, only 'such allowance' as might be made by the Joint Exchequer Board could be so regarded. The Northern Ireland government understood this to mean that although Northern Ireland would contribute rateably in common with Great Britain to the 'allowance', 'the difference between the allowance and the total increased cost would presumably be an additional charge to Northern Ireland in the Residuary Share of Reserved Taxes under section 24 of the Government of Ireland Act'.[80] However, the Northern Ireland Ministry of Finance did not force the issue but accepted that, unless and until the matter was settled with the Treasury, it could not be referred to the Joint Exchequer Board.[81] It was another example of disagreement between civil servants in London and Belfast regarding the implementation of the finer detail of financial agreements settled by the politicians in broad outline. It was also an example of an issue which remained unresolved until it was submerged within the broader settlement following the reports of the Colwyn Committee.

Following persistent requests by the Northern Ireland government for a revision of financial relations, Bonar Law's Conservative government agreed in 1923 to refer the matter to arbitration. Officially known as the Northern Ireland Arbitration Committee, it is more generally known as the 'Colwyn Committee' after its chairman, Lord Colwyn. The other two committee members appointed had been agreed following consultation between Craig and the Chancellor, Stanley Baldwin: Sir Laming Worthington-Evans and Sir Josiah Stamp. The composition of the committee was announced on 15 January 1923, and its brief was to 'consider whether, in view of the ratification of the Constitution of the Irish Free State, any alteration is needed in the present scale of the contribution of Northern Ireland to the cost of Imperial services'.[82]

Craig entrusted Pollock with the formulation of Northern Ireland's strategy and the preparation of her case for presentation to the Colwyn Committee. The Northern Ireland government attached great importance to securing a successful outcome to the committee's work: Northern Ireland was not merely seeking to improve her financial position but was attempting to find a settlement which, by rectifying the method of calculating her imperial contribution, would remove the threat of bankruptcy. Furthermore, it was necessary for the Northern Ireland

---

[80] G. C. Duggan, NI Ministry of Finance, to Niemeyer, 1 Oct. 1923, ibid.
[81] Duggan to F. G. Salter, HM Treasury, 13 Oct. 1923, ibid.
[82] Quekett, *Constitution*, i. 49.

government to secure a settlement which also provided adequate revenue to enable the development of previously neglected services.

The extent to which the Northern Ireland government was dependent on obtaining a favourable report from the Colwyn Committee is shown in the Cabinet's attitude to the Education Bill. The government had inherited an education service which was in a deplorable state owing to years of neglect by the British Government. Without delay, Craig's new administration tackled the problem by preparing legislation to reform the education service and improve its facilities and so place education on a par with that in Great Britain. Adopting all the measures proposed in the draft Education Bill would have cost the Northern Ireland government at least £500,000 per year. Craig realized that 'it would be impossible for the Northern Ireland government to provide this sum unless the Colwyn Committee accepted the representations being made by the Minister of Finance'.[83]

Although as Minister of Finance Pollock was to present Northern Ireland's case to Lord Colwyn, the main responsibility for preparing it fell to Clark, whose first task was to attempt to define exactly what was 'relative taxable capacity'. As noted earlier, he was concerned that this term as used in Sections 23(3) and 23(4) of the Government of Ireland Act was accompanied by a definition 'not one man in a thousand can explain or define unaided'.[84] In a detailed memorandum prepared for Pollock, Clark suggested that the proper definition of taxable capacity was:

what proportion of a given sum of necessary taxation ought to be raised from Great Britain and what proportion from Ireland in order that the burden of the taxation upon the community of residents in Great Britain may, in relation to the means to bear it be equal, and neither greater nor less than the burden upon the community of residents in Ireland.[85]

Clark believed, however, that the Treasury intended to propose that taxable capacity should be measured by fixing a ratio between the two countries using some economic comparison. He assumed that the Treasury would seek to produce a comparison along similar lines to those adopted by the Financial Relations Commission in its attempt

---

[83] Cabinet Conclusions, 13 Mar. 1923, PRONI CAB4/74/20. These conclusions also reveal that the Northern Ireland government hoped to fund the improvements in the education service by persuading the Colwyn Committee that Northern Ireland should receive as a free gift the land revenues totalling nearly £600,000 per year (taking into account the sinking fund).

[84] Memo: 'Taxable Capacity', prepared by Clark, c.Aug. 1921, PRONI CAB5/5.

[85] Memo by Clark entitled 'Probable Arguments which will be advanced by the Treasury Regarding Taxable Capacity', c.Jan. 1923, Colwyn Arbitration Committee Papers, PRONI FIN11/2.

to settle in 1894–6 how to measure relative taxable capacity. Clark rejected the Treasury's view, as he believed that the proper expenditure on behalf of a government ought to be in direct relation to the proper incidence of the tax. Explaining this by a simple example, he asked Pollock to consider two communities, one of two persons with £300 per annum each, and one of three persons with £200 each, and to suppose that the minimum living level is £100 for each person. Then in the case of the first community, although the total on net assessments for income tax is the same, the absolute capacity is £400, whereas in the second case it is only £300. As the net assessment of tax did not take into account the graduation of tax according to the amount of income, Clark regarded it as only a half-way house towards the yield of tax basis. He was convinced that the tax yielded following two identical assessments on 'different parts of a country under the present system will show the relative capacity, taking into account all the economic principles allowed for in levying that tax'.[86] He was able to point to Ireland's financial history following the Act of Union to illustrate the dangers of endeavouring to fix too rigidly a taxable capacity based on an economic ratio.[87]

Sir Josiah Stamp had written an article in September 1921 for the journal of the Royal Economic Society about the taxable capacity of Ireland. In it, he denied the reliability of the Financial Relations Commission's 1896 report for assessing taxable capacity in 1921. He also queried whether the commission was absolutely sure of its first principle of capacity being related to the income of inhabitants. The commissioners, he claimed, appeared to shift from the premiss that taxable capacity ought to be measured by the incomes of the inhabitants towards the premiss that it should be measured by what is produced by the country. With the development of progressive taxation, Stamp felt that the commissioners' report was completely out of date, as 'the whole conception of taxable capacity has altered since 1894. We had then a flat rate of tax with just an exemption minimum.'[88] Believing that it was persons, not countries, who paid taxation, Stamp regarded the most logical test for assessing taxable capacity to be the total resources of the residents of the country. That Stamp, as a member of the Colwyn Committee, should hold such views was most fortunate for Northern Ireland.

Clark regarded gross taxable capacity as the taxation raised in

---

[86] Ibid.

[87] Memo by Clark entitled 'The Union Attempt to estimate Taxable Capacity', ibid.

[88] Sir J. Stamp, 'The Taxable Capacity of Ireland', *The Economic Journal*, 31: 123 (Sept. 1921).

Northern Ireland on the same basis as Great Britain. The power to contribute was only the power of gross taxable capacity less obligations on the gross sum raised. As he considered that the Colwyn Committee had to deal with the power of Northern Ireland to contribute and not with the power to raise taxation, the 'taxable capacity of Northern Ireland must have regard to the disproportionate costs in Ireland of benefit and administration of such things as education, old age pensions, unemployment and health insurance'.[89] The kernel of the argument presented by the Northern Ireland government was that it should make an imperial contribution according to taxable capacity based upon a capacity to raise revenue on the same basis as Great Britain and after having met local expenditure. Any balance in the Northern Ireland budget should be handed over under agreed conditions, one of which was a surplus of a definite amount.

Northern Ireland did not accept that taxable capacity as denoting ability to pay imperial contribution could be fixed in relative amounts. While the amount which could be contributed by one country might remain constant, the amount contributable by the other country could vary. Although the taxable capacity of Northern Ireland was more or less certain, that of Great Britain was far from being so. Under the Irish Free State (Consequential Provisions) Act, Great Britain and Southern Ireland were treated as one unit from the point of view of taxable capacity. The Northern Ireland government was convinced that the taxable capacity of Great Britain when united with Ireland as a whole would diminish in proportion as the Free State became more overloaded with debt. The result would be to increase Northern Ireland's taxable capacity.

The solution was to find the proportion of revenue which one country ought to contribute when the other country contributes a certain portion. Clark recognized that if this principle was accepted then a standard had to be fixed for one example of relative proportions to be contributed. From this standard it would be possible to fix the rate at which proportions vary in relation to each other, by ascertaining limits for the values of the proportions. Yet it was vital to ensure that a standard year was agreed upon to ensure that no abnormal expenditure was perpetuated in a formula. The situation was further complicated by the impracticability of relating expenditure on specific services in Great Britain to that of Northern Ireland. Even where comparable, the services did not exist in the same degree in the two countries. For example, police only constituted 3 per cent of the total local expenditure in

---

[89] Memo (undated) entitled 'Arguments in support of . . . [Northern Ireland's] Taxable Capacity alternative', PRONI FIN11/2.

Great Britain, but 10 per cent in Northern Ireland. Thus, a reduction 'in the rate of local expenditure in Great Britain would, if applied to the local expenditure in Northern Ireland, reduce the police expenditure there by a ratio not applied to the police expenditure in Great Britain'.[90]

Clark told a colleague that in seeking to establish a standard year, the Northern Ireland government had to 'make estimates of what will automatically come into expenditure in the future in a greater proportion in Northern Ireland than in Great Britain'.[91] On 14 April 1924 he wrote to all of the permanent secretaries of Northern Ireland departments asking them to list departmental activities and to indicate variation in normal expenditure. Although he recognized that expenditure for services initiated by the Northern Ireland government were unlikely to be accepted by the Colwyn Committee, he asked each permanent secretary to list these and to give rough estimates of the amount involved in each case. He later asked the permanent secretaries to classify expenditure according to whether it was on purely temporary services or extensions of services; or whether it was for services temporarily running at abnormal cost (too low or too high) as compared with the same services prior to transfer, and which might be expected ultimately to revert to normal. They were also asked to distinguish services not yet in existence or not fully operative in 1923/4 but which would become operative as a result of legislation by the British parliament. Northern Ireland legislation creating services by duplication of imperial legislation was to be distinguished from legislation by the Northern Ireland parliament initiating new services. Following representations from Northern Ireland, the Colwyn Committee had agreed to regard the year 1923/4, with some modifications, as the standard year from which to work.[92]

In working out the standard year Clark also considered the increased cost of reserved services resulting from the creation of the Irish Free State and the increase of imperial expenditure caused by the non-payment of the Irish Free State's contribution towards debt and pensions. The loss 'thus incurred for the United Kingdom is possibly in the region of five millions, of which the Northern Irish share is at least £50,000'.[93] In preparing his case for a standard year, he examined every

---

[90] Memo: 'Taxable Capacity by relation to necessities in Expenditure', 3 Apr. 1923, ibid.

[91] Clark to Bullwinkle, 14 Apr. 1924, PRONI FIN11/4.

[92] Clark to each Permanent Secretary of a Northern Ireland department, 14 Apr. 1924, ibid.

[93] Memo: 'Reserved Services which may have been liable to increase on account of the setting up of the Irish Free State', 23 Jan. 1924, ibid.

aspect of local expenditure to ascertain beyond doubt what was normal
or abnormal expenditure. The London Treasury was to object to some
of his calculations, believing that he inflated standard local expenditure so as to reduce Northern Ireland's contribution liability. The
disagreement between Belfast and London over the numbers of police
which Northern Ireland should be allowed to claim as part of normal
expenditure is a good illustration of how detailed the negotiations
became. It also showed how intense the negotiations could become,
with Clark angrily dismissing Treasury claims as 'untenable'.[94]

The first meeting of the Colwyn Committee was held on 23 February
1923, and Northern Ireland was represented by Hugh Pollock, supported
by Clark who, in turn, was assisted by J. I. Cook. The London Treasury
was represented by G. C. Upcott, R. G. Hawtry, A. P. Waterfield, and
F. G. Salters. Opening for Northern Ireland, Pollock declared that,
although it was common practice to make larger claims than expected
or needed, he had decided only to submit 'such claims as we feel
we can honestly ask and finally maintain'.[95] Pollock emphasized the
seriousness of Northern Ireland's financial position by informing the
committee that when he presented his first budget, not only was there
no surplus but he had had to assume a reduction of £2 million in
Northern Ireland's imperial contribution simply to balance the budget.
As he admitted, he 'had no right to do so, but was driven to desperation'.
The Colwyn Committee met on a further five occasions until a sub-
committee was appointed in the autumn of 1923 to explore any common
ground for reaching a decision about the 1923/4 imperial contribution
and finally agreeing a future contributions formula.

As the expenditure in a standard year was the foundation on which
the formula was to be built, the importance of having an accurate
standard year could not be overestimated. Although the British Treasury
wanted 1920/1 to be regarded as the standard year, the Northern Ireland
government managed to ensure that 1923/4 was adopted instead.
Northern Ireland regarded 1920/1 as an exceptional year, with revenue
and expenditure both abnormal; indeed, the fact that the Treasury had
miscalculated Irish revenue by almost £7 million appeared to prove
beyond doubt that year's financial abnormality.[96] As Clark was to recall
some years later, the Northern Ireland formula was devised 'to calculate

[94] Minute by Clark, 'Royal Irish Constabulary Statistics', 21 Dec. 1923, ibid.

[95] Minutes of meeting of the Special Arbitration Committee, 23 Feb. 1923, PRONI
FIN11/40.

[96] Estimated revenue for Ireland in 1920/21 was £22,353,900 while the actual was
£15,745,090. For details see PRONI FIN11/6, which provides an analysis of the Financial Relations Return, Cmd. 207, 1922.

revenue in each year as though raised in Northern Ireland entirely at the British ratio and to allow local expenditure to vary from the standard year by the population proportion of the British variation in any year'.[97]

The revenue to be considered was thus the actual amount attributable of reserved revenue along with a proportion of the transferred revenue in the standard year, the proportion 'being in the ratio of Great Britain's taxes other than reserved taxes in the future year, as compared with the standard year'.[98] The calculation for local expenditure in Northern Ireland in the coming year was to be on the basis of the local expenditure per head in Northern Ireland as in the standard year. Meanwhile, the method of attributing revenue and apportioning costs of services was to remain as in the standard year. Clark maintained that if the standard year was adopted as the basis and any variation made according to the change per head of the cost of local expenditure, then Northern Ireland would enjoy equality of taxation. He contended that this method of allowances for local expenditure retained the standardized expenditure of each country on the same basis. Having thus ascertained the standardized revenue and expenditure for Northern Ireland in the coming year, he claimed that 'the balance remaining after deduction of the expenditure from the revenue represents [Northern Ireland's imperial] contribution'.[99] This, then, was the formula by which the Northern Ireland government sought to have the imperial contribution as a last, not a first, charge on its exchequer. The essence of the Northern Ireland formula, as Clark informed the secretary of the Colwyn Committee, was that Northern Ireland assumed 'equality of burden by respect of the total imposition at the present time—or rather, at the time of the standard year, ie we assume that the existing burdens are equitable by relation to the taxable capacity of the persons who pay them'.[100]

The British Government's case was presented to the Colwyn Committee in a twenty-nine-page Treasury memorandum. This rejected Northern Ireland's formula, regarding it as being based on 'misconceived assumptions'. The Treasury believed that if the Northern Ireland claim was accepted by the Colwyn Committee,

it would enable the Northern Irish Government and Parliament by their own volition to reduce the contribution by any amount they pleased, and to that

[97] Unpublished autobiographical notes written by Sir Ernest Clark about 'The Financial Relations of Great Britain and Northern Ireland', Clark Papers, PRONI D1022/2/22.
[98] Memo containing briefing for Sir Ernest Clark for meeting of the Arbitration Committee on 3 and 4 June 1924, PRONI FIN11/22.
[99] Memo: 'Formula for calculation of Northern Ireland's Contribution in Future Years', c.Oct. 1923, PRONI FIN11/7.
[100] Clark to William Piercy, 16 July 1923, PRONI FIN11/7.

extent the British Parliament would in effect be called upon to provide for local expenditure in regard to which it has no voice or control.[101]

The British Treasury refused to accept Northern Ireland's claim that she had been prejudicially affected in financial terms by the establishment of the Irish Free State. Consequently, it did not consider that there were any grounds for modifying the basis of the financial contribution as fixed by the 1920 Act.

The Government of Northern Ireland had stressed from the beginning that the Colwyn Committee must be unhampered by the Government of Ireland Act, 1920, and:

that it is open to them, should they consider it necessary, to suggest drastic alterations therein (to which the British Government is pledged to give parliamentary consent), just as it is open to them to suggest an interpretation of the sections of the original Act.[102]

The Treasury continued to argue that it was essential not to lose sight of the financial provisions of the 1920 Act and repeatedly stated that it was 'neither practicable nor desirable to adopt a rigid formula, which is to be regarded as binding upon the Joint Exchequer Board'.[103] Although the Northern Ireland government accepted that the Joint Exchequer Board would each year determine the actual amount of contribution, it insisted that the Colwyn Committee should deal with the formula question. While the committee was only to deal with the general principles, the government maintained that adopting a formula to guide the Joint Exchequer Board was merely a method of embodying principles.

Believing that Northern Ireland would gain a fair deal from the Colwyn Committee, Clark advised Pollock that it would be better to have the issue settled by it rather than by the Joint Exchequer Board.[104] At a meeting on 3 June 1924 Clark reminded the committee of the undertaking given by Stanley Baldwin in his letter of 27 November 1922 that, if it made recommendations involving legislation, the necessary steps would be taken. The Colwyn Committee accepted Northern Ireland's basic point that it had the right to adopt a formula which would guide the Joint Exchequer Board's fixing of the imperial contribution. Forced to come to terms with the reality that a formula was going to be adopted, the Treasury had to counter the particular one proposed by Northern Ireland.

[101] Treasury memo submitted to the Arbitration Committee, PRONI FIN11/16.

[102] Memo by Clark, 'Future Contribution', c.Jan. 1923, PRONI FIN11/2.

[103] Memo by Mr Hawtrey, British Treasury, 'Contribution of Northern Ireland: The Use of Formulas', 27 May 1924, PRONI FIN11/7.

[104] Clark to Pollock, 5 Oct. 1923, ibid.

The formula which the Treasury was to submit to the Colwyn Committee would have led, Clark thought, to Northern Ireland's bankruptcy.[105] Rather than taking the actual amount raised from reserved taxes, the Treasury sought to calculate the amount to be raised by a formula based on the possible yield of reserved taxes. In the Treasury formula the first step was to select certain reserved taxes and then, having arrived at the probable yield of each selected tax, to apply it to the yield in Great Britain of each tax in the standard year. Northern Ireland objected to the Treasury's selecting only certain taxes since transferred taxes might in the future have differential rates, while the various reserved taxes might not have been included in the selected taxes. Meanwhile, applying the yield of each selected tax to the yield in Britain of each tax in the standard year was felt by Northern Ireland to ignore 'the law of diminishing returns and it does not provide for differences in administration or scope of the tax'.[106] This was the main principle in the Treasury's formula and one which Clark regarded as hopelessly flawed. Both the Northern Ireland formula and the Treasury formula attempted to calculate a supposititious revenue and local expenditure for a future year by relation to the revenue and local expenditure ascertained for the standard year. The 'difference between the supposititious revenue and the supposititious local expenditure [would be] the imperial contribution'.[107] However, as both formulae used different methods of calculating the contribution, different sizes of contribution were likely to be suggested by London and Belfast.

Clark endeavoured to prove the proposed Treasury formula wrong not only in theory but also in practice. He realized that there would be difficulties in applying it and felt it would not stand the acid test when applied to real figures. Applying the formula to 1919—the year chosen by the Treasury as a base in its White Paper—Clark calculated that Ireland would have had to contribute £38,667,000. When the Northern Ireland formula was used, the contribution from Ireland fell to £21,172,000. In actual fact, Ireland had contributed £21,394,000, which Clark believed demonstrated that the Treasury formula was 'utterly worthless'.[108] As Northern Ireland had to pay 44 per cent of the imperial contribution due from Ireland, this would have meant that under the Treasury formula she would have to contribute £16,720,000, and that from an estimated total revenue of £16 millions! Clark could

---

[105] Clark to Piercy, 16 July 1923, ibid.

[106] Briefings for meeting of the Colwyn Committee, 4, 8, and 9 Oct. 1923, PRONI FIN11/20.

[107] Ibid.

[108] Minutes of preparatory meeting of Northern Ireland negotiators prior to the meeting of the Special Arbitration Committee, 4 Oct. 1923, ibid.

confidently inform the Colwyn Committee that, even if the Northern
Ireland formula was not absolutely right, it could not be far out, whereas
the Treasury formula was 'hopelessly wrong', and it seemed 'almost [a]
waste to argue further on these formulae'.[109]

The Colwyn Committee presented its first report to the Chancellor
of the Exchequer, Stanley Baldwin, on 4 September 1923. The report
recommended a reduction of the imperial contribution of £7.9 million
for the years 1922/3 and 1923/4 as provided for in the 1920 Act. On
the basis of the preliminary account for 1922/3, the committee suggested that the contribution should be £5,854,674. The contribution
for 1923/4 was also to be fixed by the Joint Exchequer Board as the
surplus of revenue over expenditure after excluding on the one side the
Land Purchase Annuities, and 'provided that the Joint Exchequer Board
is satisfied that the remaining expenditure represents the cost of normal
economical administration, and that there is nothing exceptional about
the expenditure or the revenue receipts'.[110]

The Colwyn Committee did not accept Northern Ireland's claim
that the whole of the properties, assets, and rights used in connection
with the Irish services should be valued and apportioned between
Northern Ireland and the Irish Free State. It did, however, award
Northern Ireland a grant of £400,000 towards the cost of a new teacher-
training college, police depot, and increased expenditure for prisons
and asylums. The Northern Ireland government had also made a claim,
strongly opposed by the Treasury, for £1,000,000 towards the cost of
malicious damage. The Treasury reasoned that Craig's government had
to accept liability as it had been responsible since November 1921 for
the maintenance of law and order within its own border. However, the
Colwyn Committee awarded £500,000 as a final contribution towards
the settlement of all claims in respect of malicious injuries inflicted on
Northern Ireland property and people. Northern Ireland had claimed
that the £500,000 Unemployment Relief Grant should be treated as an
out-and-out non-returnable grant. The Colwyn Committee directed
that the grant should be limited to £300,000, but suggested that this
should be allowed irrespective of the financial years into which the
expenditure fell.

The first report of the Colwyn Committee had been, from a Northern
Ireland point of view, most favourable. However, the Northern Ireland
government was concerned about some of the wording in the report,
which could

[109] Ibid.
[110] *The First Report of Northern Ireland Special Arbitration Committee*, 4 Sept.
1923, PRONI FIN11/25.

deny to Northern Ireland any autonomy in her own transferred services in the future by the inherent threat of absolute bankruptcy, since no new or improved services can be allowed as chargeable against revenue, the balance of which, after deduction of standard expenditure, would be appropriate to imperial contribution.[111]

William Piercy, secretary of the Colwyn Committee, informed Clark that the committee in its first report was only concerned to determine the contributions for 1922/3 and 1923/4, and that it had yet to con-sider the 'method for the determination of the contribution or any element affecting the contribution in years subsequent to these'.[112] Pollock considered Piercy's reply, 'without its unnecessary verbiage', to be most satisfactory.[113]

The second, and final, report of the Colwyn Committee was presented on 1 December 1924 to Winston Churchill, then Chancellor of the Exchequer. It recommended that the 'extent to which the total revenue exceeds the actual and necessary expenditure in Northern Ireland shall be taken as the basic sum for determining the contribution'.[114] Local expenditure was to be a first charge on the Northern Ireland exchequer, with the imperial contribution a last charge. Furthermore, the imperial contribution was to be 'related not to the services enjoyed but based upon the difference between Northern Ireland's revenue and its actual and necessary expenditure'.[115] To avoid any possible misinterpretation by the Joint Exchequer Board, the report spelled out in detail how revenue and local expenditure were to be calculated.[116] There was continued discussion between Belfast and London to remove any ambiguity in the wording, and so it was not until 10 March 1925 that the report was presented to the Westminster parliament by the Chancellor.

---

[111] Clark to Piercy, 20 Sept. 1923, PRONI FIN11/25.

[112] Piercy to Clark, 16 Oct. 1923, ibid.

[113] Pollock to Clark, 19 Oct. 1923, ibid.

[114] The Final Report of Northern Ireland Special Arbitration Committee, 1 Dec. 1924, PRONI FIN11/55.

[115] Harkness, *Northern Ireland*, 31.

[116] The report declared that revenue and local expenditure were to be calculated as follows: '(a) *Revenue*: i. the actual amount of revenue attributable from reserved rev-enues, plus ii. the amount of transferred revenues in the standard year multiplied by (1) the ratio of the yield of revenue (other than reserved revenues) in Great Britain in the year of contribution to the yield of such revenues in the standard year and (2) the ratio of the proportion which the yield of reserved taxes in Northern Ireland bears to the yield of reserved taxes in Great Britain in the year of contribution to such proportion in the standard year. (b) *Local Expenditure*: The local expenditure per head in Northern Ireland in the standard year, plus or minus the increase or decrease per head of local expenditure in Great Britain in the year of contribution as compared with the standard year, multi-plied by the estimated number of the population of Northern Ireland in the year of contribution.' PRONI FIN11/55.

It was clear that the report, by making the imperial contribution a last as opposed to a first charge on the Northern Ireland exchequer, had conceded to Craig's government what it wanted. However, even with the publication of the final report, the Treasury was reluctant to admit defeat, stating that: 'the financial effect of the report has yet to be worked out and it is clearly undesirable to give any calculations before those have been arrived at by the [Joint] Board. Any references can therefore only be in very general terms.'[117] No doubt the Colwyn Committee had prided itself on its independence from the Treasury and its impartiality, and thus acted to rectify the injustice of the financial provisions in the 1920 Act. As Clark had warned the Colwyn Committee during its deliberations, 'Northern Ireland cannot continue unless on a basis of financial stability and this can only be secured if the contribution is fixed within the powers of the province to pay'.[118]

The Colwyn Committee was also aware that a Northern Ireland beset by impossible financial pressures would create serious political problems. In addition, London would have to deal with the practical issue of finance in a Northern Ireland reabsorbed into the general financial system of the United Kingdom. While the Colwyn Committee may have been, to an extent, influenced by these political and financial considerations, Clark's personal role in securing a report favourable to Northern Ireland was immensely important. It was he more than anyone who ensured that Northern Ireland's case was meticulously researched, convincingly presented, and forcibly argued at the Colwyn Committee. Clark's practice of working to the point of exhaustion has already been mentioned, but this characteristic is most clearly seen in regard to these negotiations, when, in addition to fulfilling his duties as head of the Northern Ireland Civil Service—most exacting in themselves—he undertook responsibility for overseeing the detailed preparation of Northern Ireland's case. To complete this task successfully, he worked, as his diary for 1923 reveals, astonishingly long hours.[119]

Although some officials in the British Treasury regarded the Colwyn Report as a spendthrift's charter, it was 'not a licence for free spending in Northern Ireland'.[120] By making its imperial contribution a residual sum upon its exchequer and so removing the threat of bankruptcy, the Colwyn Report helped secure Northern Ireland's existence. However,

[117] Telegram from Treasury to Clark, 9 Mar. 1925, ibid.
[118] Brief for Clark, 3 June 1924, PRONI FIN11/22.
[119] The rather fragmentary entries in his diary for 1923 reveal that on most days, including Saturdays and Sundays, Clark was in his office by 7 a.m. and worked until late in the evening: PRONI D1022/8/25.
[120] Buckland, *Factory of Grievances*, 92.

by defining what expenditure was 'actual and necessary', the Colwyn Committee

effectively decreed that *per capita* social service expenditure after 1924 should increase in the province only at the same rate as in Britain, a decision that profoundly affected a backward region, as only a higher rate of expenditure could have permitted the 'leeway' to be made up and comparable levels of service attained.[121]

John Andrews, the Minister of Labour, was adamant that not only was it essential that Northern Ireland bring its services up to the existing level in Great Britain, but it was vital to maintain parity with any future British improvements. Andrews was a conscientious and humane minister who wanted to ensure that the workers of Northern Ireland did not suffer lower social standards because of local autonomy. However, given that the Joint Exchequer Board was to satisfy itself that expenditure in Northern Ireland represented 'the cost of normal economical administration and that there is nothing exceptional about the administration or the revenue receipts', the Northern Ireland government had very little room for manœuvre.[122] Andrews's efforts to extend social services met with 'opposition from Pollock and his officials obsessed with the need to balance the budget and keep on good terms with the imperial Treasury and suspicious that labour was being pampered at the expense of employers'.[123]

In seeking to maintain parity of social services with Great Britain, Andrews was guided as much by political considerations as by his own compassionate nature. He believed that many working-class unionists would cease to support the Ulster Unionist Party should it fail to protect their social interests. During the deliberations of the Colwyn Committee he had warned Pollock that 'unless we get a settlement which will secure to our people the same social standards as their fellow citizens in Great Britain the political future of Northern Ireland will be seriously endangered'.[124] Even had it wanted to, Northern Ireland lacked the financial ability to develop social services or to adopt radical economic policies: simply maintaining parity with Great Britain for basic services almost overwhelmed it. This is most clearly illustrated by the difficulties faced by the government in keeping the Unemployment Insurance Fund in a solvent state. The survival of this fund, which provided the poorest in society with very basic support, was frequently in doubt.

[121] Harkness, *Northern Ireland*, 31.
[122] Clark to Spender, 9 Jan. 1924, PRONI CAB9A/3/1.
[123] Buckland, *Factory of Grievances*, 13.
[124] Andrews to Pollock, 21 July 1924, PRONI FIN11/25.

The deterioration in the economic climate had reduced the revenue available for the fund in Northern Ireland but at the same time increased the demands on it. In addition, Andrews was convinced that in Northern Ireland sickness made greater numbers unfit for work than in Britain. He blamed this partly on the climate, which he felt predisposed people to illness, and partly on the number of workers involved in unhealthy occupations, combined with poor wage levels. This, Andrews maintained, forced the Northern Ireland workers to 'adopt rather a lower standard of living which gives them less reserve power when bad health comes'.[125] When the government assumed responsibility for the Unemployment Insurance Fund in 1921, it had immediately to grapple with a deficit. Indeed, the Minister of Labour was only able to keep it solvent by obtaining grants for 1921 of some £530,000.[126]

Disagreement between Andrews and Pollock about how the Unemployment Insurance Fund should be financed strained relations between them and even created bitterness.[127] Relations reached an all-time low in September 1923 when Pollock compiled and circulated to the Cabinet a memorandum about the insolvency of the Northern Ireland Unemployment Insurance Fund without having first informed Andrews. It was only through the intervention of Craig as mediator that the divisions in the Cabinet were healed. Andrews managed to have the rate of unemployment benefit raised in line with increases in the rate in Britain. He did not feel that such rises were 'unreasonable or socialistic'.[128] However, the deepening economic depression and the growing deficit in the Unemployment Insurance Fund made it increasingly difficult for Northern Ireland to continue payment of benefit.

A confidential actuarial report on the position of the Northern Ireland Unemployment Fund presented to Pollock on 28 August 1923 had indicated that it was

impracticable to continue to pay in Northern Ireland the [same] benefits as those paid in Great Britain out of similar contributions to those imposed in that part of the Kingdom, because the average rate of unemployment in Northern Ireland is, and has been for many years, at least 50% more than that of Great Britain.[129]

The Cabinet accepted Andrews's view that, as benefits were already the minimum payments necessary for the maintenance of the unemployed, they should not be reduced. In addition, the Cabinet objected

---

[125] Ibid.   [126] Spender to Andrews, 21 Dec. 1921, PRONI CAB9C/1/1.
[127] See correspondence between Andrews and Pollock in PRONI CAB9C/1/1.
[128] Andrews to Craig, 9 May 1924, ibid.
[129] Clark to Piercy, 5 Sept. 1923, PRONI FIN11/12.

in principle to what it regarded as the compulsory imposition of a relatively lower social condition on the citizens of Northern Ireland than on the rest of the United Kingdom. By June 1923 the accumulated deficiency in the Northern Ireland Unemployment Fund was £5 7s. 0d. per head of the insured population, as compared with a deficit in the British fund of £1 8s. 0d. per head. The Northern Ireland government wrote to the Colwyn Committee on 23 September 1923 and asked that it consider the financial results arising from the division of the United Kingdom Unemployment Insurance Fund.

Craig's government was very anxious to achieve a sympathetic settlement from the Colwyn Committee on this issue. The abnormally high unemployment (even by Northern Ireland levels) necessitated advances in 1922/3 of nearly £1,000,000 to aid the Fund.[130] A deficit of such proportions brought the threat of bankruptcy not merely to the Unemployment Fund but to the Government of Northern Ireland itself. The magnitude of the deficit problem was such that Clark told Pollock that a favourable settlement from the Colwyn Committee on this matter was of 'greater importance to us than the Special Constabulary seeing that it is possible to control the latter expenditure more easily than the former'.[131]

Andrews was unhappy with the Ministry of Finance's presentation of Northern Ireland's case to the Colwyn Committee. He felt that the government should stay away from a mathematical theory based on population and instead seek 'equal taxation, equal social standards for the individual throughout the United Kingdom'.[132] He was worried that Pollock might compromise with the British Treasury on the Unemployment Insurance Fund as part of an overall financial settlement. He warned Pollock that, 'under no circumstances should we agree to accept even a temporary advantage at the expense of sacrificing our claim that equal taxation with Great Britain should bring about equal benefits to our people'.[133]

The Colwyn Committee refused to consider the government's claim regarding the Unemployment Insurance Fund, as the British Government would not agree to the matter being discussed. The committee suggested that the Government of Northern Ireland seek a settlement directly with the British Government. Although unsuccessful in its efforts with the Colwyn Committee in relation to this issue, the government's overall success partly compensated for this shortfall.

---

[130] Memo: 'Unemployment Relief Grant', c.May 1923, PRONI FIN11/13.
[131] Clark to Pollock, 21 Aug. 1924, PRONI FIN11/12.
[132] Andrews to Pollock, 21 July 1924, PRONI FIN11/25.
[133] Andrews to Pollock, 18 Aug. 1924, ibid.

Pollock believed that there were certain advantages in having the allowance for local expenditure based on the total expenditure on social services in the year. He hoped that the excess on the one set of services would be made good by savings on others. However, he declined to give an undertaking to the Cabinet that it would be possible to maintain parity of services, stating that he 'could not be a party to allowing Northern Ireland to get into a serious financial position which would impair its credit'.[134] Indeed, in a major memorandum about parity of services circulated to the Cabinet, Pollock questioned the desirability of following exactly the policies adopted in Britain. He claimed that the 'people of Northern Ireland can never have social standards identical with those of Great Britain, because their requirements are not the same', and advocated that the Cabinet should 'judge every [British] reform strictly on its own merits in relation to Northern Ireland', to ensure that no reform was adopted which would be harmful to their economic well-being.[135] However, Andrews had no patience with Pollock's view that Northern Ireland ought to stand on its own financial feet, arguing that it was simply not financially independent of Britain.

Anxious to prevent the Northern Ireland Unemployment Insurance Fund collapsing under the burden of debt, Craig suggested to the British Government that it be amalgamated with the British fund. The accumulated deficit by 1925 was £3.6 million, an enormous sum for a Northern Ireland whose domestic budget was then less than £6 million.[136] To safeguard the existence of Northern Ireland, Craig's government was prepared to give up responsibility for its own unemployment fund. The British Cabinet established a committee under Lord Cave, the Lord Chancellor, to consider Craig's request, and this in turn established a committee of officials headed by Sir John Anderson to examine the practical problems of amalgamation.

The committee also considered how an amalgamation of the unemployment funds would 'relate to the provisions of the Government of Ireland Act and to the spirit as well as the letter of the Irish Treaty Settlement'.[137] Lord Cave's committee recommended that the Northern Ireland fund continue to be separate, but that there should be a partial amalgamation of responsibility for the deficit.[138] This led to the Unemployment Reinsurance Agreement, which meant that as from

[134] Cabinet Conclusions, 16 Sept. 1924, PRONI CAB4/121/16.
[135] 'Memorandum by Minister of Finance on Special Expenditure', 1925, PRONI CAB9C/11/1.
[136] Buckland, *Factory of Grievances*, 85.
[137] Rt. Hon. Stanley Baldwin to Craig, 2 July 1925, PRONI CAB9C/1/6.
[138] 'Unemployment Insurance Fund: Scheme to be recommended to Imperial Cabinet by the Lord Chancellor's Committee', c.July 1925, ibid.

1 October 1925 the Northern Ireland government undertook to provide 'equalization' payment 'to the Unemployment Fund in Northern Ireland to such an extent that the deficit on the Fund, after making such contribution, will be in relation to the deficit on the British Fund in the ratio of the insured population'.[139] In the event of Northern Ireland's equalization payment per head of population exceeding the corresponding British payment in any one year, the British Treasury was to meet three-quarters of the excess. The Northern Ireland government had, however, to accept responsibility for the large debt incurred by the Unemployment Insurance Fund up to 1 April 1925. The net deficit of £2,490,000 was to be repaid by an 'annuity at 4½% per annum over a period of 20 years', and 'the annual charge would be approximately £190,000 for that period'.[140]

Although the Reinsurance Agreement did rescue the Northern Ireland Unemployment Insurance Fund from bankruptcy, it was far from ideal. Northern Ireland obtained substantial payments from the British Treasury in the late 1920s, but there was always the possibility that the latter might attempt to end its commitment. In addition, there remained the usual method of helping Northern Ireland out of its financial difficulties through a series of *ad-hoc* arrangements. The discussions that preceded each payment from London to Belfast not only presented the British Treasury with an opportunity to interfere in Northern Ireland's financial affairs, but also had potential for disagreement and even ill feeling. Indeed, Northern Ireland's first application to London (in 1926) for financial assistance under the new agreement irritated Winston Churchill, the Chancellor of the Exchequer. The three-quarters of the equalization payment due from the British Treasury was £1,311,260, but Churchill claimed that in agreeing to help Northern Ireland, he thought 'that my liability would be limited to a maximum of £650,000 a year and no figure in excess of this has ever been mentioned to me, or by me to my colleagues'.[141] Once again it took all of Craig's political and diplomatic skills to ensure that Northern Ireland obtained what he considered was due to her. Even then, however, 'the way was not smooth. The hands of Treasury officials were still tied by law, constitutional practice and the possible implications of any concession for imperial policy towards the Free State.'[142]

Northern Ireland had managed to survive the immediate financial

---

[139] 'Memorandum explanatory of the proposed Reinsurance Scheme', c.July 1925, PRONI CAB9C/1/6.
[140] Ibid.
[141] Rt. Hon. Winston Churchill MP to Craig, 29 Jan. 1926, PRONI CAB9C/1/6.
[142] Buckland, *Factory of Grievances*, 94.

threats to her existence, but she remained weak in financial and economic matters. In addition, the government had little effective power or financial ability to tackle the socio-economic problems afflicting the province, for it

could not make use of the techniques which sovereign countries use to sustain economic independence. It was prohibited from establishing separate tariffs and legislation for external trade. It had no power to follow an independent monetary or fiscal policy, and it had few effective powers of taxation.[143]

With the main powers of economic management reserved to Westminster, the Northern Ireland government was obliged to toe the British line on many issues. Expenditure in Northern Ireland on services such as old-age pensions and unemployment benefit rose as Craig's government attempted to maintain equality of standards with Britain, but revenue to fund the development of services fell away, 'determined for the most part by the Chancellor of the Exchequer against the background of Britain's rather than Ulster's needs'.[144] Consequently, even in those areas in which Northern Ireland had power, the government's policy and administrative options were limited. The one overriding objective of the government's financial policy was a fiscal stability which could secure the existence of Northern Ireland. By achieving this objective, the government's financial policy was a success, but it was a success accomplished at a cost, an acceptance of a financial basis for Northern Ireland's system of devolved government which denied freedom for financial or economic development.

[143] D. Birrell and A. Murie, *Policy and Government in Northern Ireland: Lessons of Devolution* (Dublin, 1980), 22.
[144] Lawrence, *Government of Northern Ireland*, 47.

7

Preserving Self-Government

The treaty for securing a political settlement signed on 6 December 1921 by the British Government and Sinn Fein outraged Ulster unionists. They were particularly alarmed by the provisions for a Boundary Commission to modify the border between Northern Ireland and the new Irish Free State. Just as the treaty created an expectation among nationalists 'that Northern Ireland would soon disappear and a notion that its territory was a legitimate target for seizure', so it 'heightened apprehensions among Unionists, particularly those living in border areas, who were alarmed to the point of panic at the possibility of being transferred to the Free State'.[1]

In an attempt to ease communal tensions and reduce sectarian violence, Craig and Collins met in London on 24 January 1922 for discussions. A surprising measure of agreement was reached, it being decided that the boundary question should not be dealt with by the commission proposed in the treaty, but as a 'matter for mutual agreement' between their governments.[2] On 2 February they met once again (this time in Dublin) but failed to come to terms on the border issue. Lloyd George had assured Craig that a settlement of the boundary question would only involve rectification of the border, but at the Dublin meeting Collins 'produced large maps, showing that he wanted half of Ulster saying that Lloyd George had told him that he would get that'.[3]

Craig 'made it clear that unionists would never abandon places such as Derry city and Enniskillen and stressed their historic and sentimental importance to protestants'[4] and declined to have any further discussions with Collins. Collins may have hoped that the British Government would force Craig into making concessions and, indeed, Lloyd George and Churchill—anxious to patch up the peace-pact—both attempted to do so. Craig, however, remained 'completely adamant' that he would not compromise the integrity of Northern Ireland's territory.[5] Any further attempts to resurrect the peace-pact were dashed by a new wave

[1] P. Buckland, A History of Northern Ireland (Dublin, 1981), 38–9.
[2] Text of Craig–Collins pact, NAI S 1834A.
[3] Entry in Lady Craig's diary, 2 Feb. 1922, Craigavon Papers, PRONI D1415/B/38.
[4] M. Laffan, The Partition of Ireland 1911–1925 (Dundalk, 1983), 93.
[5] Entry in Lady Craig's diary, 6 Feb. 1922, PRONI D1415/B/38.

of IRA raids across the border on the night of 7/8 February, which intensified sectarian strife in Northern Ireland.[6]

Not until 29 March 1922 was it possible to bring Craig and Collins together in London for another conference in a fresh attempt to agree a new pact. On 30 March Churchill announced that the two leaders had signed a new peace agreement which was more detailed and far-reaching than the first. It was hoped that the pact would cure unrest and disorder in Northern Ireland by securing Roman Catholic co-operation in the maintenance of law and order. However, it also included a clause for further discussion, to ascertain 'whether agreement can be arrived at on the boundary question otherwise than by recourse to the Boundary Commission outlined in Article 12 of the Treaty'.[7] Unfortunately, the pact did not fulfil the high expectations it created. As IRA attacks against and within Northern Ireland continued, communal tensions remained high and in turn provided an atmosphere which enabled lawlessness to continue. In such a situation progress on the boundary question was scarcely possible.

In August 1922 the Provisional Government began a comprehensive re-examination of its relations with Northern Ireland in general and with Craig's government in particular. Ernest Blythe, a staunch republican of Ulster Protestant background, prepared a memorandum which became the blueprint for the Provisional Government's policy towards the North. Scathing in his criticism of the previous Provisional Government's policy of supporting IRA action and economic boycott against Northern Ireland, he emphasized that Ulster unionists could not be forced into accepting a united Ireland.[8] The failure of the existing policy and the death of Collins on 22 August cleared the way for the Provisional Government's formal adoption of Blythe's peace policy on 26 August 1922.[9]

However, this did not mean that the Provisional Government abandoned the ideal of Irish unity. Rather, it now placed increased emphasis on the Boundary Commission as envisaged by Article 12 of the Anglo-Irish Treaty. It was felt that once stability was restored to Southern Ireland, the government in Dublin would be able to pressurize the British Government into implementing the Boundary Commission clause, which was 'portrayed as a step towards unity since the Boundary

---

[6] Laffan, *Partition of Ireland*, 93.

[7] Clause 7 of the 'Heads of agreement between the Provisional Government and Government of Northern Ireland': *The Times*, 31 Mar. 1922.

[8] Memo by Ernest Blythe, 'Policy in regard to the northeast', 9 Aug. 1922, Blythe Papers, UCDAD P24/70.

[9] Minutes of Provisional Government, 26 Aug. 1922, NAI G1/3.

Commission would so reduce the area of Northern Ireland as to make its separate existence impossible and thereby end the state of Partition'.[10] Grass-roots nationalists in Northern Ireland, particularly those along the border, pinned all their hopes on the Boundary Commission's transferring their territory to the Free State.[11] The Provisional Government still appeared to believe that it would win Ulster unionist acceptance of a united Ireland, but Dublin's goodwill—be it sincere or only a tactic—failed to make 'the slightest difference to unionist intentions'.[12]

The Irish Free State came into formal existence on 6 December 1922 with the Westminster parliament's passing of the Irish Free State Constitution Act, 1922, which ratified the treaty agreement between the British Government and Sinn Fein. Next day the Northern Ireland parliament exercised its treaty right to petition the King for the powers of the Free State not to extend to Northern Ireland. The separation of Northern Ireland from the parliament in Dublin was thus reaffirmed. To Ulster unionists Northern Ireland's opting out of the Irish Free State was crucial. As early as March 1922 the Northern Ireland Cabinet approved a draft motion, prepared by the Parliamentary Draftsman, enabling Northern Ireland to vote herself out of the Free State.[13] In moving the address to the King, Craig believed that the Ulster unionists were simply fulfilling their old determination to remain a separate people.

By opting out of Dublin's jurisdiction, the Ulster unionists automatically activated the treaty provisions relating to the Boundary Commission. Conscious of this, Craig stated that the Government of Northern Ireland would not be 'dragged' into the Commission and denounced the power given to its chairman. He commented that: 'it was unthinkable that the fixing of the boundary should rest in the hands of one man . . . who might by a stroke of the pen hand over the houses, the homes, the cottages of those gallant men who had spilled their blood for the safety of their own country.'[14] Craig's speech was enthusiastically welcomed by Ulster Unionist back-bench MPs, who regarded it as the most forceful one he had ever delivered.

Anticipating Northern Ireland's voting to opt out of the Free State and thus necessitating the establishment of the Boundary Commission, the Provisional Government made preliminary moves to prepare its

[10] J. B. Dooher, 'Tyrone Nationalism and the Question of Partition 1910–25' (M.Phil. Thesis, University of Ulster, 1986), 444.
[11] P. Shea, *Voices and the Sound of Drums: An Irish Autobiography* (Belfast, 1981), 95.
[12] R. Fanning, *Independent Ireland* (Dublin, 1983), 38.
[13] Cabinet Conclusions, 13 Mar. 1922, PRONI CAB4/35/5.
[14] *Parl. Deb.* (House of Commons), ii, 7 Dec. 1922, col. 1152.

case. On 2 October it decided that its Assistant Legal Adviser, Kevin O'Shiel, a solicitor from Omagh in Northern Ireland, should be 'responsible for the collection and compilation of data in connection with the forthcoming Boundary Commission, and that he should submit reports at frequent and regular intervals to the Government'.[15] Cosgrave was therefore able to announce, in October 1922, the establishment of the North-Eastern Boundary Bureau, headed by O'Shiel, to compile Dublin's case to the Boundary Commission, but the Dublin authorities took no further action in relation to the Commission until the civil war ended in May 1923.

Within the North-Eastern Boundary Bureau O'Shiel created a Research Division staffed by personnel from the Free State Constitution Office. There was also to be a North-Eastern Local Division, and legal agents were to be appointed for various districts within Northern Ireland. Mainly solicitors from Northern Ireland's nationalist community, these agents were each to receive from the Free State government a fee of 60 guineas (£63) and any 'reasonable expenses' incurred in preparing the case for the commission. O'Shiel also formed a Publicity Division within the bureau, believing that propaganda was 'even more important than ever in view of the political crisis and the likelihood of a general election and the return of a "Die-hard" government in Great Britain'.[16]

Although the North-Eastern Boundary Bureau began without delay the preparation of the Free State case, Cosgrave did not press the British Government for the formation of the Boundary Commission. Northern nationalists lobbied him to do so as a matter of urgency, lest postponement enabled the Northern Ireland government to consolidate its grip over all its territory, but given the continuing civil war in the Free State, Cosgrave, on the advice of O'Shiel, was against an early formation of the commission. In the event of its being established amid continued civil war, O'Shiel believed that the Free State case would be weakened as it would be easy 'to imagine the flamboyant contrast that would be drawn between the chaos and horrors of the South and the peaceful and law-abiding conditions in the North'.[17] Also, Lloyd George's coalition government was replaced, in November 1922, by a new Conservative administration headed by Andrew Bonar Law, an old friend of the Ulster unionists. O'Shiel believed that the sympathies

[15] Minutes of the Provisional Government, 2 Oct. 1922, NAI G1/3.
[16] Kevin O'Shiel to Liam Cosgrave TD, 21 Oct. 1922, NAI S4 743.
[17] Memo: 'Alleged delays in holding of the Boundary Commission: Should the Boundary Commission be held now?', O'Shiel to the Irish Executive Council, 7 Feb. 1923, Mulcahy Papers, UCDAD P7/B/101.

of the British Government now lay with Northern Ireland and were reinforced by the prevailing violence in the Free State.

Cosgrave believed that it was a good tactical ploy to delay the appointment of the Boundary Commission until the new customs barrier between Northern Ireland and the Irish Free State took effect. O'Shiel contended that it would not be long before economic hardship compelled traders in Northern Ireland to seek an end to political and customs partition.[18] In this he was overly optimistic: although a customs barrier caused economic dislocation to Northern Ireland traders, particularly those in border towns, it did not drive them towards accepting rule from Dublin.[19] Nationalists in Northern Ireland might feel let down by the failure of the Free State government to press for the early formation of the Boundary Commission, but for Cosgrave, victory over the Irregulars remained his government's overriding aim and rendered all other issues secondary.

In response to charges from Northern Ireland nationalists of inactivity in relation to the Boundary Commission, Cosgrave's Cabinet claimed that it had 'been making active unceasing preparations for the Commission, and would take the necessary decisive action at the psychological moment. They were not prepared, however, to allow themselves to be stampeded into any hasty action.'[20] But the pressure from northern nationalists meant that the Free State government had at least to be seen to be making some moves on the border question. Meanwhile, the situation in Northern Ireland had been so calm and the prospect of the Boundary Commission so far removed that Craig felt able to spend long periods at his home at Streatley-on-Thames in England.[21] Indeed, so secure did Craig feel, that he considered there was 'no necessity for the Ulster Association to take notice of the [propaganda] articles issued by the North Eastern Boundary Bureau'.[22]

O'Shiel had informed Cosgrave on 12 May 1923 that the preparation of the Free State case for submission to the Boundary Commission was 'practically complete'. The Irish Cabinet, therefore, resolved to request the British Government to establish the Boundary Commission.[23] By 5 June 1923 O'Shiel was able to give Cosgrave's Cabinet a detailed

[18] Memo: 'Customs on the Irish–British Land Frontier', O'Shiel to the Irish Executive Council, 19 Feb. 1923, NAI S2 027.

[19] Memo: 'Fiscal Independence and Customs barrier', O'Shiel to the Irish Executive Council, ibid.

[20] Minutes of the Irish Executive Council, 14 May 1922, NAI G2/2.

[21] For details, see correspondence between Craig and his private secretary in PRONI PM9/8.

[22] Craig to Spender, 2 July 1923, PRONI PM9/8.

[23] Minutes of the Irish Executive Council, 12 May 1923, NAI G2/2.

briefing setting out the Free State's territorial claims. Meanwhile
Cosgrave moved to place the boundary question firmly in the centre of
the political stage by writing to Stanley Baldwin—by then British Prime
Minister—calling for the establishment of the Commission forthwith.
Although Craig was disappointed that the boundary question had been
raised again, he confided to his brother Charles, an Ulster Unionist
MP at Westminster, that 'perhaps on the whole it will be better to get
the wretched bogy settled and done with'.[24]

Craig and Cosgrave met in London on 17 July and, among other
business, discussed the proposed commission. Building on the friendly
relations established at an earlier meeting on 10 November 1922, they
discussed matters amicably. Although Craig was prepared to give
'sympathetic consideration' to Cosgrave's representations for the release
of IRA members held in custody in Northern Ireland, he was not
prepared to make any deals on the Boundary Commission.[25] On his
return to Dublin, Cosgrave discussed the situation with his Cabinet
and then informed the Dail that he was appointing Dr Eoin MacNeill,[26]
the Minister of Education, as Free State representative to the Boundary
Commission.[27] No doubt, given the impending General Election,
Cosgrave was anxious to appear active on the boundary issue, and
indeed his 'continued insistence upon the commission was a feature of
the Free State general election of August 1923'.[28]

Although Cosgrave was calling for the immediate establishment of
the Boundary Commission, no pains were spared by the British
Government in the exploration of alternative avenues. There was by
now a shared conviction 'that mutual consent, not legal force, was
required between Dublin and Belfast, and perhaps, too, a shared fear of
a commission decision that might prove difficult to enforce and which
might, whatever its findings, renew bloodshed and ill-feeling in Ireland'.[29]
On 22 September the British Government invited the Government of

[24] Craig to Charles Craig MP, 20 June 1923, Cabinet Secretariat, PRONI CAB9Z/
3/1.
[25] Minutes of the Irish Executive Council, 18 July 1923, NAI G2/3.
[26] Eoin MacNeill was vice-president of the Gaelic League and first Professor of Early
Irish History at University College Dublin. He served as Chief of Staff of the Irish
Volunteers and was elected as a Sinn Fein MP in 1918. He acted as Speaker of the Dail
during the Treaty debates and was Minister without Portfolio in the Provisional Government. He became Minister of Education in August 1922, a post he held until obliged
to resign in November 1925 after leaks about the proposed report of the Boundary Commission caused political uproar: J. McColgan, *British Policy and the Irish Administration
1920–1922* (London, 1983), 167.
[27] Entry in Lady Craig's diary, 20 July 1923, PRONI D1415/B/38.
[28] D. Kennedy, *The Widening Gulf: Northern Attitudes to the Independent Irish State
1919–49* (Belfast, 1988), 135.
[29] D. Harkness, *Northern Ireland Since 1920* (Dublin, 1983), 38.

Northern Ireland to attend a tripartite conference in London to discuss the boundary question. The invitation was accepted and Craig, Lord Londonderry, and Richard Best, the Attorney-General, were nominated as Northern Ireland's representatives.[30] However, owing to Craig's ill health, the proposed conference had to be cancelled, but the British Government continued to correspond with the Government of Northern Ireland in the hope that approval could be secured for a voluntary commission to be established by agreement between Craig and Cosgrave.

The Northern Ireland campaign for the Westminster General Election in November 1923 had been dominated by the boundary issue[31] and Ulster unionist fears of boundary revision were heightened by the election of the first Labour government in Britain. Most Ulster unionists regarded the Labour Party as sympathetic to Irish nationalism and opposed to partition, and the fact 'that it was a minority government very heavily dependent on the Liberals did not improve matters from the Unionists' point of view, since they distrusted the Liberals as well'.[32]

The fact that no party had won an overall majority in the Westminster election meant that six weeks of confusion, uncertainty, and negotiations followed before Ramsay MacDonald's Labour administration took office on 22 January 1924. During the negotiations, Northern Ireland's anxiety about the boundary issue was somewhat eased, since the whole matter disappeared from the London political agenda amid the national political manœuvring. However, fears soon reappeared as the new Labour government immediately gave a high priority to the boundary question: in only its second week in office it summoned the delayed tripartite conference. The British Government met Cosgrave, accompanied by O'Higgins and Hugh Kennedy (the Irish Attorney-General), in London on 2 February, and MacDonald proposed that

the Westminster parliament relinquish its Council of Ireland services in Northern Ireland (ie control of railways, fisheries and animal diseases) to the joint administration of Dublin and Belfast ministers under legislative powers conferred by the Dublin and Belfast parliaments sitting together (alternately in both cities) for a trial period of twelve months.[33]

During these twelve months it was envisaged that Dublin would refrain from seeking the establishment of the Boundary Commission, while the Belfast government would postpone its plans to abolish proportional representation for parliamentary elections.

[30] Spender to Oscar Henderson, Private Secretary to Governor of Northern Ireland, 8 Oct. 1923, PRONI CAB9Z/3/1.   [31] Kennedy, *Widening Gulf*, 135.
[32] M. Farrell, *Arming the Protestants: The Formation of the Ulster Special Constabulary and the Royal Ulster Constabulary 1920–27* (London, 1983), 210.
[33] Fanning, *Independent Ireland*, 88.

Although Craig was sympathetically disposed towards MacDonald's proposals, his Cabinet colleagues regarded the idea of joint meetings of the two parliaments as 'unthinkable'.[34] Cosgrave's Cabinet looked on MacDonald's scheme as derisory in relation to its aspirations for a united Ireland and rejected the proposals.[35] The Irish Free State then called for the immediate resumption of boundary talks, but the Government of Northern Ireland asked for the conference to be delayed for two or three months, again owing to Craig's ill health.[36] It has been suggested that the Ulster unionists were only seeking to stall the conference,[37] but such a view ignores the seriousness of Craig's illness. He had 'never fully recovered from a disease, akin to spotted fever, which had befallen him in the spring of 1915. The illness had kept him in bed for months, and he probably would have died but for the unremitting care of a certain Ulster bacteriologist.'[38] Craig's hectic life in 1921–2 had taken its toll on his health; by February 1924 his medical adviser warned him that he was 'running grave risks' unless he took a complete rest.[39] The Northern Ireland Cabinet was conscious that, in the event of negotiations with the Free State about the boundary question breaking down, it would be faced 'with a very grave crisis, in which the guidance of the Prime Minister would be of very great importance'.[40] Consequently, Craig's colleagues did not want to enter into any negotiations unless he was able to take the lead.

J. H. Thomas, the British Colonial Secretary, was 'most anxious' that the boundary question should not be left in abeyance for three months and wanted further exploratory meetings to be held. Spender, the Secretary to the Northern Ireland Cabinet, believed that a month's cruise in the Mediterranean would sufficiently restore Craig's health as to enable the conference to take place in April.[41] This compromise proved acceptable to the British Government, but it kept the pressure on Northern Ireland to reach a deal with the Free State. As has already been stated,[42] the British Government attempted to secure political conformity by financial blackmail. At a meeting on 11 April between Pollock and Philip Snowden (the Chancellor of the Exchequer) and J. H. Thomas, grant-aid from London for the Ulster Special Constabulary was directly linked to the Northern Ireland government's attitude to the boundary question.[43]

[34] Farrell, *Arming the Protestants*, 217.   [35] Fanning, *Independent Ireland*, 89.
[36] Cabinet Conclusions, 16 Feb. 1924, PRONI CAB4/100/29.
[37] Farrell, *Arming the Protestants*, 218.
[38] P. Buckland, *James Craig* (Dublin, 1980), 117.
[39] Cabinet Conclusions, 16 Feb. 1924, PRONI CAB4/100/29.   [40] Ibid.
[41] Cabinet Conclusions, 29 Feb. 1924, PRONI CAB4/102/14.   [42] See Chap. 6.
[43] 'Notes of interview in the Chancellor of the Exchequer's Room, House of Commons', by Clark, 11 Apr. 1924, PRONI CAB4/109/1.

The tripartite conference was eventually held on 24 April 1924 in London,[44] but it failed to reach a settlement on the boundary question.[45] On 26 April the Free State government informed the British Government that no hope remained of finding an amicable agreement with Northern Ireland and formally requested the establishment of the Boundary Commission. The British Government then publicly announced that the commission, as envisaged by the treaty, would have to go ahead and invited the Government of Northern Ireland to appoint a representative.[46] The matter was thoroughly discussed by the Northern Ireland Cabinet at a meeting on 5 May 1924, when Craig informed his colleagues that Thomas, the Colonial Secretary, held the 'view that the Boundary Commission is merely concerned with an adjustment of the actual boundary'.[47] The British Government clearly hoped to secure Craig's government's participation in the commission by persuading it that the latter was only concerned with rectification of the border and therefore posed no threat to the existence of Northern Ireland. However, speaking to the Northern Ireland parliament, on 6 May 1924, Craig declared that he was unable to nominate a representative to the Boundary Commission and the following day his Cabinet voted to inform MacDonald of its decision.[48]

Following this decision the British Cabinet resolved, on 21 May, to refer to the Judicial Committee of the Privy Council the question of London's appointing a representative on behalf of Northern Ireland.[49] The Privy Council ruled in July that such an appointment was beyond the legislative competence of the British Government. The British Home Secretary and Colonial Secretary visited Dublin to discuss the situation with Cosgrave, and Thomas informed Westminster on 6 August that it was proposed to introduce legislation at the end of September enabling the British Government to appoint a Northern Ireland member of the Commission.[50]

The pressure on the Northern Ireland government to nominate a representative was meanwhile sustained. MacDonald asked Lady Londonderry—with whom he had developed a close relationship—

[44] Craig and Richard Best represented Northern Ireland while Cosgrave and O'Higgins attended on behalf of the Irish Free State. J. H. Thomas and Arthur Henderson, the British Home Secretary, were present on behalf of the British Government, but officials 'were kept out, because, if brought in, Spender, an Ulster "die-hard", would have to be in': K. Middlemas (ed.), *Thomas Jones Whitehall Diary: Ireland 1918–1925* (London, 1971), 229.

[45] Rt. Hon. Arthur Henderson MP, Home Secretary, to the Duke of Abercorn, Governor of Northern Ireland, 29 Apr. 1924, PRONI CAB9Z/3/1.

[46] Cabinet Conclusions, 5 May 1924, PRONI CAB4/112/12.   [47] Ibid.

[48] Cabinet Conclusions, 7 May 1924, PRONI CAB4/113/9.

[49] Middlemas, *Thomas Jones Diary*, 232.   [50] Farrell, *Arming the Protestants*, 221.

to do her 'best to get . . . [the Northern Ireland Cabinet] to meet us reasonably within the period between now and the end of September'. He told her that only rectification of the boundary was contemplated, but for his government to say this in public would 'only be jumping out of the frying pan into the fire'.[51] Although the Conservatives are regarded by some commentators as sympathetic to the Ulster Unionist Party, they too applied pressure on the Northern Ireland government to participate in the Boundary Commission.[52] Meanwhile Churchill advised Craig that his fears were unfounded and criticized the Free State for laying claim to whole tracts of Northern Ireland's territory.

Further attempts in September 1924 to reach a voluntary settlement of the boundary question failed when Cosgrave declined to accept Craig's preconditions for talks. Craig had wanted Cosgrave to give up his rights to a formal commission under Clause 12 of the treaty.[53] The Northern Ireland Cabinet provided support for Craig in his stance,[54] but he came under renewed pressure to compromise, on this occasion from the King. Lord Stamfordham, the King's private secretary, wrote to Craig that His Majesty watched developments with 'anxiety' and hoped that Craig would continue to work for an agreement with Cosgrave. Once again, as in July and November 1921, Craig found his government pressurized by the British establishment to compromise with Dublin, and frankly admitted to Stamfordham that 'these are the most difficult times I have experienced since accepting my present office'.[55]

The British Government indicated that it intended to appoint Lord Carson as the Northern Ireland representative to the Boundary Commission. Craig supported this proposal, believing that the participation of a public figure of the stature of Carson could influence the outcome of the commission's deliberations. There was, however, strong opposition in the Northern Ireland Cabinet to any endorsement of Carson's appointment, with Richard Best, the Attorney-General, warning that 'our people will certainly not believe that we did not support [his] nomination'.[56] Back-bench Ulster Unionist MPs fiercely attacked the idea of supporting Carson's appointment, while some prominent Orangemen even criticized Carson himself, claiming that, having betrayed the nine-county Ulster in 1920, he might sell out the

[51] H. Montgomery Hyde, *The Londonderrys: A Family Portrait* (London, 1979), 159.
[52] For details, see correspondence in PRONI CAB9Z/3/2.
[53] Middlemas, *Thomas Jones Diary*, 233.
[54] Cabinet Conclusions, 16 Sept. 1924, PRONI CAB4/121/16.
[55] Craig to Lord Stamfordham, 20 Sept. 1924, PRONI CAB9Z/3/2.
[56] Cabinet Conclusions, 30 Sept. 1924, PRONI CAB4/122/1.

six counties now. Lord Londonderry believed that Craig was 'rattled' by the intensity of the opposition, and told his wife that he believed his premiership was shaken in the Cabinet and party.[57] Craig, in close contact with Carson about the boundary question, now advised him against accepting appointment to the commission as it could cause a 'crisis' in Northern Ireland.[58] When the Northern Ireland parliament reassembled on 7 October, Craig vigorously denounced moves to form the Boundary Commission. His wife, rather relieved, noted in her diary that his speech was received with enthusiasm.[59] He declared that if the Boundary Commission produced a report hostile to Northern Ireland, he would

resign and place myself at the disposal of the people, no longer as Prime Minister but as their chosen leader to defend any territory which we may consider has been unfairly transferred from under Ulster, Great Britain, and the flag of our Empire. That will be my duty, and that duty will be faithfully performed and that is the policy of a unanimous cabinet.[60]

The legislation enabling the British Government to appoint a rep-resentative on behalf of Northern Ireland was introduced at Westmin-ster on 1 October, with the Conservatives offering only limited resistance and most of the front-bench abstaining in the final vote. Although Craig's Cabinet had wanted the Conservatives to oppose the Bill, it recognized that it would be for them to decide whether or not to defeat the Bill since the consequence could be the downfall of the minority Labour government.[61] Baldwin did not want to go to the country on the boundary issue, and so the Conservatives confined themselves to putting forward an amendment specifying that the commission could make only minor rectifications of the border. The amendment was defeated by the combined votes of the Labour and Liberal MPs. The Ulster Unionist MPs at Westminster, as directed by the Northern Ire-land Cabinet, then pressed for the defeat of the Bill. They were unsuc-cessful, but Conservative and Unionist peers in the House of Lords managed to pass a resolution during the Second Reading of the Boundary Bill, declaring that Article 12 of the treaty had 'contemplated nothing more than readjustment of boundaries and that no other interpretation is acceptable or could be enforced'.[62]

On 5 June 1924 the British Government announced the appointment

---

[57] Hyde, *The Londonderrys*, 162.
[58] Craig to Carson, 7 Oct. 1924, PRONI CAB9Z/5.
[59] Entry in Lady Craig's diary, 7 Oct. 1924, PRONI D1415/B/38.
[60] *Parl. Deb.* (Commons), iv, 7 Oct. 1924, col. 1207.
[61] Cabinet Conclusions, 16 Sept. 1924, PRONI CAB4/121/16.
[62] D. Macardle, *The Irish Republic* (London, 1937), 797.

of Mr Justice Richard Feetham of the South African Supreme Court as chairman of the Boundary Commission. The British Government had initially wanted to appoint Sir Robert Borden, but he declined the invitation unless Northern Ireland willingly participated in it.[63] As chairman Feetham would undoubtedly be the most important member of the commission, and some writers have questioned his impartiality.[64] Geoffrey Hand, however, believes that Feetham's 'later opposition to the apartheid regime in South Africa (he died as recently as 1965) suggests a conscientious lawyer with a keen analytical mind, courageous in standing for Christian and liberal ideas'.[65] Such a person was unlikely to be other than independent in his approach to the boundary question.

Membership of the Boundary Commission was completed on 24 October with the appointment by the British Government of J. R. Fisher as representative for Northern Ireland. A Belfast barrister and former editor of the unionist *Northern Whig* newspaper, Fisher favoured a two-way transfer of territory between Northern Ireland and the Free State. He felt that east Donegal and north Monaghan should come into Northern Ireland while south Armagh should be transferred to the Free State. Fisher had told Craig in 1922 that if such a settlement was achieved, Northern Ireland 'should have a solid ethnographic and strategic frontier to the South, and a hostile "Afghanistan" on our north-west frontier would be placed in safe keeping'.[66] Craig was content with Fisher's appointment and, although he was not consulted about it by the British Government, he was aware from Fisher of the moves to appoint him.[67] His appointment meant that Northern Ireland's interests on the Boundary Commission would be safeguarded while, at the same time, the Northern Ireland government was in 'the happy position not to be implicated in any agreement with either the British Government or the Free State'.[68]

The appointment of Fisher was one of the last acts of the Labour government which, defeated in parliament on 8 October, had to face the election it had called for 29 October. The Ulster Unionist Party, realizing that once again voting in the Fermanagh and Tyrone constituency would be seen as a border plebiscite, maximized their support

[63] Cabinet Conclusions, 12 May 1924, PRONI CAB4/114/9.

[64] Macardle, *The Irish Republic*, 797.

[65] G. J. Hand, *Report of the Irish Boundary Commission 1925* (London, 1969), p. x.

[66] St John Ervine, *Craigavon: Ulsterman* (Aberdeen, 1949), 481–2.

[67] Lady Craig noted in her diary that Fisher 'is a most excellent choice, as he will have our interests absolutely at heart, and be as firm as a rock . . . James is really delighted with the appointment': Lady Craig's diary, 31 Oct. 1924, PRONI D1415/B/38.

[68] Craig to Spender, 17 Sept. 1923, PRONI PM9/8.

and 'helped by a nationalist split took both seats in those two counties, and indeed won all the Northern Ireland seats. To add to the Unionist euphoria, Labour was defeated overall, thus, marginally at least, reducing the threat to Ulster.'[69] The election of a Conservative government was a 'welcome relief' for the Northern Ireland government, and Craig hurried to London to meet Stanley Baldwin, the new Prime Minister.[70] Although Baldwin had strong 'die-hard' sympathies, the Irish Free State Cabinet realized that the constraints of office would make 'it utterly impossible for the Conservatives to adopt a strong pro-Ulster and anti-Irish attitude as their party is . . . pledged to carry out the Treaty in good faith'.[71]

The Boundary Commission held its first session on 6 November 1924 and continued to deliberate in secret for a year. The story of its workings is well known and well told, and need not detain us.[72] On 13 November Spender wrote to F. B. Bourdillon, Secretary of the commission, that the Government of Northern Ireland did not wish to present to 'the Commission any statement with reference to the work with which the Commission is charged, nor to appear before the Commission by Counsel, or by other accredited representatives, nor to submit to the Commission any evidence dealing with the question'.[73] However, in July 1924 Craig had met Feetham in Belfast on two occasions to explain 'the gravity of the question which he was handling and the very grave dangers which would ensue from any mistakes'. At their meeting on 3 July Craig informed Feetham that he would 'facilitate' a boundary settlement which transferred to the Irish Free State those Roman Catholics who wished to live under the rule of the Dublin parliament. He also made clear that he 'could never be a party to the compulsory transfer of any loyalists or of any Roman Catholics against their wish'.[74]

Feetham proposed that the Colonial Secretary summon a meeting with Craig and Cosgrave, with their respective attorneys-general present, to ascertain whether there was any possibility of agreement in respect of the areas on each side of the border where the inhabitants could be consulted as to their views. Feetham suggested that he also attend the without-prejudice meeting, and in the event of acceptance the Boundary Commission would merely register the decision arrived at. Craig

---

[69] Kennedy, *Widening Gulf*, 136.
[70] Cabinet Conclusions, 3 Nov. 1924, PRONI CAB4/127/17.
[71] Memo: 'The Boundary Issue', from O'Shiel to each member of the Irish Free State Cabinet, 29 May 1923, NAI S2 027.
[72] See Hand, *Boundary Commission Report*.   [73] Ibid. 7.
[74] Cabinet Conclusions, 4 July 1924, PRONI CAB4/117/4.

indicated his willingness to participate in this open conference, but the Dublin government found Feetham's proposal unacceptable.[75] On 5 September Cosgrave's Cabinet decided instead to demand a plebiscite 'according to District Electoral Divisions, over all the Poor law Unions which showed a Catholic—and presumably, a Nationalist—majority in the last census'.[76] However, by September, when the British Government was preparing amending legislation to enable it to appoint a boundary commissioner on behalf of Northern Ireland, the proposal for a plebiscite was not attractive to Craig, who had always opposed any move which could result in a large-scale transfer of loyalists to the Irish Free State.

Although the Government of Northern Ireland had decided that it should not officially co-operate with the Boundary Commission, it was anxious that the loyalist case should be properly prepared and presented. The Cabinet agreed that the Ulster Unionist Council was the most appropriate organization to co-ordinate the compilation of evidence from the loyalist community.[77] The Chief Whip of the Ulster Unionist Parliamentary party, Captain Herbert Dixon, undertook responsibility for overseeing at Unionist Headquarters the co-ordination of the preparation of evidence and, by virtue of being Parliamentary Secretary to the Ministry of Finance, was also able directly—albeit unofficially—to liaise with the Cabinet.[78]

Craig and two Cabinet colleagues were members of Ulster Unionist constituency associations which included disputed border areas,[79] and these associations were directly involved in preparing material for submission to the Boundary Commission.[80] The Northern Ireland Cabinet was thus able, through the constituency associations, to guide loyalist attempts to influence the commission without having—as a government—to co-operate formally. Not only were Ulster Unionist Associations encouraged to submit evidence to the commission, but Craig felt that those public bodies controlled by Ulster Unionists should be discreetly encouraged to do the same. He believed that the submission of evidence by loyalist-controlled public bodies would not embarrass

[75] Minutes of the Irish Free State Executive Council, 10 July 1924, NAI G2/3.

[76] Minutes of the Irish Free State Executive Council, 5 Sept. 1924; ibid.

[77] Cabinet Conclusions, 16 Sept. 1924, PRONI CAB4/121/16.

[78] Spender to Wilson Hungerford, Secretary of the Ulster Unionist Council, 11 Dec. 1925, PRONI CAB9Z/2/2.

[79] Sir James Craig and John Andrews as the local MPs were prominent in County Down Joint Unionist Association, as was Edward Archdale in the Fermanagh and Tyrone Joint Unionist Association.

[80] For details of correspondence between these associations and Unionist HQ, see material on the Boundary Commission in Ulster Unionist Council Papers, PRONI D1327/24/3.

his government, since it would still be 'free to take action found necessary when the [Boundary] Report is issued'.[81]

After hearing legal submissions at the beginning of December 1924, the Boundary Commission spent a fortnight touring the border area. It then invited and considered written evidence. Between March and July 1925 it held formal sessions in Northern Ireland to hear oral evidence from public bodies and delegations of local citizens. Although the Government of Northern Ireland did not officially co-operate with the Boundary Commission, it did afford police protection to the commissioners and their staff to ensure that they were not attacked by any militant grass-roots unionists. By escorting the commissioners during their visit to the border areas, the police were also able to report their movements to Craig's government, including whom they met in the different localities.[82] There was no violence towards the Boundary Commission from unionist supporters, and the Free State government made special efforts to ensure that there was no cross-border violence, since it had long recognized the importance of being able to demonstrate that it was 'in a position to maintain public order and to guarantee the protection of the lives and property of possibly future citizens'.[83]

Although Northern Ireland was spared IRA violence during 1924/5 and her people (in contrast to 1921/2) were able to enjoy a peaceful existence, the Boundary Commission—in the eyes of the Ulster unionists—continued to cast a shadow over the future. By appearing to constitute a 'mortal danger' to Northern Ireland, the commission contributed to the unionist siege mentality.[84] The growing fears among grass-roots unionists were reflected by the electoral decline of the local Labour Party in 1924. Perceiving a threat, and with passions inflamed, the Protestant working class rallied to the Ulster Unionist Party, believing that it was best able to safeguard their position.[85] There were also strong calls from the unionist grass-roots for the Northern Ireland government to strengthen the Ulster Special Constabulary while the boundary question remained unresolved. It was not only the working-class unionists who were frightened by the commission but also many middle-class unionist businessmen. The Belfast Wholesale Merchants'

[81] Spender to Hungerford, 11 Dec. 1925, PRONI CAB9Z/2/2.

[82] District Inspector E. Gilfillan, RUC HQ, to Samuel Watt, Permanent Secretary to Ministry of Home Affairs, 15 Jan. 1925, PRONI CAB9Z/2/2.

[83] Memorandum from Kevin O'Shiel to Secretary of Irish Free State Executive Council, 7 Feb. 1923, NAI S2/027.

[84] Laffan, *Partition of Ireland*, 92.

[85] G. S. Walker, *The Politics of Frustration: Harry Midgley and the Failure of Labour in Northern Ireland* (Manchester, 1985), 34–6.

Association, for example, was so concerned at the situation that it believed an outbreak of war between Northern Ireland and the Free State was a possibility.[86]

Anxious to show solidarity with the Ulster unionist people living in disputed border areas, Craig embarked on a series of visits along the border which were designed to boost morale and restore the confidence of the local inhabitants. Under strong police escort he visited most loyalist border communities, making speeches pledging his government to stand by them. Although, as Lady Craig noted in her diary, his cavalcade and speeches were resented by nationalists, they did bring 'delight' to the local loyalists. The Free State government was concerned about the success of Craig's border tours, in that it could 'be made [to] appear that the pro-Free State are either converted to the law and order of the north or are so apathetic that they do not make any demand for joining the Free State'.[87] However, the Free State government realized that violent protests in the border areas against Craig's visits would be counter-productive, and organizers might well be promptly arrested and probably interned.

The Northern Ireland government had moved, in 1923, to reduce the Ulster Special Constabulary in response to the decline in IRA violence. The formation of the Boundary Commission and its threat— or at least perceived threat—to the territorial integrity of Northern Ireland prompted Craig's government to halt the proposed retrenchment of its security forces. Despite the financial burden, the Cabinet decided to 'make no reduction in the Special Constabulary . . . unless the whole Boundary question is settled'.[88] Not only was the run-down of the USC halted but a Civil Service committee was established to review plans for the mobilization of 'B' Specials and the 'C1' force. Test mobilizations were held, and on 16 September 1924 the Cabinet approved a recommendation from the Inspector-General that local County Commandants should be authorized to mobilize their local forces in case of an emergency. The Cabinet also agreed to the purchase of another 150 Lewis guns and an additional five million rounds of ammunition.[89] The head of the Northern Ireland Civil Service, Sir Ernest Clark, was worried by these preparations, believing that the extra ammunition alone would be enough for a 'small war'. He suggested that the 'preparations were

---

[86] See correspondence between Belfast Wholesale Merchants' Association and the Government of Northern Ireland in PRONI CAB9F/42/1.

[87] E. M. Stephens, Secretary of North-Eastern Boundary Bureau, to C. McCann, 30 July 1923, NAI S4 743.

[88] Spender to Clark, 23 Apr. 1925, Treasury Division Papers, PRONI FIN18/5/151.

[89] Cabinet Conclusions, 16 Sept. 1924, PRONI CAB4/121/16.

either to resist the award of the Boundary Commission or for show, partly to intimidate the Commission and the Dublin government and partly to reassure the government's own followers'.[90] Clark felt that attempting to resist the implementation of the Boundary Commission's award would lead Northern Ireland forces into conflict with British troops.

The Northern Ireland Cabinet had actually considered at its meeting on 11 August 1924 the possibility of having to oppose the British Government in the event of the latter's attempting to enforce the transfer of territory from Northern Ireland to the Irish Free State. However, it had deferred making a policy-decision as it believed that the time had not yet arrived to discuss such a momentous issue. This did not stop J. M. Andrews, the Minister of Labour, telling a rally in Newry that the government would not concede the town to the Free State even if the Boundary Commission recommended it.[91] It is questionable whether the Northern Ireland government would have engaged the forces of the British Government, as it was well aware of its own limitations and of its dependence upon the British for financial support of the USC. Drawing upon its own resources, the Northern Ireland government could not even afford a sustained mobilization of the 'B' Specials.[92]

It is more probable that the Northern Ireland government was attempting to carry out an elaborate game of bluff, and Kevin O'Higgins, a minister in the Free State government, was later to complain that the Boundary Commission 'took the line of least resistance; where the Special police were thick in the North, the Commission sheered away . . . the Commission has been influenced by Specials standing with their fingers on the triggers'.[93] Clark had suspected that the Northern Ireland government was perhaps making preparations not with any intention of putting them into effect but purely as a political demonstration. His concern was that the government 'might be mobilizing and making more effective forces which it would ultimately be unable to control',[94] but the government was rather attempting to reassure its own supporters who, feeling threatened, might otherwise have taken the law into their own hands.

As tension mounted[95] Craig's government wanted to prevent the

---

[90] Farrell, *Arming the Protestants*, 224. [91] Ibid.
[92] Clark to O. E. Niemeyer, HM Treasury, 12 July 1922, PRONI FIN18/1/862.
[93] Farrell, *Arming the Protestants*, 248. [94] Ibid. 224.
[95] The RUC Inspector-General's office informed the Permanent Secretary of Home Affairs, for example, that for the Westminster General Election held on 29 Oct. 1924, it was necessary to mobilize 528 'B' Specials, 'in view of the circumstances under which the election is taking place': 24 Oct. 1924, Police Administration, PRONI HA4/1/251.

slide back into inter-communal conflict as in July–September 1920 and
February–June 1922, when loyalists had engaged in sustained sectarian
violence as a response to the perceived threat of the IRA. The border
represented a defensive rampart to Ulster unionists, and thus any attempt to alter it undermined the unionist sense of communal security
and territorial integrity. The Northern Ireland government was
genuinely concerned that, pending the report of the Boundary Commission, attempts would be made either by the Free State army or by
Irregulars to seize some of its territory.[96] That this concern was genuine
and not just a tactic to win additional funding from the British
Government for the USC is shown by the detailed mobilization plans
made by the Inspector-General for the defence of Northern Ireland
against invasion.[97] The Northern Ireland Cabinet was acutely conscious
that the Irish Free State was equipped with artillery and aeroplanes,
and that there was 'no warlike material in Northern Ireland competent
to meet and cope with these instruments of war'.[98]

Referring to maps and diagrams, Kevin O'Shiel had explained to the
Free State Cabinet on 5 June 1923 exactly what territory in Northern
Ireland it should claim. In researching and drafting the Free State's
submission, O'Shiel prepared maximum and minimum boundary claims.
If the Free State secured its maximum claim, Northern Ireland would
only consist of Belfast, County Antrim, a small portion of County
Londonderry, less than half of County Armagh, and less than half of
County Down. This maximum claim would considerably disrupt the
Northern Ireland railway system, cut off Belfast from its water supply
in the Mournes, and place some 263,938 Protestants as 'unwilling citizens' under the Dublin government. The Free State privately conceded
that it 'cannot be maintained that the maximum line is altogether in
accordance with the wishes of the inhabitants'.[99] The Boundary Bureau
also acknowledged that the maximum line was 'not the best' from an
economic and geographical point of view, and it 'could only be defended
on the ground that the area excluded constitutes a solid block of territory
whose inhabitants are unwilling to come into the Free State'.[100]
    In presenting the minimum boundary line as a second choice, O'Shiel

    [96] Cabinet Conclusions, 11 Aug. 1924, PRONI CAB4/119/16.
    [97] Sir Arthur Hezlet, *The 'B' Specials: A History of the Ulster Special Constabulary*
(London, 1972), 96.
    [98] C. Blackmore to S. G. Tallents, Imperial Secretary, 11 Aug. 1924, PRONI CAB4/
119/3.
    [99] Memo prepared by North-Eastern Boundary Bureau for the Irish Free State Executive
Council, 'Report on Possible Boundary Lines', NAI S2 207.
    [100] Ibid.

emphasized that it was 'the minimum claim of the Free State beyond which they could not recede'.[101] If the Free State only secured its minimum claim, then Northern Ireland would comprise Belfast, County Antrim, more than two-thirds of County Londonderry, one-third of County Tyrone, two-thirds of County Armagh, and more than three-quarters of County Down. The minimum claim, if successful, would diminish the area of Northern Ireland by about a third and its population by about a fifth. Some 179,421 'unwilling citizens' would be placed under the Dublin government, but 266,135 people who favoured the Free State would remain under the Belfast government.

The task of the Boundary Commission was to 'Determine in accord-ance with the wishes of the inhabitants, so far as may be compatible with economic and geographic conditions, the boundaries between Northern Ireland and the rest of Ireland'.[102] In opposing the territorial claims of the Irish Free State, the Ulster unionists laid particular stress on economic reasons for not transferring such areas from Northern Ire-land. This approach enabled the unionists to present a strong argument against the transfer of certain areas where, on a purely numerical basis, the nationalists constituted a majority. In Newry and Warrenpoint, for example, the majority of the inhabitants were presumed to favour in-corporation in the Irish Free State. However, the unionist businessmen in the area stated to the Boundary Commission that, should the area

be taken from its natural geographical and economical position, wherein is its trade, and handed over to another country with whom they do little business, [there would exist] a condition of affairs too serious from every point of view to even for a moment contemplate, knowing it would mean great loss of trade and cause largely increased unemployment in this town and district.[103]

In an age when the rights of property were still regarded by con-servatives as almost as important as the rights of man, it was incon-ceivable that the economic and financial arguments used by the Ulster unionists should not strike a chord with the Boundary Commission. The Ulster unionists, therefore, insisted that the commission should attend to the rights and wishes of the majority of ratepayers as well as the rights of the simple political majority in a locality. This was a particularly important argument as regards Fermanagh and Tyrone where, while the nationalists enjoyed a numerical majority, the union-ists constituted the bulk of ratepayers and owned most of the property.

---

[101] Minutes of the Irish Free State Executive Council, 5 June 1923, NAI G2/2.
[102] Art. XII of the Anglo-Irish Treaty, 1921, PRONI CAB9Z/3/1.
[103] Copy of submission prepared by Newry Chamber of Commerce for the Boundary Commission and forwarded by F. D. Russell, Warrenpoint, to Craig, 12 Jan. 1925, PRONI CAB9Z/1/3.

In preparing their case against the transfer of Fermanagh to the Free State, the Ulster unionists claimed that they paid over 75 per cent of rates and over 90 per cent of all income tax in the county.[104] But the Fermanagh unionists did recognize the validity of some rectification in the boundary, conceding that chunks of Fermanagh south of the Erne might pass to the Free State. The unionists realized that the transfer of nationalist areas would strengthen the precarious unionist electoral position in the rest of the county.[105] Meanwhile, in Tyrone the unionists also claimed that the county could not be transferred to the Free State simply because the nationalists had a numerical majority. Research by unionists revealed that they owned property to the value of £280,663, while nationalist-owned property was worth only £146,100; unionists paid annual rates of £54,495 and nationalists paid £25,090.[106]

Fisher and MacNeill to a large extent cancelled out one another's influence, and Feetham dominated the discussions among the commissioners. Thomas Jones, who was assistant secretary to Lloyd George's Cabinet in December 1921 when the treaty between the British Government and Sinn Fein had been signed, has observed that the treaty was not drafted in the meticulous manner of an Act of Parliament.[107] Consequently, the rather imprecise language used in Clause 12—relating to the boundary question—made the problem of interpretation very difficult for the members of the commission. Feetham believed that the commission's task was only to rectify the boundary, and while historians have differed as to whether Feetham's interpretation was correct, it is beyond argument that during treaty negotiations 'the Irish delegation thought the Article would give very substantial areas of Northern Ireland to the Free State and that Conservative spokesmen, in particular, in Britain soon began to press a restrictive interpretation'.[108]

Feetham has been strongly criticized by Free State politicians and writers for having been swayed by the pressure for a restrictive interpretation, but the evidence for his independence of mind and legal acumen suggests that allegations of his partisanship are without foundation. In a memorandum to his fellow commissioners, Feetham declared that the

---

[104] James Cooper MP to Craig, 3 Nov. 1921, PRONI CAB9Z/4/2.
[105] See correspondence between Cooper and Spender, Feb. 1924, in PRONI CAB9Z/1/1.
[106] H. de F. Montgomery, Fivemiletown, to Hungerford, 3 Nov. 1921, PRONI CAB9Z/4/2.
[107] Middlemas, *Thomas Jones Diary*, 234.
[108] Hand, *Boundary Commission Report*, p. xiii.

term 'Northern Ireland' as used in Article XII clearly means not some vague indefinite area in the north of Ireland, but the Northern Ireland established and defined by the Government of Ireland Act, 1920, and it is the boundary between this 'Northern Ireland' and 'the rest of Ireland' which is to be 'determined', or in effect, as there is clearly an existing boundary, redetermined.[109]

The nationalists hoped that following the implementation of the Boundary Commission's report, the 'mutilated Northern Ireland that remained would prove economically unviable, would atrophy and also ultimately be incorporated in the Free State'.[110] That Feetham referred to a redetermined boundary indicates that he envisaged the continued existence of Northern Ireland.

As the Boundary Commission managed to conduct its deliberations in strict secrecy for almost a year, there was no indication as to the likely outcome, and Craig's government was initially worried that there could be significant territorial loss from Northern Ireland. Unionists' fears were fuelled by the Dublin government's propaganda among its supporters, which asserted that Northern Ireland would be so reduced as to force the rump into the Irish Free State. In private, the Free State Cabinet was aware that it was 'absurd' to hope for Northern Ireland's being reduced to an uneconomic area, unable to sustain a separate government. O'Shiel acknowledged that

there are states in America and Australia and provinces in Canada which, with a population very considerably less than the population to which Northern Ireland would be reduced by the proposed line, nevertheless maintain provincial governments with powers at least as great as those of the government of Northern Ireland.[111]

The Publicity Division, established by O'Shiel within the North-Eastern Boundary Bureau, waged a hostile propaganda campaign against Northern Ireland, using press reporters from the Free State to 'work up' negative aspects of Craig's government.[112] As part of the propaganda offensive, the Boundary Bureau carried out extensive research on the various post-Versailles Treaty border-changes between new states in Europe, and published it as a major handbook in which it was maintained that the Boundary Commission should follow the European precedents and ascertain the 'wishes of the inhabitants of the disputed areas' so as to 'give effect to the principle of self-determination'.[113] The Boundary Bureau also published a *Weekly Bulletin*, distributed to

---

[109] Ibid. 37.   [110] Fanning, *Independent Ireland*, 24.
[111] Memo: 'Report on Possible Boundary Lines', NAI S2 027.
[112] Memo: 'The Boundary Issue', NAI S2 027.
[113] North-Eastern Boundary Bureau, *Handbook of the Ulster Question* (Dublin, 1923), 151.

politicians and pressmen in Britain and various other countries, in an effort to win support for the territorial claims of the Irish Free State.

In his propaganda campaign O'Shiel gave particular importance to the wooing of the Dominions because of the influence they could bring to bear on the British Government through the Imperial Conference. He felt that it

should not be too difficult to get Dominion opinion overwhelmingly behind us on this matter, as they will be directly concerned both because of analogous problems of a similar nature (eg Rhodesia, Newfoundland) and because of the power of the Irish in these countries.[114]

O'Shiel also emphasized the damage to Commonwealth relations in the event of the British Government's failing to carry through the report of the Boundary Commission. He claimed that it was the Dublin government which had done most to maintain the integrity of the Commonwealth by successfully carrying out a war against the Irregulars. The Free State attempted to depict Craig as a threat to the strategic interests of the Empire, claiming that it was he and Sir Edward Carson who 'by their unwise and foolish pronouncements and illegal actions in 1912–14 were the main causes of [the] modern physical force movement in Ireland and contributed more than any other persons to the destruction of the Union in Ireland'.[115]

Of necessity such claims had to ignore the fact that it was the governing party in the Irish Free State which, campaigning for separation from Britain, had supported the violence of the IRA. The Irish propaganda did, however, impress many non-conservative imperialists in the British establishment. Such people, whose ideas found powerful expression through the magazine *Round Table*,[116] believing that the Empire and Commonwealth could be held together by consensus, sought to balance the differing—and sometimes competing—interests of the individual Dominions. The Ulster unionists' opposition to the Boundary Commission thus found little sympathy among the liberal imperialists who, concerned for the overall imperial interest, wanted to prop up the pro-treaty (and apparently pro-Commonwealth) government in Dublin.[117] The Free State government realized that even a Conservative

[114] Memo: 'The Boundary Issue', NAI S2 027.   [115] Ibid.

[116] *Round Table* consistently favoured good relations with the Irish—it had been an early advocate in 1921 of a negotiated settlement with the establishment of a Dominion —and its editor, John Dove, kept in regular contact with the Free State government: Middlemas, *Thomas Jones Diary*, 227.

[117] The Irish Free State's membership of the British Commonwealth was in reality far from enthusiastic, and at times Irish resentment at the role of the Crown caused relations to be greatly strained. For further details, see D. Harkness, *The Restless Dominion* (London, 1969).

government in Britain would not wish to offend it over the boundary question, and O'Shiel believed that a 'little bit of the Ulster dourness and thick headedness at this stage will produce excellent results. Legally and morally we will be in the right and Craig will be in the wrong, and we should use this card for all we are worth.'[118]

The Government of Northern Ireland was concerned that the propaganda of the Irish Free State would influence British opinion on the boundary question and was convinced that the loyalist case needed to be presented as a counter-attack. Craig's government was particularly stung by the Free State's portrayal of Northern Ireland as the threat to the unity of the Empire, and reminded the British establishment that 'The people of Ulster have always been very tenacious of their rights as citizens of the United Kingdom and hold fast by the Union Jack and other symbols of loyalty to the Crown and to British traditions.'[119] The Northern Ireland government sought to justify its opposition to the possible transfer of Fermanagh and Tyrone to the Free State by claiming that it was only 'very largely, as a result of casualties in the war incurred by the loyalist population, [that] the previous loyalist majority [in the two counties] has been temporarily reduced to a slight minority'.[120] Northern Ireland's case on the mainland was promoted by the Ulster Association (whose notepaper had the slogan 'Save Ulster for the Empire'). By emphasizing their true commitment to the Empire, the Ulster unionists managed to reduce the impact of Free State propaganda and struck a chord with die-hard conservative imperialists. One die-hard wrote that, 'like many others I regard Ulster as the key question of the Empire's maintenance. Once weaken there and we are done. For one, I am ready at anytime to volunteer to fight for Ulster if she should be compelled to resist the vile intrigues employed against her.'[121]

Nationalists in Northern Ireland looked to the Boundary Commission to transfer to the Free State those areas where they predominated. Conversely, unionists in border districts on the Free State side hoped that the Boundary Commission would transfer to Northern Ireland those areas where they formed a majority. The unionists in eastern Donegal—where there was a strong Protestant community—were particularly active in lobbying the Northern Ireland government to

[118] O'Shiel to Cosgrave, 17 Apr. 1923, NAI S2 027.
[119] Briefing notes prepared by the Government of Northern Ireland about its attitude to the boundary question, 1924, PRONI PM4/11/2.
[120] Ibid.
[121] W. Comyns Beaumont, London, to Viscount Templeton, who forwarded it to Craig, 17 May 1924, PRONI PM4/11/2.

support their wish to be transferred from the Irish Free State. Although Craig lamented the inclusion of loyalist people in the Free State, he felt unable to take up the representations of the Donegal loyalists with the Boundary Commission because of his declared policy of non-co-operation with it.[122] He did, however, encourage the unionists in Donegal to present evidence to the Boundary Commission independently, but some were afraid to do so lest they be victimized by the nationalists in the Free State. They were also concerned that, in the event of the Boundary Commission's deciding to award east Donegal to Northern Ireland as part of a settlement, Protestant property would be subject to a campaign of looting and arson in the period before Craig's government assumed control of the area.[123]

On 3 April 1925 the people of Northern Ireland went to the polls in a General Election which Craig specifically made a border election, 'thus ensuring, or seeking to ensure maximum Unionist solidarity at a time when his administration was coming under a deal of criticism over education and other administrative matters'.[124] Craig campaigned under the slogan 'Not an inch', and in the four border counties of Armagh, Fermanagh, Londonderry, and Tyrone the Ulster Unionist Party slightly increased its vote. His party enjoyed 'a majority of almost 17,000 in the four counties taken as a whole, though the nationalists still won a slender majority in the joint constituency of Fermanagh and Tyrone'.[125] However, in Belfast, where the Boundary Commission was no longer perceived as an immediate threat, the election was fought on social and economic issues and the Unionist Party lost seven seats to Labour and Independent Unionists, while in County Antrim it lost a seat to a farmers' candidate.[126] Working-class Protestants who voted against the Ulster Unionist Party did not feel that they were weakening the loyalist bloc vote, in that the Independent Unionists strongly protested their 'loyalty' on the boundary question.[127]

The anti-unionists won only twelve seats—the same ones they had captured in 1921—with Sinn Fein doing poorly and losing four of its six seats to the moderate nationalists led by Joseph Devlin. The decision by the Nationalist members to take their seats in the Parliament of Northern Ireland was regarded by the Ulster Unionists with delight, since they felt that it signalled the failure of the non-recognition

---

[122] Spender to Captain Scott, Secretary of Donegal Unionist Association, 11 June 1923, PRONI PM4/11/1.

[123] Captain Scott to Spender, 11 Nov. 1925, PRONI CAB9Z/4/1.

[124] Kennedy, *Widening Gulf*, 137.	[125] Farrell, *Arming the Protestants*, 240.

[126] For details of the 1925 Northern Ireland General Election, see Appendix 2.

[127] Farrell, *Arming the Protestants*, 240.

campaign. Despite the loss by the Unionist Party of seats to Labour and the Independents, the loyalists as a community were still resolved to oppose a hostile report from the Boundary Commission, and Craig was therefore able to use the election as a mandate to reaffirm his government's opposition to any large-scale transfer of Northern Ireland territory. As the Boundary Commission continued its deliberations through 1925, speculation mounted among the Ulster unionists as to its recommendations. Letters continued to pour in to Craig from frightened border loyalists, urging him to stand fast against any proposals to transfer territory to the Free State.[128] Such intensity of opposition left Craig with very little room for manœuvre, and he declared at a rally that 'if the necessity arose he would no more hesitate than he did in 1914 to fight in the open against their enemies who would take away the loved soil of Ulster'.[129] Craig was conscious that, in addition to being Prime Minister of Northern Ireland, he was the leader of the Ulster loyalists and had a duty to 'safeguard the interests of the loyalist [people] throughout the length and breadth of . . . Ulster'.[130]

On 17 October 1925 the Boundary Commission decided its award, one which would have 'shortened the complex border by some 51 miles (from 280 down to 229), transferred 183,290 acres and 31,319 persons (27,843 being Roman Catholics) to the Free State and transferred in the opposite direction 49,242 acres and 7,594 persons (2,746 being Roman Catholics)'.[131] On 7 November the Tory newspaper the *Morning News* carried an accurate leak of the commissioners' recommendations. The reaction in Northern Ireland was cautious, 'though there were signs that the changes proposed were rather pleasing to the Unionists. Caution turned into something like delight as Southern discomfort over the findings became evident.'[132] The Free State had always officially argued that the Boundary Commission had no power to transfer any of its territory to Northern Ireland, and inexpressible

amazement and indignation were felt in the threatened areas and throughout the Free State. The [nationalist] people . . . determined to resist being handed over to . . . Belfast, demanded protection from the Free State Government, [and] Cosgrave was called upon to burst up the Commission without a moment's delay.[133]

As outrage increased in the Irish Free State, the pressure on its boundary commissioner, Eoin MacNeill, to resign became overwhelming,

---

[128] For details, see correspondence in PRONI CAB9Z/1/3.
[129] Farrell, *Arming the Protestants*, 245–6.
[130] *Parl. Deb.* (Commons), v, 10 Mar. 1925, col. 19.
[131] Harkness, *Northern Ireland*, 40.   [132] Kennedy, *Widening Gulf*, 137.
[133] Macardle, *The Irish Republic*, 807.

and he did so on 20 November. He later also resigned from the
government, 'in recognition of the embarrassment he had caused by
participating in a commission which had produced so unsatisfactory a
report'.[134] Cosgrave may have thought that MacNeill's resignation would
mean the end of the Boundary Commission's report, but Feetham and
Fisher indicated that they intended to proceed with an award which
would be binding once promulgated. Cosgrave seems to have panicked;
crossing to London he met Stanley Baldwin, the British Prime Minister, about the 'serious and difficult situation'. Cosgrave urged that the
Boundary Commission should not issue its report, which 'served to
bring the Free State to support Baldwin's wish to bury the Commission's report altogether—a solution which presented the least number
of unpleasant disadvantages'.[135] Cosgrave attempted to win some concessions from Northern Ireland to sweeten the pill of defeat, but Craig
would only agree to the release of the remaining IRA prisoners held
since the 1922 troubles. The Dublin Cabinet, however, refused to
endorse Cosgrave's acceptance of Baldwin's offer as it feared it could
not hold the confidence of the Dail on the issue.[136]

In an effort to secure a better settlement on the boundary question,
the Free State sent to London its Minister for Justice, Kevin O'Higgins,
and its Minister for Commerce, Patrick McGilligan. Cosgrave, accompanied by John O'Byrne, the Attorney-General, joined them after a
few days and there followed intensive negotiations with the British
Government. Craig, accompanied by the Secretary to the Northern
Ireland Cabinet, Charles Blackmore, also crossed to London and a
tripartite conference was held at Chequers on 29 November. Recognizing
that the Boundary Commission had failed to meet their expectations—
and more importantly from an electoral point of view, the expectations
of their supporters—the Irish Free State delegation attempted to secure
political and financial concessions. Craig rejected requests for political
reforms (such as the restoration of proportional representation for local-
government elections) to appease the nationalist minority in Northern
Ireland, but stated that he was anxious for all citizens to receive fair
and equal treatment. He promised to consider sympathetically any
practical suggestion Cosgrave might make for improving relations within
Northern Ireland and which would make his government more acceptable to the nationalist minority. Craig's firm line 'won not only the
gratitude of his own supporters but also the respect of Free State
ministers'.[137] In the absence of concessions from Craig, O'Higgins sought

---

[134] Fanning, *Independent Ireland*, 91.   [135] Middlemas, *Thomas Jones Diary*, 238.
[136] Farrell, *Arming the Protestants*, 248.   [137] Buckland, *James Craig*, 96.

the cancellation of the Free State's liability under Article 5 of the 1921 treaty, for a portion of the British war debt.[138]

On 3 December 1925 an agreement was signed in Baldwin's room at the House of Commons between the governments of the Irish Free State, Northern Ireland, and Britain. The report of the Boundary Commission was suppressed and the existing border confirmed; the Irish Free State was released from its obligations under Article 5 of the treaty, but undertook to accept financial liability for malicious damage caused in the IRA campaign since 1919.[139] The Free State also agreed to increase by 10 per cent the compensation paid for damage caused to property during the civil war (much of it owned by the small Protestant minority). All the powers of the Council of Ireland relating to Northern Ireland, given it by the Government of Ireland Act, were transferred to the Parliament and Government of Northern Ireland. It was also agreed that the Belfast and Dublin governments would meet 'as and when necessary, for the purpose of considering matters of common interest arising out of, or connected with, the exercise and administration of the said powers'.[140] Related to the agreement was an undertaking that the British Government would review the cases of IRA prisoners in Northern Ireland, and that the decision in each case would be accepted by the Government of Northern Ireland. Following the review, thirty-four of the thirty-seven IRA prisoners held were released in January 1926.[141]

Also linked to the agreement, though not a formal part of it, was the decision of the British Government to waive payment of £700,000 due from the Government of Northern Ireland for arms and equipment loaned to the USC, and to make a grant of £1,200,000 towards the current cost of the force. During the negotiations on the boundary question O'Higgins had pressed for the abolition of the Special Constabulary, and Churchill, 'anxious to get an agreement on the boundary, put considerable pressure on Craig to agree to a speedy disbandment of the USC and made it a condition of renewing the grant for 1925–26'.[142] Craig's government, unable to sustain the USC from its own resources, was forced to move quickly to disband the full-time 'A' Specials and 'C1' force. Although the 'B' Specials were retained, Craig had to deal with the barrage of criticism from Independent Unionist

[138] Middlemas, *Thomas Jones Diary*, 243.
[139] For the full text of the agreement see Cabinet Conclusions, 7 Dec. 1925, PRONI CAB4/155/21.
[140] Cabinet Conclusions, 7 Dec. 1925, PRONI CAB4/155/21.
[141] Minutes of Irish Free State Executive Council, 21 Jan. 1926, NAI G2/4.
[142] Farrell, *Arming the Protestants*, 253.

MPs and overcome opposition from within the Ulster Special Constabulary to make even those cuts which his government imposed.[143]

Before the end of 1925 the agreement on the boundary had been ratified by Westminster, the Dail, and the Parliament of Northern Ireland.[144] There was some grumbling by Ulster unionists 'over the generosity to the Free State of the financial terms of the new agreement—Carson said these constituted a gift of £300 million to Dublin'[145]—but on the whole there was something like general rejoicing in loyalist Ulster. A great and enthusiastic crowd received Craig on his return to Northern Ireland after signing the boundary agreement, and praise continued to be heaped on him when the agreement was debated in the Northern Ireland parliament.[146] However, as late as 17 November 1925, when Craig still had no official indication of how the Boundary Commission would report, the Government of Northern Ireland was considering the administrative difficulties it would have to face should moves be made to transfer any of its territory to the Free State.[147]

Although they would have like to have gained east Donegal, the confirmation of the existing border delighted the Ulster unionists. By contrast, the implications for Cosgrave's government were 'damning', since it could no longer 'even try to claim that the treaty by which they set such store would serve as an instrument for the re-unification of Ireland'.[148] Some suggest that Cosgrave was wrong to rush into negotiations with the British Government following the leak by the *Morning Post*, believing that had he waited, 'the British Government might have made an offer considerably in advance of what was ultimately achieved'.[149] Dooher acknowledges that the agreement signed was a victory for Craig and the Ulster unionists, which no doubt is why nationalists and republicans 'believed the settlement "a farce", "terrible", "a debacle", worse still, some described it as a "sale"'.[150] One republican writer feels that the Roman Catholic minority in Northern Ireland was 'thrown to the wolves'.[151] Although northern nationalists had begun to fear that the Boundary Commission would not make

---

[143] Cabinet Conclusions, 17 Dec. 1925, PRONI CAB4/157/20 and *Parl. Deb.* (House of Commons), vi, 15 Dec. 1925, cols. 1991–3.

[144] For details of the legislation passed to give force of law to the agreement, see A. S. Quekett, *The Constitution of Northern Ireland*, 3 vols. (Belfast, 1928–46), ii. 231–42.

[145] Kennedy, *Widening Gulf*, 138.

[146] *Parl. Deb.* (Commons), vi, 9 Dec. 1925, cols. 1853–95.

[147] See memo prepared by the Ministry of Home Affairs, 17 Nov. 1925, PRONI CABZ/2/2.

[148] Fanning, *Independent Ireland*, 91.   [149] Dooher, 'Tyrone Nationalism', 535.

[150] J. Bowman, *De Valera and the Ulster Question 1917–1973* (Oxford, 1982), 92.

[151] Macardle, *The Irish Republic*, 813.

sweeping transfers of territory to the Free State, few had suspected that failure to secure their aspirations would be so complete.[152] The nationalists in Northern Ireland were further upset that Cosgrave did not consult them before he signed the agreement ratifying the existing border.[153] However, it is perhaps fair to say that Cosgrave hurried things in an effort, as he saw it, to limit the damage by having the report suppressed.

During the negotiations which led to the boundary agreement, Craig had been accompanied by Charles Blackmore, the Secretary to the Northern Ireland Cabinet. In recognition of his hard work for Northern Ireland since 1921, Craig invited Blackmore to sign the agreement with him on behalf of Northern Ireland. Lord Londonderry, who had been in London during the negotiations, was deeply offended at his exclusion, which he considered a deliberate slight. A few weeks later he resigned from Craig's Cabinet, pleading that it was necessary for him to devote more time to his business interests. Being excluded by Craig from the negotiations and from the signing of the boundary agreement was not the sole reason for Londonderry's resignation, but it undoubtedly acted as the trigger.[154]

It has been suggested that the 'Ulster Unionists emerged as the only clear winners in the forty-year struggle which began with the first home rule bill in 1886 and ended with the consolidation of two separate Irish states in 1925'.[155] Although the fear of territorial loss to the Free State was largely removed, the Northern Ireland government still had to come to terms with the large nationalist minority in its midst. There were 'indications that the government was anxious to act responsibly and on behalf of the whole community',[156] but perhaps, given the painful birth of Northern Ireland, 'it was now too late to accommodate minority view-points and the character-lines of the new state had been drawn already in indelible ink'.[157] The nationalist minority was still to decide

---

[152] Dooher, 'Tyrone Nationalism', 535–6.

[153] *Parl. Deb.* (Commons), vi, 9 Dec. 1925, col. 1869.

[154] Lord Londonderry's main achievement as a member of the Northern Ireland Cabinet was the introduction of a major education bill. His Education Act (Northern Ireland), 1923, restructured primary and secondary education in an effort to improve educational facilities and standards. However, it also attempted to promote an interdenominational system by making religious education only a voluntary appendage to secular teaching. Under strong pressure from the various churches, the Government of Northern Ireland introduced amending legislation in 1925 to strengthen the religious-education element in state schools. Londonderry had opposed the amendment of his Act and undoubtedly was greatly upset by his inability to prevent any amendment. For details of the dispute over Londonderry's educational policies see D. H. Akenson, *Education and Enmity: The Control of Schooling in Northern Ireland 1920–50* (Newton Abbot, 1973), 39–88.

[155] Laffan, *Partition of Ireland*, 106.

[156] Buckland, *A History of Northern Ireland*, 56.

[157] Harkness, *Northern Ireland*, 42.

whether to accept its position within Northern Ireland or remain 'an embittered and potentially dangerous irredentist minority'.[158] Had the threat of Dublin completely disappeared, the differences between Northern Ireland and Britain could have widened steadily, but

Northern Ireland was to find itself still subject to the political and economic currents swirling around it . . . [and] too dependent on the succour of a Westminster often careless of its condition, and too open to a Dublin irredentism of unpredictable conviction, ever to relax fully in the years ahead.[159]

Inter-communal tensions within Northern Ireland were never properly resolved, and there was no sustained growth in friendly relations between Northern Ireland and the Irish Free State, despite their declaration in the 1925 boundary agreement 'to aid one another in a spirit of neighbourly comradeship'.[160] Explanations as to the failure to secure improved relations are outside the scope of this work, and it need only be said that in 1925 there was a real expectation that relations would improve. The predominant mood in Northern Ireland was one of confidence, with the Ulster unionists conscious that through their single-minded determination they had secured the existence of their state. Celebration among the unionist people culminated with a national day of thanksgiving in Northern Ireland on Sunday, 6 December organized by the Protestant churches, and 'Christmas 1925, complete with snow in Belfast, was the happiest for five years'.[161]

[158] Dooher, 'Tyrone Nationalism', 539.   [159] Harkness, *Northern Ireland*, 42.
[160] Cabinet Conclusions, 7 Dec. 1925, PRONI CAB4/155/21.
[161] Kennedy, *Widening Gulf*, 138.

8

Conclusion

The fact that the public sector is today the largest employer in Northern Ireland, or that the public purse primes some 80 per cent of total expenditure, can conceal the modest (and recent) origins of the state. Indeed, prior to the establishment of devolved government in 1921, not only were there no organs of statehood in Northern Ireland but Northern Ireland as a political entity and administrative unit did not exist. Apart from some junior- to middle-ranking civil servants administering public services such as revenue collection, agriculture, national insurance, and labour exchanges, there was no central government presence in Belfast. All the senior civil servants responsible for policy formulation were based either in Dublin or in London, as were the bulk of officers who administered the services affecting the people in what was to become Northern Ireland. The Government of Ireland Act, 1920, did not so much establish a devolved government in Northern Ireland as create the entity called Northern Ireland. Unlike the United Kingdom state, which evolved over centuries, Northern Ireland was conceived and born in a matter of months.

Apart from the exercise of limited power in the local-government arena, the people of Northern Ireland had never managed their own affairs. True, they also returned Members of Parliament to Westminster, but they were, generally speaking, peripheral to the political and administrative decision-making—a point exemplified by Westminster's neglect of education in Belfast. The establishment of a devolved parliament in Northern Ireland granted legislative and executive authority to a people which not only had no direct experience of self-government but also had to operate institutions of state devoid of administrative roots in the soil of political society. Indeed, the institutions of state had in themselves to be created before self-government could begin to become a reality. Transferring experienced officers from the imperial civil service provided the means to plan and construct the new institutions. The appointment in September 1920 of Sir Ernest Clark to head the new Belfast branch of the Chief Secretary's Office was therefore an essential step towards the creation of Northern Ireland as a distinct entity. The opening of the Belfast office 'not only presaged partition four months before the 1920 Act became law, but initiated it in a practical way by the establishment of central administrative apparatus working in the interests of the prospective Northern Ireland government'.[1]

In establishing the Special Constabulary by devising the framework for the new force and overseeing recruitment to it, Clark made a significant contribution to the creation and consolidation of Northern Ireland. The Special Constabulary provided the Government of Northern Ireland with a defence force composed of Ulstermen who regarded themselves as concerned for Ulster's future, loyal to the Government of Northern Ireland, and pledged to the protection of the Ulster people. In security matters the Government of Northern Ireland was (apart from the financing of its forces) almost self-sufficient, and hence in large measure able to pursue an independent defence policy against the IRA. However, it is unlikely that the London government envisaged such independence of action when it created the Special Constabulary in 1920. Probably it merely thought that it would help to placate and quieten the loyalists as well as contributing to the restoration of law and order, providing an auxiliary force to assist the police (and at lower cost than that of regular troops). Furthermore, it allowed for a reduction in the number of troops, who, thus released from duty in Ireland, could be deployed to help Britain fulfil her other world commitments—such as those in Egypt, India, Russia, and Mesopotamia—at a time of troop shortage.

In laying the administrative foundations of Northern Ireland, Clark played an invaluable role in constructing the edifice of the new state. Quite simply, without his efforts the election to the first Parliament of Northern Ireland could not have been held when it was, nor could the Government of Northern Ireland have been formed or able to assume office when it did. Devising the organizational structure of the Northern Ireland Civil Service and making preparations to secure for it the necessary accommodation, furniture, stationery, and staff; liaising with Dublin Castle and Whitehall about the separation of the administration of Northern Ireland's reserved services from Dublin; and co-ordinating efforts to create a new parliamentary forum: these achievements turned Northern Ireland's nominal existence into a reality. Clark was 'maid-of-all-work', and declared that it was a 'more trying job to help in the creation of the Government of a new Province than in the creation of its Police, especially as that new Province has not grown but is to come suddenly into being'.[2] Yet Northern Ireland

---

[1] J. McColgan, *British Policy and the Irish Administration, 1920–1922* (London, 1983), 132.

[2] Sir Ernest Clark to General Macready, 4 Feb. 1921, Treasury Division Papers, PRONI FIN18/1/188.

was to enjoy a basic continuity in the administration of its services which helped ensure there was no breakdown in the machinery of government and contributed to the stability of society and survival of the state. This continuity in the public services related both to the practices and procedures of the British Civil Service and, more importantly, to its values and traditions. That Clark managed to graft the principles of political impartiality and administrative professionalism on to the new Civil Service in Northern Ireland was perhaps his greatest achievement. It enabled the Civil Service to act as a strong anchor to the executive authority when beset by storms in the turbulent waters of Ulster politics.

In the context both of history and of political developments, the question is whether the establishment of Northern Ireland is something to celebrate. Some writers believe that, in 'a very definite sense the history of the current Northern Ireland problem does date from the setting up of a separate government and parliament in 1921'.[3] Others go further, suggesting that the existence of Northern Ireland is 'at the root of the problem'.[4] However, the emergence of Northern Ireland as a separate entity was a result, and not the cause, of the problem, and it merely recognized the reality of the bitter divisions between loyalist Ulster and nationalist Ireland. The Government of Ireland Act, 1920, attempted to find a broadly acceptable compromise between the conflicting aspirations of loyalism and nationalism: the former resolved to secure self-determination, and the latter to secure self-government.

Once the Liberal peer Lord Crewe had moved an amendment in 1912 to exclude part of Ulster from an all-Ireland Home Rule parliament, the Irish question was dominated by attempts to find a satisfactory form of exclusion. The 1920 Act reflected the effort of Lloyd George's post-war coalition government to honour its election pledge that, while it would seek to meet the desire in Ireland for self-government, it would not coerce the Ulster unionists into accepting a Dublin parliament. The overwhelming Conservative composition of the coalition meant that Lloyd George's Cabinet accepted many of the representations from Ulster Unionist MPs about the provisions to be included in the legislation. However, this is not to suggest—as some nationalists did —that the 'government in Belfast was established for the purpose of keeping that part of the country [as] a stepping-off ground for the

<hr>

[3] P. Buckland, *The Factory of Grievances: Devolved Government in Northern Ireland 1921–39* (Dublin, 1979), 277.

[4] M. Farrell, *Arming the Protestants: The Formation of the Ulster Special Constabulary and the Royal Ulster Constabulary* (London, 1983), 291.

reconquest of Ireland should British policy dictate that at any time'.[5] Weary of the Irish question and alarmed at the rising level of violence, the British political establishment wanted to disengage from Ireland, and granting Home Rule to a partitioned island appeared to be the best method of doing so.

The creation of Northern Ireland was not a price nationalist Ireland was prepared to pay for Home Rule. It attacked the destruction of the 'ancient historical unity' of Ireland and denounced the 1920 Act as a 'desecration of the traditions and history of Ireland'.[6] However, the Act did provide for a Council of Ireland as a unifying link between north and south. Apart from creating the mechanism for unity, the Act was also politically and psychologically slanted towards Irish unity. It was the rejection of the Act by nationalist Southern Ireland, and the consequent failure to operate the Council of Ireland, which achieved real partition between north and south. Once the London agreement transformed Southern Ireland (a constituent part of the United Kingdom) into the Irish Free State (an independent state), partition was confirmed. The boundary between Northern Ireland and the rest of the island became an international frontier. The erection by the Irish Free State of customs posts along the border gave substance to the feeling that travelling from Northern Ireland into the Irish Free State involved moving from one country to another; Ireland was indeed fully partitioned. Nevertheless, it would be quite wrong to attribute the origins of partition to the 1920 Act and the political reaction to it. The emergence of Northern Ireland and of the Irish Free State as two distinct, self-governing entities was the culmination of a forty-year clash between Ulster unionism and Irish nationalism, a clash which was a manifestation of deeper divisions in society.

The almost exclusively Protestant unionists—descended from various waves of British settlers, many of whose families had arrived in the seventeenth century—were a geographically scattered minority in the south of Ireland, concentrated mainly among the upper classes. Only in north-east Ulster did the Protestants form a distinct community embracing all socio-economic classes. The difference between Protestant and Roman Catholic was much deeper and more complex than a mere difference in professed creed. It involved a profound difference of culture and of approach to nearly every undertaking in life. Economic developments accentuated these divisions, with Ulster, in contrast to

    [5] C. O'Halloran, *Partition and the Limits of Irish Nationalism* (Atlantic Highlands, NJ, 1987), 6.
    [6] P. Colum, *Arthur Griffith* (Dublin, 1959), 251.

the rest of Ireland, enjoying considerable prosperity as a result of major industrialization. In their whole outlook, their way of life, their loyalty, and their sense of history, the Ulster Protestants were distinctively British and saw the Gaelic, Roman Catholic Irish as being—in varying degrees—anti-British. From the time of O'Connell Irish nationalism had broadly equated religious affiliation with nationality, thus excluding the Ulster Protestants from any effective role in the creation of a new united Irish nation.[7] For at least a century before the creation of Northern Ireland a partitionist mentality existed whereby Ulster was commonly, and pejoratively, referred to by Roman Catholic Ireland as the 'black north' and, despite 'the rhetoric of "one nation", nationalists had long been forced to acknowledge in practice the reality of division'.[8] As has been stated:

Irish nationalists—as one of them admitted—often excluded northern unionists from the Irish nation: 'We have had a habit, when it suited a particular case, of saying they were Irish, and when it did not suit a particular case, of saying they were British or planters or the seed of planters.'[9]

While Sinn Fein did not emphasize that Roman Catholicism was an integral part of Irish nationalism, it did insist that the Gaelic language was of the very essence of Irish nationhood. To the Ulster unionists, 'pro-Gaelic' and 'anti-British' were virtually synonymous terms, and the Gaelic language 'quickly became an exclusive emblem the force of which in a divided community was inevitably divisive rather than healing'.[10] As Kennedy has observed, Sinn Fein simply did not even begin to comprehend the nature and depth of the Ulster unionist objections to the language issue. But that failure was merely part of a greater failure, the inability to begin to understand Ulster unionism. Only crisis could force the Sinn Fein leadership to pay sufficient attention to Ulster issues, and the Dail Cabinet acted as if the Ulster Question were one to be avoided for as long as was possible. Indeed, the minutes of meetings of the Dail Cabinet reveal that during 1919–20 there was practically no discussion about the Ulster unionists, and it was only with the moves to establish Northern Ireland that attention increasingly focused on them.[11] The adoption of an economic boycott of Belfast as an official policy of Dail Eireann deepened divisions and increased the bitterness between Ulster unionists and Irish nationalists. It was for

[7] D. G. Boyce, *Nationalism in Ireland* (London, 1982), 144.

[8] O'Halloran, *Partition*, 5.

[9] J. Bowman, *De Valera and the Ulster Question 1917–1973* (Oxford, 1982), 20.

[10] L. M. Cullen, 'The Cultural Basis of Modern Irish Nationalism', in R. Mitchison (ed.), *The Roots of Nationalism: Studies in Northern Europe* (Edinburgh, 1980), 101.

[11] Minutes of the Dail Cabinet, 1919–20, NAI DE1/1, 1/2, and 1/3.

this reason that Arthur Griffith had hesitated in imposing the boycott, fearful that it would place the Ulster unionists 'outside' the Irish nation. However, to northern nationalists, Ulster unionists 'rather than the British were the hereditary enemy and there could be no meaningful attempt to woo them from the enemy camp and assimilate them into the nationalist cause'.[12]

Against a background of ethnic tension, hostility, and violence, the Government of Ireland Act, 1920, can be seen as an attempt to deal with conflicting political ambitions and national aspirations. While the Act represented an effort by the British Government to come to terms with the desire of Irish nationalists for Home Rule, it failed to take cognizance of the growth of Sinn Fein with its demands for Irish separation. Once the local-government elections of January 1920 confirmed the political dominance of Sinn Fein in nationalist Ireland, Lloyd George moved quietly to lay the foundations for a rapprochement with it. Following the appointment to Dublin Castle in the spring of 1920 of various officials of distinctly liberal outlook, the administration underwent a metamorphosis in attitude. Although the coalition government remained in public committed to the establishment of devolved government in both Northern and Southern Ireland, behind the scenes its civil servants were making peace overtures to Sinn Fein and promising that Ireland could enjoy dominion status if the IRA ended the violence. By December 1920 when the Government of Ireland Act, 1920, became law, Lloyd George was ready publicly to offer Ireland dominion status as the basis of a political settlement with Sinn Fein. However, as conditions for a truce could not be agreed, it proved impossible to find a framework within which negotiations could take place. In the absence of a viable alternative policy, the British Government proceeded with plans to implement the 1920 Act. Given the hostility of nationalist Ireland to partition, the pursuit of a peace policy towards Sinn Fein posed a major threat to the emerging Northern Ireland.

Attempts to postpone the election to the Parliament of Northern Ireland, to slow down the administrative preparations, and then— following the achievement of a truce and pending negotiations with Sinn Fein—to delay the transfer of power to Craig's government, showed that the British Government did not regard its interests as being identical to those of the Ulster unionists. Fearful that their newly acquired structures of self-government would be sacrificed to facilitate an overall

[12] J. B. Dooher, 'Tyrone Nationalism and the Question of Partition 1910–25' (M.Phil. Thesis, University of Ulster, 1986), 307.

settlement, the Ulster unionists withdrew behind their psychological ramparts. Isolated and alienated from the policy-makers in London, and threatened by the ambitions of Irish nationalism, the new Government of Northern Ireland took office uncertain of its future and unsure of its friends. That it survived was mainly due to the resolute leadership of Sir James Craig and the determination of the Ulster unionists who had, in the last analysis, the 'solidarity and the moral justification for pursuing an independent line in opposition to Irish nationalism'.[13] Other factors contributing to Northern Ireland's survival were the instability of Lloyd George's coalition (which faced disintegration if it attempted to coerce the Ulster unionists) and the willingness of Sinn Fein to allow the transfer of services to the government in Belfast. It is clear that the Sinn Fein negotiators failed to appreciate the importance of their concession, for 'the significant result of the transfer of services was that partition was now achieved in the practical sense: the establishment in June 1921 of the state, Parliament and government of Northern Ireland was now consolidated in November by vesting that government with administrative powers'.[14]

As Sinn Fein began to comprehend the reality of Northern Ireland's existence, it sought to block any steps strengthening the Belfast administration. Collins, urged on by northern nationalists, tried to use his power as head of the Provisional Government to prevent the transfer of civil servants and records from Dublin to Belfast. He also prohibited any co-operation between his departments and Craig's government, and backed a policy of administrative obstruction which extended to financial support for northern nationalists who refused to recognize the Government of Northern Ireland. Not only did Collins's policy fail to prevent the consolidation of Northern Ireland but it actually reinforced partition. Community relations within Northern Ireland deteriorated as the Ulster unionists, seeing themselves as under administrative siege, once again adopted a siege mentality. Meanwhile the refusal by the Provisional Government to allow cross-border co-operation on matters such as education merely emphasized the administrative division between Southern and Northern Ireland. Although all shades of nationalist opinion regarded the Treaty provisions for a Boundary Commission as a means of securing a unitary Ireland, none grasped that the Treaty in itself deepened partition. By making Southern Ireland a dominion, the border with Northern Ireland became an international frontier, the administration of reserved services for

---

[13] P. Buckland, 'Irish Unionism and the New Ireland', in D. G. Boyce (ed.), *The Revolution in Ireland, 1879–1923* (Dublin, 1988), 90.

[14] McColgan, *British Policy*, 133.

Northern Ireland was removed from Dublin, and the proposals for a Council of Ireland became impractical. Sinn Fein won Irish independence at the cost of partition. However, if nationalist Ireland did not grasp the implications of the Treaty, no more did the Ulster unionists, who believed that the Treaty represented a serious threat to Northern Ireland, and their feelings of insecurity rose as their lack of confidence reached new depths.

IRA attacks against and within Northern Ireland increased very soon after the signing of the Treaty. While there was some reduction in the number of incidents following the attempts by Craig and Collins in January and March 1922 to secure a peaceful settlement, the general pattern was one of increased violence. The peak was reached in May 1922 when the IRA launched a major offensive intended to produce anarchy and thus prevent the Government of Northern Ireland from consolidating its authority. Record levels of murders, bombings, shootings, and arson attacks almost overwhelmed Craig's government, and Northern Ireland came close to falling into a pit of sectarian violence of unprecedented intensity and viciousness. The Ulster Special Constabulary and the Civil Authorities (Special Powers) Act, 1922, provided the Government of Northern Ireland with blunt weapons with which to oppose the IRA, while Craig and Bates, Minister for Home Affairs, demonstrated that they had the will to win. However, the defeat of the IRA was a tribute to the determination of the Ulster unionist people as a whole, since it was as a people that the government, security forces, and general population sought to preserve their state against subversive attack.

Some believe that the tough security measures adopted by the Government of Northern Ireland alienated the Roman Catholic minority and left it 'with no belief in the legitimacy of the new state'.[15] However, the Roman Catholic community in Northern Ireland was never attached to the institutions of the new state, being opposed to its very existence. Furthermore, it can be argued that the Roman Catholic community was not alienated by the government's counter-insurgency policy, but rather by the sectarian attacks made by elements of the Protestant community. Nevertheless, the alienation of the minority cannot be ignored. The Roman Catholic community believed itself to be under attack, and the fact that more Roman Catholics than Protestants were killed in the violence in 1920–2 appeared to substantiate its fears. The security forces of the new state were not regarded as impartial but as accessories to the violence committed by the

[15] Farrell, *Arming the Protestants*, 287.

Protestant community from whom they almost exclusively drew their personnel. However mistaken the perceptions, the reality of Northern Ireland's survival was that the price of Ulster unionist self-determination was its denial to northern nationalists.

Matching the minority's feelings of alienation and embitteredness were those of the Ulster unionists, who had also suffered from the violence. While unionists have frequently been accused of having a siege mentality, this—as Buckland has pointed out—does require besiegers as well as the besieged. With the IRA terrorist campaign and the republican doctrines of Sinn Fein, unionist Ulster did not lack besiegers. One Ulster Unionist MP, referring to the border area, stated that it was 'infested by those we call our enemies. We have the entire border encircled by those who are hostile to us.'[16] Ulster unionist fears were increased by the feeling of isolation resulting from what they regarded as their abandonment and betrayal by a British Government which showed not the slightest sympathy for their difficult position. Worst of all, the unionists could not even feel safe within their own siege-walls; they were aware that the population was not homogeneous and that many opposed the existence of Northern Ireland. Stewart suggests that the presence of those whom Ulster unionists regard as an enemy in their midst is 'the very essence of what is called the Ulster problem'.[17] He argues that the Protestants suffer from a chronic insecurity dating back to the 1641 rebellion, when the Irish committed atrocities against the Protestants' ancestors. He maintains that the memory of that rebellion has survived in the Protestant subconscious, and it is therefore not surprising to find Robert Lynn, an Ulster Unionist MP, warning in 1922 that 'the spirit that underlay the attack made on Protestants of Ulster in 1641 is the spirit that animates the attack that is being made on Ulster today'.[18]

The ending of the IRA campaign against the Government of Northern Ireland brought relative peace, but it did not bring a spirit of reconciliation to the two communities in Northern Ireland nor between the governments in Belfast and Dublin. Memories of inter-communal violence were too recent and the scars too deep to allow reconciliation within Northern Ireland. Meanwhile, cross-border relations remained cool, with the Government of Northern Ireland still wary of the political ambitions of the Irish Free State. Although the latter had abandoned its support for hostilities against Northern Ireland in August 1922,

[16] *Parl. Deb.* (House of Commons), ii, 15 Mar. 1922, col. 46.
[17] A. T. Q. Stewart, *The Narrow Ground: Aspects of Ulster, 1609–1969* (London, 1977), 47.
[18] *Parl. Deb.* (House of Commons), ii, 23 May 1922, col. 614.

it did little to normalize relations with Craig's administration and took
no meaningful action to win over the Ulster unionists, as Blythe had
urged, by the adoption of a 'friendly disposition'.[19] Instead, the Dublin
government concentrated on securing a victory in the Irish civil war
against the Irregulars and ignored Northern Ireland. It was only with
the emergence of the boundary question on to the political stage in
1924 that Northern Ireland became a major consideration for Cosgrave's
Cabinet. However, the Boundary Commission was not likely to enhance
cross-border relations or engender improved community relations within
Northern Ireland. Indeed, inter-communal tensions rose once again as
fear gripped the Ulster unionists, particularly those along the border,
that the integrity of their territory was under threat. Unlike 1920–2,
the rise in tension in 1924–5 did not lead to widespread violence, partly
because of the desire of the Dublin government to preserve the existing
peaceful conditions, but to a greater extent because of the greatly
expanded Northern Ireland security forces.

Anticipating possible difficulties arising from the Boundary Commission, and anxious to deter cross-border attacks, reassure its grass-roots
supporters, and prevent sectarian violence, the Government of Northern
Ireland had steadily built up its security forces. That substantial amounts
of additional arms and ammunition were obtained and the numerical
strength of the USC increased was made possible by financial grants
from the London government. An adequate supply of funds for its
security forces was as important to Northern Ireland as an adequate
water supply is to a besieged garrison. However, the source of Northern
Ireland's funding was not within its own control, and with future grants
always uncertain, Craig's government was unsure whether it could
sustain its security forces. The unpredictability of financial support added
to the feelings of anxiety experienced by the Ulster unionists. The use
made in 1924 by the Labour government of withholding grants until,
and unless, the Northern Ireland government co-operated on the
boundary question illustrated the vulnerability of Craig's administration.
This in turn increased the sense of siege again being felt by the Ulster
unionists. The London government could not use its financial weapon
to force the Government of Northern Ireland into political submission
since, in the event of the latter resigning, the entire Irish question
would have been reopened—a negative development which London
was keen to avoid. Nevertheless, London sought to provide financial
support on an *ad-hoc* basis in an attempt to keep Northern Ireland in
a weakened and dependent state.

[19] Memo by Ernest Blythe, 'Policy in regard to the northeast', 9 Aug. 1922, Blythe
Papers, UCDAD P24/70.

If, as mentioned earlier, Sinn Fein secured Irish independence at the cost of partition, then it can be said that Ulster unionists secured the survival of Northern Ireland at the cost of deepened divisions. Although Northern Ireland inherited (rather than created) these divisions, its establishment did bequeath to future generations a legacy of increased bitterness. While the continued existence of the state in itself was a source of antagonism to the nationalist community, the sectarian violence of 1920–2 had scarred the minority's collective conscious-ness and contributed to the creation of a ghetto mentality. Yet the nationalists did not have a monopoly of suffering from violence, and the sense of siege experienced by the Ulster unionists as a result of administrative, security, financial, and territorial threats did not incline them to make political concessions to the minority. This narrowed the room the unionist leadership had for compromise or even for seeking to reach an accommodation with the nationalist community, and required that government decisions, no matter how politically neutral, had to be presented in a partisan manner. This is understandable in the period 1920–2 when Ulster unionists believed that their backs were to the wall, or in 1924–5 when once again they regarded themselves as being in a corner, but it is highly regrettable that they did not later seek to improve relations. An opportunity of immense potential future importance was missed, and all in Northern Ireland, nationalist and unionist, have lived with the consequences.

Having finally secured the consolidation of Northern Ireland with the boundary agreement in December 1925, Craig's government should have made 'a sustained and imaginative attempt to win over the minority and to assuage their suspicions and fears. Whether or not such an effort would have succeeded it is impossible to say, but what is certain is that no such attempt was made.'[20] However, uncertain of London's support, fearful of renewed irredentist claims from the Irish Free State (as was to happen in the 1930s), and apprehensive of the sizeable minority within Northern Ireland, the Ulster unionists never felt secure enough to offer nationalists a greater participation in the administration of the state. The bitterness and fears of both commun-ities are at the heart of what was the Irish problem, and what is now the Northern Ireland problem. Indeed, the most marked feature in the society

is fear, mistrust and sometimes hatred by one community of the other, or of the imperial power. Catholic fears and resentments were paralleled by Protestant fears . . . The reciprocal fear and mistrust of each other by the communities

[20] Buckland, *Factory of Grievances*, 222.

results in a tendency to place the worst possible construction on the actions of the other community.[21]

Granting self-government in Ireland was a means of facilitating Irish nationalist claims to self-determination, while the establishment of Northern Ireland was an attempt to meet Ulster unionist claims for self-determination outside of an Irish state. While the 1920 Act was not the source of the Irish problem, neither was it a solution, since partition could be no more than an exercise in conflict-management. Furthermore, given that Northern Ireland did not contain a homogeneous population—and no matter how the border was redrawn, never could—further problems were being stored up for the future. To the extent that the 1920 Act served as a mechanism for conflict-management, it must be considered a success. It could never solve the problems then faced by Ireland, or today faced by Northern Ireland: how to reconcile the aspirations of two nations for statehood when those aspirations unavoidably conflict, since each nation lays claim to territory which the other regards as part of its state. As Professor Tom Wilson has observed: 'The impossibility of reconciling the different claims to self-determination has been the core of the Irish problem. It is essentially for this reason that the problem has been judged insoluble.'[22]

The problems of Northern Ireland and the broader Irish question can never be settled until what General Smuts called the 'human difficulty' has been overcome. Writing to de Valera in August 1921 after the offer of dominion status, he declared that the 'Irish question is no longer a constitutional, but mostly a human problem'.[23] It was then, and it remains so today.

---

[21] C. Palley, 'The Evolution, Disintegration and Possible Reconstruction of the Northern Ireland Constitution', *Anglo-American Law Review* (May 1972), 372.

[22] T. Wilson, *Ulster: Conflict and Consent* (Oxford, 1989), p. xii.

[23] General Jan Smuts to Eamon de Valera, 4 Aug. 1921, PRONI D1916/8.

Appendix 1. Results of the General Election (1921) to the Parliament of Northern Ireland

BELFAST, EAST
Electors: 40,198
Turnout: 89.3%

No. of Seats: 4
Quota: 7,182

Candidate	Party	Votes	Elected
Sir R. D. Bates	Unionist	10,026	1
H. Dixon	Unionist	8,849	2
T. Donald	Unionist	6,856	3
J. A. Duff	Unionist	3,585	4
A. Savage	Sinn Fein	3,573	
T. J. Campbell	Nationalist	2,373	
H. C. Midgley	Independent Labour	645	

BELFAST, NORTH
Electors: 43,194
Turnout: 92.3%

No. of Seats: 4
Quota: 7,971

Candidate	Party	Votes	Elected
L. Campbell	Unionist	12,875	1
S. McGuffin	Unionist	11,596	2
W. Grant	Unionist	6,148	3
R. J. McKeown	Unionist	3,562	4
M. Carolan	Sinn Fein	3,235	
F. P. Harkin	Nationalist	1,509	
Revd J. B. Wallace	Independent Labour	926	

BELFAST, SOUTH
Electors: 40,566
Turnout: 89.5%

No. of Seats: 4
Quota: 7,261

Candidate	Party	Votes	Elected
T. Moles	Unionist	17,248	1
H. M. Pollock	Unionist	6,334	2
Sir C. McCullagh	Unionist	5,068	3
D. Barnes	Sinn Fein	2,719	
Mrs J. McMordie	Unionist	2,372	4
B. McCoy	Nationalist	1,688	
J. Baird	Independent Labour	875	

BELFAST, WEST
Electors: 57,914
Turnout: 89.5%

No. of Seats: 4
Quota: 10,691

Candidate	Party	Votes	Elected
T. H. Burn	Unionist	13,298	1
J. Devlin*	Nationalist	10,621	4
W. J. Twaddell	Unionist	10,316	3
R. J. Lynn	Unionist	9,315	2
D. McCullough	Sinn Fein	6,270	
J. F. McEntee	Sinn Fein	2,954	
J. A. Hanna	Independent Labour	367	
R. Byrne	Nationalist	311	

*Also elected for Antrim.

ANTRIM

Electors: 93,566   No. of Seats: 7
Turnout: 85.5%   Quota: 9,994

Candidate	Party	Votes	Elected
J. M. Barbour	Unionist	17,735	1
R. W. H. O'Neill	Unionist	16,681	2
G. B. Hanna	Unionist	12,584	3
J. Devlin*	Nationalist	9,448	7
R. D. Megaw	Unionist	8,326	5
R. Crawford	Unionist	5,976	4
L. J. Walsh	Sinn Fein	4,951	
J. F. Gordon	Unionist	2,967	6
J. Connolly	Sinn Fein	1,281	

*Also elected for Belfast, West.

ARMAGH

Electors: 53,977   No. of Seats: 4
Turnout: 86.2%   Quota: 9,307

Candidate	Party	Votes	Elected
R. Best	Unionist	15,988	1
M. Collins	Sinn Fein	12,656	2
D. G. Shillington	Unionist	9,730	3
J. D. Nugent	Nationalist	6,857	4
F. Aiken	Sinn Fein	1,301	

DOWN

Electors: 93,138   No. of Seats: 8
Turnout: 87.2%   Quota: 9,021

Candidate	Party	Votes	Elected
Sir J. Craig	Unionist	29,829	1
E. de Valera	Sinn Fein	16,269	2
J. M. Andrews	Unionist	12,584	3
P. O'Neill	Nationalist	7,317	8
Hon. H. G. H. Mulholland	Unionist	4,665	5
R. McBride	Unionist	3,297	6
T. R. Lavery	Unionist	2,863	4
T. W. McMullan	Unionist	2,692	7
A. Adams	Independent Labour	1,188	
P. Lavery	Sinn Fein	327	
P. M. Moore	Sinn Fein	149	

FERMANAGH AND TYRONE
Electors: 95,272   No. of Seats: 8
Turnout: 87.9%   Quota: 9,306

Candidate	Party	Votes	Elected
A. Griffith	Sinn Fein	21,677	1
E. M. Archdale	Unionist	10,336	2
W. Coote	Unionist	9,672	3
W. T. Miller	Unionist	9,165	5
J. Cooper	Unionist	8,754	6
T. J. S. Harbinson	Nationalist	7,090	8
J. P. Gillin	Nationalist	5,591	
J. O'Mahoney	Sinn Fein	4,979	7
K. O'Shiel	Sinn Fein	4,464	
J. Milroy	Sinn Fein	1,846	4
J. F. McEntee	Sinn Fein	179	

LONDONDERRY
Electors: 62,111   No. of Seats: 5
Turnout: 86.9%   Quota: 8,999

Candidate	Party	Votes	Elected
Sir R. H. Anderson	Unionist	13,466	1
J. McNeill	Sinn Fein	11,866	2
Mrs D. Chichester	Unionist	8,709	3
J. M. Mark	Unionist	8,155	4
G. Leeke	Nationalist	6,298	5
J. Walsh	Sinn Fein	4,020	
H. W. Shields	Nationalist	1,474	

QUEEN'S UNIVERSITY
Electors: 2,528   No. of Seats: 4
Turnout: 76.2   Quota: 386

Candidate	Party	Votes	Elected
J. Campbell	Unionist	835	1
J. H. Robb	Unionist	368	3
Prof. R. J. Johnstone	Unionist	279	2
H. S. Morrison	Unionist	243	4
J. B. Dolan	Sinn Fein	201	

ELECTION SUMMARY

Party	Total votes	% share of total votes	Candidates	MPs elected
Unionist	341,622	66.9	40	40
Nationalist	60,577	11.8	12	6
Sinn Fein	104,716	20.5	20	6
Independent Labour	4,001	0.8	5	0
TOTAL	510,916	100.00	77	52

Source: S. Elliott, *Northern Ireland Parliamentary Election Results 1921–1972* (Chichester, 1973), 2–20.

Appendix 2. Results of the General Election (1925) to the Parliament of Northern Ireland

Abbreviations used:

Ind. Un.	Independent Unionist
NILP	Northern Ireland Labour Party
TT	Town Tenants Association
UTA	Unbought Tenants Association

BELFAST, EAST

Electors: 44,400   No. of Seats: 4
Turnout: 73.5%   Quota: 6,525

Candidate	Party	Votes	Elected
J. Beattie	NILP	9,330	1
H. Dixon	Unionist	8,508	2
J. W. Gyle	Ind. Un.	5,997	3
Sir R. D. Bates	Unionist	5,744	4
T. Donald	Unionist	1,900	
J. A. Duff	Unionist	1,142	

BELFAST, NORTH

Electors: 47,228   No. of Seats: 4
Turnout: 71.1%   Quota: 6,720

Candidate	Party	Votes	Elected
T. Henderson	Ind. Un.	10,306	1
W. Grant	Unionist	6,610	3
S. Kyle	NILP	5,915	2
L. Campbell	Unionist	5,421	4
J. W. Nixon	Unionist	4,068	
H. T. Whitaker	Unionist	1,276	

BELFAST, SOUTH

Electors: 43,164   No. of Seats: 4
Turnout: 67.3%   Quota: 5,813

Candidate	Party	Votes	Elected
P. J. Woods*	Ind. Un.	8,814	1
T. Moles	Unionist	7,756	2
H. M. Pollock	Unionist	4,291	3
W. Magill	TT	3,320	
A. Black	Unionist	3,176	4
Sir C. McCullagh	Unionist	1,707	

*Also elected for Belfast, West.

BELFAST, WEST
Electors: 66,550   No. of Seats: 4
Turnout: 75.5%   Quota: 9,897

Candidate	Party	Votes	Elected
J. Devlin	Nationalist	17,558	1
P. J. Woods*	Ind. Un.	9,599	2
Sir R. J. Lynn	Unionist	8,371	3
T. H. Burn	Unionist	4,808	
J. McConville	Republican	3,146	
R. Dickson	Unionist	3,133	
W. McMullen	NILP	2,869	4

*Also elected for Belfast, South.

ANTRIM
Electors: 98,278   No. of Seats: 7
Turnout: 65.4%   Quota: 8,040

Candidate	Party	Votes	Elected
J. M. Barbour	Unionist	13,499	1
R. W. H. O'Neill	Unionist	12,579	2
T. S. McAllister	Nationalist	11,857	3
R. Crawford	Unionist	7,310	4
G. B. Hanna	Unionist	6,524	5
G. Henderson	UTA	4,866	6
R. D. Megaw	Unionist	4,362	
J. F. Gordon	Unionist	3,318	7

ARMAGH
Electors: 54,082   No. of Seats: 4
Turnout: 78.8%   Quota: 8,520

Candidate	Party	Votes	Elected
R. Best	Unionist	15,969	1
D. G. Shillington	Unionist	10,575	2
E. Donnelly	Republican	5,788	3
J. H. Collins	Nationalist	5,272	4
J. D. Nugent	Nationalist	4,991	

DOWN
No. of Seats: 8 (all candidates returned unopposed)

Candidate	Party
J. M. Andrews	Unionist
Sir J. Craig	Unionist
E. de Valera	Republican
T. R. Lavery	Unionist
R. McBride	Unionist
T. W. McMullan	Unionist
Hon. H. G. H. Mulholland	Unionist
P. O'Neill	Nationalist

FERMANAGH AND TYRONE
Electors: 96,388   No. of Seats: 8
Turnout: 85.8%   Quota: 9,193

Candidate	Party	Votes	Elected
A. E. Donnelly	Nationalist	12,098	1
E. M. Archdale	Unionist	11,834	2
R. Elliott	Unionist	10,115	3
W. T. Miller	Unionist	9,593	4
C. Healy	Nationalist	9,191	5
J. Cooper	Unionist	8,923	7
T. J. S. Harbinson	Nationalist	8,257	6
J. McHugh	Nationalist	6,584	8
T. Larkin	Republican	4,483	
J. O'Mahoney	Republican	1,652	

LONDONDERRY
Electors: 63,174   No. of Seats: 5
Turnout: 79.7%   Quota: 8,391

Candidate	Party	Votes	Elected
G. Leeke	Nationalist	13,671	1
Sir R. H. Anderson	Unionist	12,085	2
J. M. Mark	Unionist	8,804	3
Mrs D. Chichester	Unionist	8,261	4
C. MacWhinney	Republican	5,546	
B. McGuckin	Nationalist	1,973	5

QUEEN'S UNIVERSITY
No. of Seats: 4 (all candidates returned unopposed)

Candidate	Party
Sir J. Campbell	Unionist
J. H. Robb	Unionist
Prof. R. J. Johnstone	Unionist
H. S. Morrison	Unionist

ELECTION SUMMARY

Party	Total votes	% share of total votes	Candidates	MPs elected	Unopposed returns
Unionist	211,662	55.0	40	32	10
Ind. Un.	34,716	9.0	4	4	0
Nationalist	91,452	23.8	11	10	1
Republican	20,615	5.3	6	2	1
NILP	18,114	4.7	3	3	0
TT	3,320	0.9	1	0	0
UTA	4,866	1.3	1	1	0
TOTAL	384,745	100.0	66	52	12

Source: S. Elliott, *Northern Ireland Parliamentary Election Results 1921–1972*
(Chichester, 1973), 3–20.

Bibliography

A. Primary Sources

(a) MANUSCRIPT MATERIAL

Public Record Office of Northern Ireland (PRONI)

(i) Private Records

Crawford Papers, D640

Crawford's journal and his correspondence with Carson, Craig, and Wickham provide useful insights into how Ulster Unionists perceived the IRA threat in 1920–2.

Clark Papers, D1022

Clark's autobiographical reminiscences of his time as Assistant Under-Secretary are an extremely important source of information regarding the planning and preparation which led to the establishment of Northern Ireland.

Spender Papers, D1295 and D1633

The correspondence by Spender with various individuals, and his wife's diary, detail the re-formation of the UVF and moves towards the formation of the Special Constabulary in 1920.

Ulster Unionist Council Papers, D1327

The correspondence of the UUC Secretary forms part of the extensive addition to this archive which, having been only recently deposited, has not been examined by other researchers. The correspondence reveals the private attitudes of the UUC to the Government of Ireland Act, 1920, and the Boundary Commission, 1924/5.

Craigavon Papers, D1415

Lady Craig's diary and the albums of press cuttings which she prepared, 1920–6, are useful sources of information about the difficulties Craig had in balancing Ulster Unionist interests with those of the British Government.

(ii) Official Records

Assistant Under-Secretary's Papers, AUS

These files are extremely useful in indicating how Clark, as Assistant Under-Secretary, had to create the foundations which enabled the new Northern Ireland administration to be established.

Cabinet Conclusions, CAB4

The minutes of each Cabinet meeting and the related memoranda provide invaluable insights into the deliberations of the Government of Northern Ireland

and reveal how it approached all the major problems which threatened its existence.

Cabinet Secretariat, CAB5, 6, 8, 9, and 11

The registered and unregistered subject files of the Cabinet Secretariat are an essential source for anyone seeking to trace and understand the formulation of policy by the Government of Northern Ireland. The files—particularly those in CAB9 which are subdivided by ministry—relate to all major issues of an administrative, political, financial, and security nature. The telegrams in CAB11 indicate how strained the relations between the governments in Belfast, Dublin, and London became in 1922.

Colwyn Arbitration Committee Papers, FIN11

These files, previously unused by any researcher, are indispensable to anyone wishing to understand the calculations and negotiations on the imperial contribution which led to the Colwyn Award.

Treasury Division Papers, FIN18

As all expenditure in every area of the Northern Ireland Civil Service had to be approved by the Treasury Division, these files relate to every aspect of government activity. They are a good source of information about the formation and development of the constabulary forces and of the administration itself.

Works Division, FIN19

These papers show efforts to secure suitable accommodation to enable the establishment of the Government of Northern Ireland and its Civil Service to proceed without delay.

Establishment Division, FIN20

These files provide useful information about staffing levels, salary scales, and other matters in the Northern Ireland Civil Service, and the 1925 Efficiency Report on it by Sir Russell Scott.

Joint Exchequer Board, FIN26

These files relate to the division of government property with Southern Ireland and to the emergence of the Northern Ireland administration.

Private Office, FIN30

These files are a good source regarding the improvements in, and formalization of, Civil Service recruitment.

Police Administration, HA4

These files are useful as a source about security-related administrative matters, including the equipping and deploying of the RUC.

Miscellaneous File Series, HA5

Among the various issues which these files provide information about is that of prison administration, including details about numbers of prisoners and internees.

Private Office, HA20

Useful for an understanding of the political sensitivities involved in the administration of law and order.

Parliamentary Questions, HA23

These indicate the range of law-and-order issues which troubled Ulster Unionist MPs at what was a very difficult time.

Provisional Government of Ireland Cabinet Committee Papers, HO5 and MIC545

Minutes of the meetings provide an extremely interesting insight into the attitude of the British Government towards the emerging governments in Belfast and Dublin.

Department of Prime Minister's Correspondence, PM1, 4, 6, 9, 10, 11, and 15

Craig's correspondence, dating from 1 January 1921, and hitherto unused by any researcher, is a rich source of information about the establishment of Northern Ireland. The correspondence also reveals the apprehensions of the Ulster Unionists, particularly among the grass roots, at the negotiations between the British Government and Sinn Fein. There are also files on a variety of miscellaneous political issues which required Craig's personal attention.

Public Record Office (London) (PRO(L))

Cabinet Conclusions, CAB23

These minutes are important for revealing that the attitude of the British Government towards the Government of Northern Ireland was subordinate to its search for a settlement with Sinn Fein.

Cabinet Memoranda, CAB24

Among the memoranda are secret reports prepared by the Chief Secretary for Ireland which interestingly detail IRA breaches of the truce.

Colonial Office Irish Papers, CO739

The correspondence in these files is an important source for shedding light on the obstructionist tactics of the Provisional Government in its attempt to prevent the consolidation of the Government of Northern Ireland.

Treasury Finance Series, T160

A few files in this series are very important in that they relate to the actual process for transferring services in 1921/2 to the Government of Northern Ireland.

Treasury Establishment Series, T162

These files provided a wealth of information about the loan and/or transfer of civil servants to the new Northern Ireland administration, and related matters such as salaries and pension-rights.

University College Dublin Archives Department (UCDAD)

Mulcahy Papers, P7

This excellent archive contains a number of important documents relating to the reorganization of the IRA during the truce, its May 1922 offensive against Northern Ireland, and the shift in strategy by IRA GHQ in Dublin away from violence.

Blythe Papers, P24

The memorandum prepared by Blythe in August 1922 advocating a peace policy towards the Government of Northern Ireland is a vital document for anyone wishing to trace the evolution of the Provisional Government's attitude to Ulster unionists.

National Archives of Ireland (incorporating what was formerly the State Paper Office of Ireland)

Dail Eireann Cabinet, DE1

The minutes of Cabinet meetings for 1919–22 are important in that they indicate the reaction of Sinn Fein to the proposed establishment of Northern Ireland.

Dail Eireann Files, DE2

This series contains a few files which are useful in explaining Dail Eireann attitudes to key issues in relation to the emerging Northern Ireland. These include the Belfast Boycott and whether Sinn Fein should contest elections to the proposed Belfast parliament.

Provisional Government Cabinet, G1

These minutes are important in plotting the rapidly changing attitudes of the Provisional Government to the Government of Northern Ireland as reflected by the two attempted peace pacts in contrast to its obstructionist campaign.

Executive Council, G2

These Cabinet minutes for 1922–6 are an important source of information about Dublin attitudes to co-operation between the Irish Free State and Northern Ireland. They also provide details about Dublin's support for a campaign of non-recognition of the Government of Northern Ireland.

Executive Council Files, 'S' series

Many of the files in this series are most informative about the role of the North-Eastern Advisory Committee, the North-Eastern Boundary Bureau, and the attitude of the Irish Free State Government to the Boundary Commission in general.

National Library of Ireland (NLI)

Thomas Johnson Papers, MS 17,143

Interesting references to the assistance provided by the Provisional Government in 1922 to the 2nd Northern IRA Division in its attacks against the Government of Northern Ireland.

Joseph McGarrity Papers, MS 17,506

Useful account of how the IRA in County Tyrone used the truce in 1921 to strengthen its organizational structure.

John Devoy Papers, MS 18,127

Important memorandum about fading expectations of the Irish Free State Government to secure major territorial gains through the Boundary Commission.

J. J. O'Connell Papers, MS 22,143

Interesting report on the deployment of Irish Free State troops along the border with Northern Ireland in 1923.

Katherine MacKenna Papers, MS 22,774

Transcript notes by Michael Collins provide an important insight into his attitude towards Northern Ireland in 1922.

(b) PRINTED MATERIAL

Parl. Deb. (House of Commons), i–iv, 1921–5.
Parl. Deb. (Senate), i–vi, 1921–5.
Belfast Gazette, Nos. 1–245, 7 June 1921–5 Mar. 1926.
Government of Ireland Bill, Outline of Financial Provisions, Cmd. 645, 1920.
Government of Ireland Act, 1920 [10 & 11 Geo. 5 Ch. 67].
Articles of Agreement for a Treaty Between Great Britain and Ireland, Cmd. 1560, 1921.
Heads of Working Arrangements for Implementing the Treaty, Cmd. 1911, 1923.
First Report of the Northern Ireland Special Arbitration Committee, Cmd. 2072, 1924.
Final Report of the Northern Ireland Special Arbitration Committee, Cmd. 2389, 1925.
Irish Boundary: Extracts from Parliamentary Debates, Command Papers, etc., relevant to Questions arising out of Article XII of the Articles of Agreement for a Treaty between Great Britain and Ireland, dated 6th December, 1921, Cmd. 2264, 1924.
Ireland (Confirmation of Agreement) Act, 1925 [15 & 16 Geo. 5 Ch. 77].
Statutory Rules and Orders Issued in the Year 1921 (London, 1922).
Statutory Rules and Orders Issued in the Year 1922 (London, 1923).
Statutory Rules and Orders Issued in the Year 1923 (London, 1924).

B. Secondary Sources

(a) BOOKS

ADAMSON, IAN, *The Identity of Ulster* (Belfast, 1981).
AKENSON, D. H., *Education and Enmity: The Control of Schooling in Northern Ireland 1920–50* (Newton Abbot, 1973).
ALCOCK, A. E., *Northern Ireland: Problems and Solutions* (Sindelfingen, West Germany, 1985).
ARMOUR, W. S., *Ulster, Ireland, Britain: A Forgotten Trust* (London, 1938).

ARTHUR, PAUL, *Government and Politics of Northern Ireland* (Harlow, 1980).

AUGHEY, ARTHUR, *Under Siege: Ulster Unionism and the Anglo-Irish Agreement* (Belfast, 1989).

BARTON, BRIAN, *Brookeborough: The Making of a Prime Minister* (Belfast, 1988).

BECKETT, J. C., *The Making of Modern Ireland 1603–1923* (London, 1966).

—— and GLASSCOCK, R. E. (eds.), *Belfast: The Origin and Growth of an Industrial City* (London, 1967).

BELL, J. B., *A Time of Terror: How Democratic Societies Respond to Revolutionary Violence* (New York, 1978).

BEW, P., GIBBON, P., and PATTERSON, H., *The State in Northern Ireland 1921–72* (Manchester, 1979).

BIRRELL, D., and MURIE, A., *Policy and Government in Northern Ireland: Lessons of Devolution* (Dublin, 1980).

BLAKE, J. W., *Northern Ireland in the Second World War* (Belfast, 1956).

BLAKE, ROBERT, *The Unknown Prime Minister: The Life and Times of Andrew Bonar Law 1858–1923* (London, 1955).

BOWDEN, TOM, *The Breakdown of Public Security: The Case of Ireland 1916–1921 and Palestine 1936–1939* (London, 1977).

BOWMAN, JOHN, *De Valera and the Ulster Question 1917–1973* (Oxford, 1982).

BOYCE, D. G., *Englishmen and Irish Troubles: British Public Opinion and the Making of Irish Policy 1918–22* (London, 1972).

—— *Nationalism in Ireland* (London, 1982).

—— (ed.), *The Crisis of British Unionism: The Domestic Political Papers of the Second Earl of Selborne, 1885–1922* (Gloucester, 1987).

—— (ed.), *The Revolution in Ireland, 1879–1923* (Dublin, 1988).

BOYLE, K., HADDEN, T., and HILLYARD, P., *Law and State: The Case of Northern Ireland* (London, 1975).

BROOKE, PETER, *Ulster Presbyterianism* (Dublin, 1987).

BRUCE, STEVE, *God Save Ulster!* (Oxford, 1986).

BUCKLAND, PATRICK, *The Anglo-Irish and the New Ireland 1885 to 1922* (Dublin, 1972).

—— *Ulster Unionism and the Origins of Northern Ireland 1886 to 1922* (Dublin, 1973).

—— *The Factory of Grievances: Devolved Government in Northern Ireland 1921– 39* (Dublin, 1979).

—— *James Craig* (Dublin, 1980).

—— *A History of Northern Ireland* (Dublin, 1981).

BUDGE, I., and O'LEARY, C., *Belfast: Approach to Crisis: A Study of Belfast Politics, 1603–1970* (London, 1973).

BURROWS, Sir ROLAND (ed.), *Halsbury's Statutes of England*, vols. 6 and 17 (London, 1948 and 1950).

CALLWELL, Sir C. E. (ed.), *Field-Marshal Sir Henry Wilson: His Life and Diaries* (London, 1927).

CALVERT, HARRY, *Constitutional Law in Northern Ireland: A Study in Regional Government* (London and Belfast, 1968).

CAMPBELL, T. J., *Fifty Years of Ulster 1890–1940* (Belfast, 1941).

CHURCHILL, W. S., *The Aftermath: A Sequel to the World Crisis* (London, 1941).

CLARK, W., *Guns in Ulster: A History of the B Special Constabulary in Part of Co. Derry* (Belfast, 1967).

COLUM, PADRIAC, *Arthur Griffith* (Dublin, 1959).

COLVIN, IAN, *The Life of Lord Carson*, vol. 3 (London, 1936).

COOGAN, T. P., *The I.R.A.* (London, 1970).

CORKEY, WILLIAM, *Episode in the History of Protestant Ulster 1923–1947* (Belfast, 1965).

CRONIN, SEAN, *Washington's Irish Policy 1916–1986: Independence Partition Neutrality* (Dublin, 1987).

CURRAN, J. M., *The Birth of the Irish Free State 1921–1923* (Birmingham, Ala., 1980).

CURTIS, EDMUND, *A History of Ireland* (London, 1936).

DEWAR, M. W., BROWN, J., and LONG, S. E., *Orangeism: A New Historical Appreciation, 1688–1967* (Belfast, 1967).

DUGDALE, B. E. C., *Arthur James Balfour*, vol. ii (London, 1936).

DWYER, T. R., *Eamon de Valera* (Dublin, 1980).

ELLIOTT, SYDNEY, *Northern Ireland Parliamentary Election Results 1921–1972* (Chichester, 1973).

ERVINE, ST JOHN, *Craigavon: Ulsterman* (Aberdeen, 1949).

FANNING, RONAN, *The Irish Department of Finance, 1922–58* (London, 1978).

—— *Independent Ireland* (Dublin, 1983).

FARRELL, MICHAEL, *Northern Ireland: The Orange State* (London, 1976).

—— *Arming the Protestants: The Formation of the Ulster Special Constabulary and the Royal Ulster Constabulary, 1920–27* (London, 1983).

FINLAY, IAN, *The Civil Service* (London, 1966).

FISK, ROBERT, *The Point of No Return: The Strike which Broke the British in Ulster* (London, 1975).

FORSYTH, MURRAY (ed.), *Federalism and Nationalism* (Leicester, 1989).

GIBBON, PETER, *The Origins of Ulster Unionism: The Formation of Popular Protestant Politics and Ideology in Nineteenth-Century Ireland* (Manchester, 1975).

GOLDRING, MAURICE, *Faith of Our Fathers: The Formation of Irish Nationalist Ideology 1890–1920* (Dublin, 1982).

HAMILTON, E. W., *The Soul of Ulster* (London, 1917).

HAND, G. J., *Report of the Irish Boundary Commission 1925* (London, 1969).

HARBINSON, J. F., *The Ulster Unionist Party, 1882–1973: Its Development and Organisation* (Belfast, 1973).

HARKNESS, D. W., *The Restless Dominion* (London, 1969).

—— *Northern Ireland Since 1920* (Dublin, 1983).

HAYES, C. J. H., *Essays on Nationalism* (New York, 1941).

HECHTER, MICHAEL, *Internal Colonialism: The Celtic Fringe in British National Development 1536–1966* (London, 1975).

HEPBURN, A. C. (ed.), *Minorities in History* (London, 1978).

—— (ed.), *The Conflict of Nationality in Modern Ireland* (London, 1980).

HESLINGA, M. W., *The Irish Border as a Cultural Divide* (Assen, 1971).

HEZLET, Sir ARTHUR, *The 'B' Specials: A History of the Ulster Special Constabulary* (London, 1972).

HYDE, H. MONTGOMERY, *Carson: The Life of Sir Edward Carson, Lord Carson of Duncairn* (Surrey, 1953).

—— *The Londonderrys: A Family Portrait* (London, 1979).

JALLAND, PATRICIA, *The Liberals and Ireland: The Ulster Question in British Politics to 1914* (Brighton, 1980).

KENNEDY, DENIS, *The Widening Gulf: Northern Attitudes to the Independent Irish State 1919–49* (Belfast, 1988).

KINNEAR, MICHAEL, *The Fall of Lloyd George* (London, 1973).

LAFFAN, MICHAEL, *The Partition of Ireland 1911–1925* (Dundalk, 1983).

LAWRENCE, R. J., *The Government of Northern Ireland: Public Finance and Public Services, 1921–1964* (Oxford, 1965).

LOUGHLIN, JAMES, *Gladstone, Home Rule and the Ulster Question 1882–93* (Dublin, 1986).

LYONS, F. S. L., *Ireland Since the Famine* (London, 1973).

—— *Culture and Anarchy in Ireland 1890–1939* (Oxford, 1979).

MACARDLE, DOROTHY, *The Irish Republic* (London, 1937).

McCOLGAN, JOHN, *British Policy and the Irish Administration, 1920–1922* (London, 1983).

MACRORY, Sir PATRICK, *The Siege of Derry* (Oxford, 1988).

MANSERGH, NICHOLAS, *The Irish Free State* (London, 1934).

—— *The Government of Northern Ireland: A Study in Devolution* (London, 1936).

MAXWELL, HENRY, *Ulster Was Right* (London, 1934).

MIDDLEMAS, KEITH (ed.), *Thomas Jones Whitehall Diary: Ireland 1918–1925* (London, 1971).

MILLER, DAVID, *Queen's Rebels: Ulster Loyalism in Historical Perspective* (Dublin and New York, 1978).

MITCHISON, ROSALIND (ed.), *The Roots of Nationalism: Studies in Northern Europe* (Edinburgh, 1980).

MOLES, THOMAS, *Lord Carson of Duncairn* (Belfast, 1925).

MONYPENNY, W. F., *The Two Irish Nations* (London, 1913).

MOODY, T. W. (ed.), *Nationality and the Pursuit of National Independence* (Belfast, 1978).

—— and MARTIN, F. X., *The Course of Irish History* (Cork, 1967).

MORTON, GRENFELL, *Home Rule and the Irish Question* (Harlow, 1980).

MOXON-BROWN, EDWARD, *Nation, Class and Creed in Northern Ireland* (London, 1983).

NELSON, SARAH, *Ulster's Uncertain Defenders: Loyalists and the Northern Ireland Conflict* (Belfast, 1984).

North-Eastern Boundary Bureau, *Handbook of the Ulster Question* (Dublin, 1923).

O'BRIEN, C. C., *States of Ireland* (New York, 1972).

O'CUNINNEAGAIN, MICHAEL, *Partition from Michael Collins to Bobby Sands 1922–81* (Donegal, 1986).

O'HALLORAN, *Partition and the Limits of Irish Nationalism* (Atlantic Highlands, NJ, 1987).

O'HALPIN, EUNAN, *The Decline of the Union: British Government in Ireland 1892–1920* (Dublin, 1987).

OLIVER, J. A., *Working at Stormont* (Dublin, 1978).

PHILIPS, W. A., *The Revolution in Ireland 1906–1923* (London, 1926).

QUEKETT, A. S., *The Constitution of Northern Ireland*, 3 vols. (Belfast, 1928–46).

REA, DESMOND (ed.), *Political Co-operation in Divided Societies* (Dublin, 1982).

REDMOND, JOHN, *Church, State, Industry, 1827–1949 in East Belfast* (Belfast, 1950).

SHEA, PATRICK, *Voices and the Sound of Drums: An Irish Autobiography* (Belfast, 1981).

SHEARMAN, HUGH, *Not An Inch: A Study of Northern Ireland and Lord Craigavon* (London, 1942).

—— *Anglo-Irish Relations* (London, 1948).

—— *Northern Ireland 1921–1971* (Belfast, 1971).

STEWART, A. T. Q., *The Ulster Crisis: Resistance to Home Rule, 1912–14* (London, 1967).

—— *The Narrow Ground: Aspects of Ulster, 1609–1969* (London, 1977).

—— *Edward Carson* (Dublin, 1981).

TAYLOR, REX, *Michael Collins* (London, 1958).

TOWNSHEND, CHARLES, *The British Campaign in Ireland 1919–1921: The Development of Political and Military Politics* (Oxford, 1975).

TRAVERS, PAURIC, *Settlements and Divisions: Ireland 1870–1922* (Dublin, 1988).

WALKER, G. S., *The Politics of Frustration: Harry Midgley, and the Failure of Labour in Northern Ireland* (Manchester, 1985).

WHITE, TERENCE DE VERE, *Kevin O'Higgins* (London, 1948).

WILKINSON, BURKE, *The Zeal of the Convert: The Life of Erskine Childers* (Gerrards Cross, 1976).

WILLIAMS, DESMOND (ed.), *The Irish Struggle 1916–1926* (London, 1966).

WILSON, TOM (ed.), *Ulster Under Home Rule* (London, 1955).

—— *Ulster: Conflict and Consent* (Oxford, 1989).

(*b*) THESES

DOAK, J. C., 'Rioting and Civil Strife in the City of Londonderry during the 19th and Early 20th Centuries' (MA Thesis, The Queen's University of Belfast, 1978).

DOOHER, J. B., 'Tyrone Nationalism and the Question of Partition, 1910–25' (M.Phil. Thesis, University of Ulster, 1986).

MAGILL, P. F., 'The Senate in Northern Ireland, 1921–62' (Ph.D. Thesis, The Queen's University of Belfast, 1965).

(*c*) ARTICLES

BOYCE, D. G., 'British Conservative Opinion, the Ulster Question and the Partition of Ireland, 1919–21', *Irish Historical Studies*, 17: 65 (1968).

CONNOR, WALKER, 'A nation is a nation, is a state, is an ethnic, is a . . .', *Ethnic and Racial Studies*, 1 (Oct. 1978).

MCVICKER, PHILIP, 'Paying for Security: A Divisive Issue within the Northern Ireland State 1925–35', *Bulletin of the Political Science Department, Ulster Polytechnic* (1980).

MURPHY, RICHARD, 'Walter Long and the Making of the Government of Ireland Act 1919–20', *Irish Historical Studies*, 25: 97 (1986).

PALLEY, CLAIRE, 'The Evolution, Disintegration and Possible Reconstruction of the Northern Ireland Constitution', *Anglo-American Law Review* (May 1972).

STAMP, Sir JOSIAH, 'The Taxable Capacity of Ireland', *The Economic Journal*, 31: 123 (Sept. 1921).

WRIGHT, FRANK, 'Protestant Ideology and Politics in Ulster', *European Journal of Sociology*, 14 (1973).

(*d*) PAMPHLETS

BROWN, TERENCE, *The Whole Protestant Community: The Making of a Historical Myth*, Field Day No. 7 (1985).

ELLIOTT, MARIANNE, *Watchmen in Sion: The Protestant Idea of Liberty*, Field Day No. 8 (1985).

MONTGOMERY, ERIC, *The Ulster Spirit* (Belfast, 1955).

National Council for Civil Liberties, *Report of a Commission of Inquiry Appointed to Examine the Purpose and Effect of the Civil Authorities (Special Powers) Acts (Northern Ireland) 1922 and 1933* (London, 1936).

TRIMBLE, W. D. (ed.), *Ulster: an Ethnic Nation* (Belfast, 1986).

Ulster Unionist Council, *Government of Northern Ireland: Its First Three Years' Record: June 1921 to July 1924* (Belfast, 1924).

WALLIS, R., BRUCE, S., and TAYLOR, D., *No Surrender! Paisleyism and the Politics of Ethnic Identity in Northern Ireland* (Belfast, 1986).

Index